Transmedia Harry Potter

ALSO FROM CHRISTOPHER E. BELL
AND MCFARLAND

*Inside the World of Harry Potter:
Critical Essays on the Books and Films* (2018, editor)

*Wizards vs. Muggles: Essays on Identity
and the Harry Potter Universe* (2016, editor)

*From Here to Hogwarts:
Essays on Harry Potter Fandom and Fiction* (2016, editor)

*Hermione Granger Saves the World:
Essays on the Feminist Heroine of Hogwarts* (2012, editor)

*American Idolatry:
Celebrity, Commodity and Reality Television* (2010)

Transmedia Harry Potter

Essays on Storytelling Across Platforms

Edited by CHRISTOPHER E. BELL

McFarland & Company, Inc., Publishers
Jefferson, North Carolina

ISBN 978-1-4766-7354-7 (softcover : acid free paper)
ISBN 978-1-4766-3702-0 (ebook)

LIBRARY OF CONGRESS AND BRITISH LIBRARY
CATALOGUING DATA ARE AVAILABLE

© 2019 Christopher E. Bell. All rights reserved

No part of this book may be reproduced or transmitted in any form or by any means, electronic or mechanical, including photocopying or recording, or by any information storage and retrieval system, without permission in writing from the publisher.

Front cover image © 2019 Tithi Luadthong/Shutterstock

Printed in the United States of America

McFarland & Company, Inc., Publishers
   Box 611, Jefferson, North Carolina 28640
      www.mcfarlandpub.com

For Megan,
the Tonks to my Lupin

Table of Contents

Introduction
    Christopher E. Bell   1

Representations of Journalism in the Potterverse
    Gabriela Gruszynski Sanseverino *and* Ana Gruszynski   7

Supplement or Supplant? How Fan Editors Contribute to Fictional Universes
    Brian P. Bernard *and* Kimberly D. Martinez   30

Harry Potter and the Development of Narrative and Media Literacies
    Alison Halsall   48

Harry Potter and the Transmediality of Artistic Expression
    Caitlin Boyle   62

Harry Potter Fandom and Narratives of Inequality in the United States Presidential Election of 2016
    Sergey Medvedev *and* Elena Pronkina   72

The Magic of Translation: An Analysis of the Brazilian Portuguese Version of *Harry Potter and the Philosopher's Stone*
    Bárbara Cardoso de Souza   88

Transmediated Weasleys: A Tale of Two Ginnys
    Christopher E. Bell *and* Celina Smith   105

Performing Memories Through Fandom Talk: What a Focus Group Interview Reveals About Growing Up with *Harry Potter*
    Bronwyn E. Beatty   118

Table of Contents

Magical and Mundane Narrative Devices
    Jørgen Riber Christensen *and* Thessa Jensen   135

The Magic of Harry Potter for Children in Care
    Sarah Jayne Mokrzycki   154

House-Elves in Harlem: Stereotyping the Other in *Fantastic Beasts and Where to Find Them*
    Kris Swank   166

Harry Potter, the Boy with Many Faces: The Illustrated *Harry Potter* Books in Transmedia Motion
    Sarah Mygind   181

About the Contributors   199

Index   203

Introduction
CHRISTOPHER E. BELL

This will be a mercifully brief introduction, as nobody picks up a book and says, "I can't wait to read the *introduction*!" You want to get to the show you came to see, so to speak, and I want to get you there as quickly as possible. However, it certainly makes sense to give you a baseline primer on the concept of transmediation before sending you on your way, so please, a brief moment of your time.

If one wants to fully understand the concept of transmediation, one reads Henry Jenkins' essential 2006 volume *Convergence Culture*. In this work, Jenkins lays out the seminal definition of transmedia:

> A transmedia story unfolds across multiple media platforms, with each new text making a distinctive and valuable contribution to the whole. In the ideal form of transmedia storytelling each medium does what it does best—so that a story might be introduced in a film, expanded through television, novels, and comics [Jenkins, 2006, p. 1].

Transmedia, then, is not simply synergy or cross-promotion. If I walk into my local Hot Topic store and purchase a *Stranger Things* t-shirt, I am not engaging in transmediation. Transmediation requires another telling of the story in an alternate medium than the original. But, beyond that, it requires that each telling of the story be able to stand on its own, without needing to access other iterations of the tale, yet all of the iterations taken as a whole must also form *one* narrative. Transmediation is the storytelling equivalent of Voltron; each telling of the story is its own independent entity, but when they come together, they form something much more powerful.

Transmediation is not new. In fact, "[people] have been transmediating texts for decades, as when teachers invite students to write poems to express their interpretations of pictures, or to use art, music, or drama to retell books or stories" (Conner-Zachocki, 2015, p. 87). Stories are heard, seen, processed, interpreted, and reimagined into new contexts and mediums all the time. Take, for example, the original *Transformers* franchise. In 1984, Hasbro released the first wave of *Transformers* toys. Simultaneously, Marvel Comics launched *The Transformers* issue #1, and Sunbow Pictures released the first episode of *The Transformers* in syndicated television. This is a classic example of transmediation.

While there has been considerable disagreement about whether or not adaptation "counts as" transmediation (see Eder 2015, Harvey 2015, Klinger 2015, Shacklock 2015, among numerous others), in the case of *Harry Potter*, it seems relatively indisputable that from novel to film to video games, the story has undergone a significant transmediating process that extends far beyond normal "adaptation." While even Jenkins himself originally rejected the idea of adaptation as transmediation, it was *Harry Potter* that forced him to concede:

> Any adaptation represents an interpretation of the work in question and not simply a reproduction, so all adaptions to some degree add to the range of meanings attached to a story.... To translate *Harry Potter* from a book to a movie series means thinking through much more deeply what Hogwarts looks like and thus the art director/production designer has significantly expanded and extended the story in the process. It might be better to think of adaptation and extension as part of a continuum [of transmediation] [Jenkins 2011].

In the case of *Harry Potter*, the transmediation from novel to screen and games provides multiple points of entry into the narrative, which has proven to be beneficial to those parts of the audience who would not have connected to (or even consumed) the text in print. Also, it is clear that transmediating the narrative has provided for much, much more economic gain—transmediation has generated an enormous amount of profit. This profit, in turn, has generated more opportunity—and, more importantly, more desire—to seek out additional transmediating possibilities.

If we accept Jenkins' suggestion of a continuum of transmediation, then it might run from something like an audiobook at one end (an audiobook being a verbatim adaptation of the work, with the addition of vocal nuance), to something like a filmic adaptation in the middle (films usually excise some material from the story and add in new material not found in the original text), to something like a role-playing game on the distant end (using the storyworld and maybe even some major characters from the original, but allowing for completely new stories to be generated in real time). These practices include both author-generated transmediated products and fan-generated transmediated products. In fact, fan-created work is often the more interesting of the transmediated products, as the insight into the way fans process the original work and make meaning for themselves is usually fascinating. For this reason, in this volume, I intended to include many, many more expressions as transmediation than traditionally included: adaptation, translation, paratextuality, fan fiction, fan editing—I am including them all. This may rankle transmediation purists a bit, but much like many topics in Harry Potter Studies, I'm willing to take us out on a limb here, perhaps all by ourselves.

The level of complexity of the original text certainly serves as a determining factor as to the scope and extent of transmediation—the more complicated the original text, the easier it is to move into other contexts. For example, a work like *Star Wars*, with its expansive universe, enormous range of characters, and an intricate web of relationships among those characters provides a rich tapestry upon which to draw. This, in turn, has led to not only the original films, but novelizations, video games, novels, graphic novels, comic book series, role-playing games, and the most extensive toy line in history, not to mention volume upon volume of fan fiction, the creation of fan reenactment groups like the 501st Legion, and multiple fan films. Contrast this with a text that is far less involved—it is highly unlikely that anyone is writing fan fiction or creating official comic books or video games based on *Saturday Night Live*. It's a straight-forward sketch comedy show, and despite a vast cast of actors over the years, it has spawned relatively few transmediated products—a few movies, but almost nothing else. The biggest *SNL* official transmediated products, such as *Wayne's World*, generated more texts in more venues; there was a *Wayne's World* video game released by THQ for both Sega Genesis and Super Nintendo, for example. But even then, the possibilities are limited. There are no *Wayne's World* novelizations, or comic books, or any other texts of that nature. The original text is a series of six- to eight-minute comedy sketches, which do not lend themselves to too many expansion or adaptation possibilities.

The target audience for the text determines its transmediation possibilities, again, due to complexity, but also due to the cognitive capabilities of the target market. An adult text can be *Game of Thrones*–level complex, with dozens of simultaneous storylines, hundreds of characters to keep track of, and a narrative that spans years. A text for children must necessarily be less complicated. In order to participate in transmedia, users "require advanced media-literacy and multiliteracy skills … to interpret and process narrative information from multiple media systems and platforms. Depending on their developmental stages, children often lack these skills and can therefore not understand or participate in transmedia experiences like adults can" (Pietschmann, Völkel & Ohler, 2014, p. 2261). However, children's franchises are still veering more and more into transmedia territory; "even *Bob the Builder* and *Sesame Street* introduce children to characters and stories extended on websites and in mobile apps with animated, sometimes interactive, picture stories and in computer games and toys" (Pietschmann, Völkel & Ohler, p. 2262).

Harry Potter sits at a sweet spot between children's media and adult media, that elusive "young adult" categorization that has spawned multiple transmedia franchises, from *A Series of Unfortunate Events* to *The Hunger Games* to *Divergent*. Most contemporary comic book franchises also fall into this particular sweet spot, like *Guardians of the Galaxy, The Avengers,* and *Wonder Woman*. Even World Wrestling Entertainment rides this fine line between programming for children (the toys marketed directly at an 8- to 12-year-old market), programming for teens (video games and comic books), and programming for adults (live events), as well as programming designed "for the whole family" (weekly television broadcasts). It makes sense that the greatest successes in transmediation would come from this multigenerational strategy—it maximizes the profitability of the text over multiple groups of buyers. The most successful of these transmediated texts—like *Star Wars* or *Harry Potter*—appeal to children, teens, and adults alike. As such, *Harry Potter* provides us with a perfect example to interrogate transmedia and the creation practices, fan usage, and applications of those texts.

Essays in this collection span considerations of a wide range of transmediating practices and uses, from adaptation to fan editing to practical application of the text. This collection just scratches the surface of the many-faceted world of transmediated storytelling in the Potterverse. Entire volumes could be written just on Wizard Rock,[1] or just on *Potter* fan fiction, or just on fan editing. This collection is meant to be a starting point; use the work within to generate your own thoughts, questions, and ideas on transmediating practices, not just within the Potterverse, but in all sorts of storytelling contexts. Use it to help define for yourself what the term "transmediation" might mean. Feel free to read the collection in any order that suits you. It is your book, after all.

Naming Conventions

For the ease of reading and for the sake of consistency, in this volume, the titles of the books/films will be abbreviated as follows:

Harry Potter and the Sorcerer's/Philosopher's Stone—SS or *PS*
Harry Potter and the Chamber of Secrets—CoS
Harry Potter and the Prisoner of Azkaban—PoA
Harry Potter and the Goblet of Fire—GoF
Harry Potter and the Order of the Phoenix—OotP
Harry Potter and the Half-Blood Prince—HBP
Harry Potter and the Deathly Hallows—DH, or *DH1/DH2*

Note

1. For a full exploration of the Wizard Rock phenomenon, see Paul Thomas, 2019, *I wanna wrock! The world of Harry Potter–inspired "wizard rock" and its fandom* (Jefferson, NC: McFarland).

References

Conner-Zachocki, J. (2015). Using the digital transmedia magazine project to support students with 21st-century literacies. *Theory into Practice, 54*, pp. 86–93.

Eder J. (2015) Transmediality and the politics of adaptation: Concepts, forms, and Strategies. in D. Hassler-Forest & P. Nicklas (Eds.), *The politics of adaptation*. London: Palgrave Macmillan.

Freeman, M. (2014, April 4). Transmediating Tim Burton's Gotham City: Brand convergence, child audiences, and Batman: The Animated Series. *Networking Knowledge: Journal of the MeCCSA Postgraduate Network, 7*(1). Retrieved from https://ojs.meccsa.org.uk/index.php/netknow/article/view/329

Harvey C.B. (2015). Of hobbits and hulks: Adaptation versus narrative expansion. In: *Fantastic transmedia*. Palgrave Macmillan, London.

Jenkins, H. (2011). Transmedia 202: Further reflections. *Confessions of an Aca-Fan*. Retrieved from http://henryjenkins.org/blog/2011/08/defining_transmedia_further_re.html

Klinger, B. (2015). Pre-cult: Casablanca, radio adaptation, and transmedia in the 1940s. *New Review of Film and Television Studies, 13*(1), pp. 45–62.

Pietschmann, D., Völkel, S., & Ohler, P. (2014). Limitations of transmedia storytelling for children: A cognitive developmental analysis. *International Journal of Communication. 8*(1), pp. 2259–2282.

Shacklock, Z. (2015). "A reader lives a thousand lives before he dies": Transmedia textuality and the flows of adaptation. In J. Battis & S. Johnston (Eds.), *Mastering the game of thrones: Essays on George R.R. Martin's A Song of Ice and Fire*. Jefferson, NC: McFarland.

Representations of Journalism in the Potterverse

GABRIELA GRUSZYNSKI SANSEVERINO *and* ANA GRUSZYNSKI

Lumos

The Harry Potter series acquired cultural capital as well as an impressive market value. The franchise started by Rowling's books has an indisputable commercial value. This is an external factor, characteristic of the dimension of the commodity, in which a cultural good becomes part of the cultural industry (literature, bestseller; cinema, blockbuster; website, number of hits; visitation park, commercial products, etc.). There is an outer dimension that places limits and conditions for the existence of cultural products in the world. This quantitative value, however, which the series came to represent, makes the Harry Potter narrative a valuable object of study in the scope of the qualitative.

There is an academic and intellectual bias with the bestseller, the massive, which sometimes denies the capacity of these narratives that have become a phenomenon to raise questions about the reality with which it works. So, the first contribution that this research effort, which has focused on Rowling's history, seeks to make to the academic field, is to demonstrate how these products, demarcated by a market interest, can provide serious reflections on our empirical universe.

Men have always needed ways to mediate their own reality and, over time, they have found ways to manipulate cultural instruments in order to analyze, reflect and transform it. Stories are able to represent reality from a specific perspective and have become constant forms of human expression, regardless of ethnic origin, primary language and enculturation (Hazel, 2007).

They are international, transhistorical, transcultural and always present, as if they had a life of their own (Barthes, 1977). Parameters created in fictional narratives mark our perception of the real world, even if they are set in an imaginary environment. We do not assume that they have the capacity to mimic the real world, but they can create spaces of reflection, debate and learning.

This essay creates a movement toward a particular element of this universe created by Rowling, journalism. In books and films, journalism and journalism are part of the universe represented. At the Pottermore site, they were part of the interaction between the network user and the fictional universe. Journalism, besides being representation, takes on a life of its own, mirroring the values of contemporary, globalized and market-based everyday life. The profession becomes a way of entering the reality of the magical world. In a way, the mediation function of the newspaper is brought to fiction, a form of access to this universe. The fictional journalism imagined in the series is a creation of Rowling, therefore it can not be seen like mirror of the real one; but is still imbued with the legitimacy of the profession as a social institutions—journalism has the credibility to inform.

The transmuted universe created by Rowling assists in our quest to interpret everyday life. The representations of journalism mark the imaginary of the profession and the reach of Rowling's work makes the image of the profession reach a wide and heterogeneous public. The author imagined a reality endowed with magic, but that reflects her view of the world and that allows the fans to trigger strategies to interpret their reality.

Throughout history, journalism has been systematically represented in fiction, and these representations point to ways of imagining it in our reality. Understanding how the idea of the journalist is disseminated in cultural products offers a unique way of assessing the public's relationship with journalism over the centuries (Ehrlich, 2004; Saltzman, 2005). The representations found in cultural products become part of the public's imaginary, and it does not matter whether these representations correspond to actual fact or not. Few people have witnessed a journalist in action, however, the public tends to have a very specific idea of what a journalist is and how they work after having read about them in novels, comic books, television shows, plays etc. (Ehrlich, 2004; Saltzman, 2005).

Harry Potter is one of these stories—a narrative that created in its fictional world a representation of journalism. As a transmedia narrative, a new form of telling stories, Harry Potter began to interpret reality in a way that allows each person to choose how they want to get involved in the plot and to what extent they want to be integrated with it (Jenkins, 2009). Transmedia storytelling involves media industry (canon) and collaborative culture (fandom) in relation to narrative and media expansion (Scolari, Bertetti & Freeman, 2014), with character-building, world-building and authorship being the essence of this kind of story (Freeman, 2017). Rowling's fictional world grew into a multimedia universe, with each new text contributing in a different way to form its own magical transmedia narrative.

In October 2011, the author announced the release of the Pottermore.com website, a portal to the magical world. Rowling wrote new material about the characters, places and objects in the stories that could be accessed in the various sections of the page. In September 2015, the website underwent a major change, and the previous one was deleted, along with all its content. The old version of the website provided an interactive story based on the seven books, retold from texts, audio, illustrations, games and animations, as well as a section called *Daily Prophet*, which contained exclusive excerpts written by the author in news format produced by well-known characters—Ginny Potter and Rita Skeeter. After Pottermore's revamp, that content no longer exists, but since digital content can be shared, copied and sent, our research was able to study the website's old version in its entirety—the interactive story as well as the *Daily Prophet* section.

Anchored in different forms of media, Rowling inserted journalism into the narrative, conferring distinct levels of importance on the development of wizarding and *muggle* societies. As a cultural product, the story not only raises criticism but also delves into the conflicts and tensions that are part of the journalistic activity. This essay proposes to identify and analyze the representations of journalism and journalists constructed in seven books, eight films and the old *Pottermore*[1] website, in order to verify how different platforms can represent the same institution: journalism. Our aim is to analyze the functions performed by journalism in the story and observe the professional *ethos* of journalists throughout the series. To do so, we used bibliographical and documentary research, as well as content analysis in a qualitative approach.

Alohomora

Transmedia stories have a high fidelization rate because they are capable of involving their consumer in a potentially infinite universe, which provides ample experience. Jenkins (2010) presents principles that characterize this kind of narrative. The sharing × depth potential is identified with popularity, which in Harry Potter's case generated the fan movement Pottermania. The strong relation between them and the plot made the story go beyond books and movies through debate and the audience's search for new ways to relate to the narrative, sharing content in social media and doing deep into web spaces created by fans, such as fan fiction and debate forums. The plot was complete and complex enough (Scolari et. al., 2014) to motivate the story's extensive sharing and its ramifications. The *Pottermore* website kept the interest of fans alive for new material and opened a portal to the public through which they could deepen their knowledge, providing engagement.

The principle of continuity × multiplicity can be observed in the coherence between different official platforms through which the audience could actively cooperate in the expansion process (Scolari, 2013). At first, Rowling was favorable to the stories' publication on the Internet (Anelli, 2011). However, when fans began to gain online space, Warner Bros. interfered and sued several pages and their owners, many of whom were children and teenagers, for the use of brand licensed terms (Jenkins, 2009). In reaction, the fan community gave way to what was called Potter Wars—a movement that fought for its freedom of speech. The franchise went through a marketing restructuring made by the company that developed the cooperative policy and began to include the immense and articulate fanbase that wished to be a part of the narrative.

The immersion × extraction principle is present mainly through amusement parks. The old version of *Pottermore* also allowed immersion into the virtual environment, as it allowed the fans to become students in a digital Hogwarts, to interact with other wizard students, cast spells and make potions. It encompassed a greater number of users, since it was free and did not required physical presence. The extraction principle, on the other hand, was accomplished by selling fans products from the series, such as shirts, backpacks and others, allowing them to live and demonstrate their connection publicly. The seriality principle is strongly present: the main story arc is shared inside different installations in one media type—a plot divided into seven books, then in eight movies etc.—with their expansion to different platforms. Seriality allows individuals without previous knowledge of the plot to jump in at any point of the story.

The franchise universe build-up had so much success that it received a name: Potterverse. Fans were able to imagine that the series' magic universe could exist parallel to our *muggle* universe. In *Pottermore*'s old *Daily Prophet* version, for example, a continuous transmission of the Quiddich Would Cup was created in parallel to the Football World Cup in the real world, encouraging fans to follow and cheer for real countries' national teams, participating in a theoretically fictitious sport.

The subjectivity principle can be noticed through *Pottermore* and other books derived from the series, since characters and secondary stories (Freeman, 2017) were explored in these new products, not only bringing about other perspectives from what happened in the stories, but also creating new narratives from the original plot.

The widening of spaces for publicizing fiction, narrative threads development possibilities were created, which, underdeveloped in the main plot, gain a new life of their own. It is the case of Ginny Potter, who in the old version of *Pottermore* gained her own space, portrayed as an adult and a professional journalist.

The performance principle, that takes from the narrative's capacity of inciting fans to produce their own content, can be observed in fandom, which is notably participative and numerous, as a Google search for Harry Potter fan fictions can demonstrate. The fandom is one of the most representative manifestations of participative culture, and is anchored in the desire to be or to feel close to others who appreciate and are willing to get involved in the same ludic universe.

It is worth noting that, although respecting transmedia narrative principles as delimitated by Jenkins (2010), the Harry Potter franchise is, according to Long's (2007) classification, a weak transmedia narrative. It was only when the first books were successful and reached the best-seller list that the secondary elements were created. It was the effect denominated by Ryan (2014) as snowball: because of the story's popularity, Rowling's narrative was widened and became transmediatic through fan identification with the universe and the possibility for monetary profit.

Aparecium

In order to conduct our research, we decided on our object of study (*corpus*) and how to proceed with our study using the method of content analysis. We determined our corpus by Bardin's (2006) three rules: *representation*, in which the sample needs to represent the universe of the object researched; *homogeneity*, in which the documents obtained must be of the same nature, genre or subject; and *pertinence*, in which the documents analyzed must be adequate to the research objective.

Considering these rules, the research *corpus* was composed by Harry Potter entire multimedia franchise, detailed in the Tables 1 to 3. They were chosen for being the primary ways of distribution and points of entry to the story, available worldwide for a major audience, allowing journalism to be identified and seen as it is portrayed in the narrative. To analyze our *corpus*, we created and applied a research instrument, represented in Table 4.

Table 1. Books That Compose the Corpus

Book	Publisher	Year	
Original	*Used edition*	*Release*	*Used Version*
Harry Potter and the Sorcerer's Stone/Harry Potter and the Philosopher's Stone	Scholastic/Bloomsbury	1997	1998

(Table 1, *continued*)

Book Original	Publisher Used edition	Year Release	Used Version
Harry Potter and the Chamber of Secrets	Bloomsbury	1998	2004
Harry Potter and the Prisoner of Azkaban	Bloomsbury	1999	2000
Harry Potter and the Goblet of Fire	Bloomsbury	2000	2001
Harry Potter and the Order of the Phoenix	Scholastic	2003	2003
Harry Potter and the Half-Blood Prince	Scholastic	2005	2005
Harry Potter and the Deathly Hallows	Bloombury	2007	2007

Table 2. Films That Compose the Corpus

Film Title	Director	Studio	Year of Release
Harry Potter and the Sorcerer's Stone/Harry Potter and the Philosopher's Stone	Chris Colombus	Warner Bros.	2001
Harry Potter and the Chamber of Secrets	Chris Colombus	Warner Bros.	2002
Harry Potter and the Prisoner of Azkaban	Alfonso Cuarón	Warner Bros.	2004
Harry Potter and the Goblet of Fire	Mike Newell	Warner Bros.	2005
Harry Potter and the Order of the Phoenix	David Yates	Warner Bros.	2007
Harry Potter and the Half-Blood Prince	David Yates	Warner Bros.	2009
Harry Potter and the Deathly Hallows—Part I	David Yates	Warner Bros.	2010
Harry Potter and the Deathly Hallows—Part II	David Yates	Warner Bros.	2011

Table 3. Website That Composes the Corpus

Website	Address	Year Release	Consult
Pottermore	https://www.pottermore.com/en-us/	2011	2015

Table 4. Instruments

Newspaper	Vehicle	Means of Communication	
	muggle	Daily Mail	No name mentioned
	wizard	Daily Prophet	No name mentioned

	Presentation modality		With highlighted news In a character's speech In the description of environment/scenery Harry Potter's thoughts Character action Journalist characterization Initial scene description Text to be explored
Magazine	Vehicle	muggle wizard	No name mentioned *The Quibbler* *Challenges in Charming* *Witch Weekly* *Transfiguration Today* *The Practical Potioneer* *Which Broomstick* No name mentioned
	Presentation modality		With highlighted news In a character's speech In the description of environment/scenery Harry Potter's thoughts Character action Journalist characterization Element to be collected
Radio	Vehicle	muggle wizard	*FM Dial* No name mentioned WWN | *Wizarding Wireless Network* *Potterwatch* No name mentioned
	Program	muggle wizard	No name mentioned *Witching Hour* *WWN News* *Christmas Broadcast* No name mentioned
Television	Vehicle Program	muggle	No name mentioned *News at Ten* No name mentioned

News

Sources		Present Not present
Presentation modality		In full In character's speech

Journalists

Presentation modality		Active role in the narrative In character speech Present in the environment/scenery

14   Transmedia Harry Potter

	Journalists (continued)	
		Inside the news
		Harry Potter's thoughts
		Initial scene description
		Text to be explored
Professionals	**muggle**	Jim McGuffin
		Mary Dorkins
		Ted
		No name mentioned
	wizard	Rita Skeeter
		Ginny
		Xenophilius Lovegood
		Barnabas Cuffe
		Bozo
		No name mentioned
	Other Journalistic Manifestation	
Occasional		In the wizard world
apparition		In the muggle world
Reference to		Print media
		Television
		Radio

To compose the *corpus* we have catalogued all mentions of journalism in the franchise (expect for the *Daily Prophet* section in the *Pottermore* website, whose content were not created directly from the main narrative); all characters that assumed roles related to journalism; characters' speech about news, journalists or journalistic media; and news written by Rowling as part of the story. In order to evaluate print newspapers, magazines, and radio's presence, we have observed the presence of muggle and wizard vehicles presented. All four categories were evaluated regarding their vehicles and programs, both named and unnamed.

For newspapers and magazines, we have also considered their presentation modalities, since print news outlets represents most of the profession throughout the narrative. These presentation modalities refer to different ways the vehicles can be inserted in the story, considering each evaluated medium's characteristics.

There are six categories common to newspapers and magazines: (a) as highlighted news—when the news is emphasized in the plot and can be clearly seen by the reader; (b) in a character's speech—when the vehicle is mentioned, debated or topic of conversation among characters; (c) in the description of the environment/scene—when the vehicle is a composing element of the story or indicated as part of the routine, not been presented as crucial the scene or even interacting with any of the characters; (d) in Harry Potter's thoughts—when the story is told from his point of view, there are moments in which his memory and imagination about the vehicles become important to the plot; (e) in a character's action—when their interaction with the environment becomes important to the plot; and (f) in the journalist's characterization—when the vehicle is used to contextualize who the journalist is to a character, as well as to the reader.

Two categories are specific to newspapers and their apparition is implied in *Pottermore*'s website interactive story. The first concerns the scene's initial description, when the vehicle mentioned in a text with the purpose of explaining the moment to be explored by the website's user, while the second concerns the text to be explored, where there is a hyperlink to be clicked and explored in certain scenes. One category is specific to magazines and also concerns their presence in *Pottermore*'s interactive story, in which there is a hyperlink to an element to be explored and collected for the user's personal collection.

To investigate the presence of journalists in the *corpus*, we have gathered all professionals, named and unnamed. The modalities were to the ones used to categorize the abovementioned means of communication: (a) when they have an active role in the narrative, being a central character in the plot, and being distinguished through their actions; (b) in a character's speech, when they are mentioned or becomes the topic of conversation; (c) present in the environment/scene, when they appear in the background of the narrative, being present in a situation, but not having any pertinent action in the story; (d) inside the news, when they are mentioned in the news presented in full throughout the story; (e) in Harry Potter's thoughts, as previously explained; (f) in the text to be explored, when they are mentioned in a hyperlink that can be clicked and explored; and (g) in a scene's initial description before an interactive story to be explored by the website's user.

To evaluate the news, we have considered: if they were fully present throughout the plot—a text transcript or a newspaper image with a highlighted clipping; if they were presented through a character's speech, who read parts of the news' text; and if a different font was used. A category concerning other manifestations was created and denominated occasional mentions, to identify the ones that occur through character speech, which, while being related to journalism, do not concern their vehicle, news or professionals. We have also evaluated if the mentions make reference to print, television, or radio.

It must be noted that in the case of the films and the *Pottermore* interactive story, there are characteristics specific to be built by images, scenery, character wardrobe, and the vehicles' graphic design present in the scene, which must be considered in order to understand the representation of journalism in the franchise. These elements were evaluated only qualitatively.

Priori Incantato

Other means of communication are presented in the same way journalism is, their output will only differ according to the resources each society has access to—while wizards have magic, *muggles* have technology. The magical community media vehicles are more relevant to the development of the story. Out of 555 mentions in the interactive story, films and books, 504 (91 percent) are from magical vehicles and 51 (9 percent) are from *muggle* ones.

Print newspaper has the more expressive number of mentions—395 (71 percent) out of 555, considering 370 from the wizarding community against 25 *muggle* titles. There are 121 magazines out of 555, considering 100 mentions related to the wizarding world and 21 from *muggles*. Radio and television have more inexpressive numbers. Radio appears 27 times in the corpus, 22 times from wizard society while only 5 are *muggle*. Television is an exclusive *muggle* medium with 12 mentions. A reasonable explanation for this is that the plot revolves around magical society, and *muggle* means of communication are only there to connect the two realities, even if it goes unnoticed by the characters. The intersection between wizard and *muggle* worlds through media can be observed from the series' very beginning.

Wizards avoid *muggle* devices as a cultural preference, which can explain the predominance of print media. The wizard community takes pride in the fact that they do not need technology, since it was only created by *muggles* to do what could be otherwise done with magic.

Television

Television the only uniquely muggle vehicle, not having any correspondence in the wizarding world and generating curiosity among several members of the magical community. The closest wizard resources are the moving photographs used by print media to illustrate stories in the newspaper. It is known in the story that a group of wizards has tried to create their own television channel, but the project was interrupted by the Ministry of Magic for risk of exposing the community to the regular world.

Out of twelve mentions, no platform or specific channel is named, despite having the denomination of a program: *News at Ten*. Journalism shows through generic news programs, always at the Dursley home. The medium is also present in the houses of other muggle characters, but no journalism-related programs are mentioned.

Radio

In the story's universe, the wizarding community appropriated radios from muggle technology legally, then modified and bewitched them for their own use. Several wizard radio stations were created and transmit regular programs. The government controls the means of communication, mainly in order to determine which means can be used by the magical society, establishing which risks of exposing the community are acceptable and which are not.

In all platforms, the radio appears for most of plot in background of everyday life, playing generic news programs. There is mention of the *WWN—Wizarding Wireless Network*—and mentions of the programs *Witching Hour*, *WWN News* and *Christmas Broadcast*. In muggle reality, the radio also appears in the background, with one named station, the FM Dial.

The *Potterwatch* radio is the main station linked to journalism in the narrative; it has 14 (64 percent) mentions in the corpus out of 22 wizarding radio mentions. The resistance movement initiates it after Voldemort seizes power. The station manages to survive by always changing location and using passwords to connect listeners to each new transmission, which limits its access. In the story, it is used to report what is not being reported in other means of communication.

Print News Outlets

Even when it was not central to the plot, print newspapers have consistently appeared in all platforms, being marked as part of the characters' routine. Out of all 395 mentions of print newspapers in the corpus, 175 (44 percent) were in the book's description of a scene or as an object in the movies, which indicated print newspapers to be a part of everyday life for muggles as well as wizards.

In muggle reality, newspapers make an appearance in the Dursley home as a part of Uncle Vernon's reading habits, with 25 mentions in movies, books and interactive stories. Of those, 24 occur through generic, unnamed vehicles, and one mention in the books indicate the vehicle *Daily Mail*.

The *Daily Prophet* is a symbol of print media in magical vehicles and is the most present, with 348 mentions out of 555 means of communication. It is the only print newspaper in Great Britain, with a headquarters in Diagon Alley and daily delivery by owls to almost all wizards resident in the United Kingdom. It has a daily edition, but, occasionally, when something particularly interesting or exciting happens in the wizard world, a special edition of the *Evening Prophet* is published.

While a plurality of means of communication is implied in muggle reality, the wizarding community presents their print media as constituting a monopoly in the information services. The *Daily Prophet* appears without competition, dominating the market. The formation of a monopoly among means of communication can affect the plurality of informative content and compromises the quality of the information distributed. In the development of the plot, it becomes clear that this monopoly of information is prejudicial to the public and that the government, when it is strong and stable, can influence what is published.

To many wizards without relations with other members of the magical community, the newspaper is their only form of connection. In an exclusive content in *Pottermore* about the *Daily Prophet*, Rowling indicates that print newspaper would continue to be favored by the wizarding society.

Print Magazines

In muggle reality, no magazines are linked to journalism, despite there being mentions of gossip publications and a crochet magazine, as opposed to the six named magazines in the wizarding community in the studied corpus.

The Quibbler appears 59 times, and is inserted in the narrative as an alternative publication. It becomes known for publishing stories considered to be rubbish, news that is not based in reality and does not have any informative value, generally assuming creative and eccentric formats. In the story, when Voldemort seizes power, the magazine changes its perspective and assumes a role in which it becomes reference of truth and coherence with reality.

Witch Weekly appears in punctual moments in the story, with 15 mentions, as a publication with big stories on subjects that receive little to no space in the *Daily Prophet*. It would be the equivalent of a gossip publication that has stories of human interest, about the characters and their personal dramas. It is easily acknowledged as a publication with ample audience that influences their readers. Characters even change their attitudes according to stories written in the magazine.

In the plot, *The Quibbler* is more relevant than *Witch Weekly*. In the context of wizarding society, however, *Witch Weekly* is shown to be more popular for its content based on soft news, bringing, for example, celebrity gossip. *The Quibbler*, despite working creatively with newsworthy texts, publishes niche content that appeals to a more specific audience.

Which Broomstick appears only in the books, with four mentions, bringing evaluations on the best brooms, mainly regarding Quidditch. There are three academic publications mentioned only in the books: the *Practical Potioneer*, dedicated to the study of potions, *Transfiguration Today*, with five mentions, and *Challenges in Charming*, with two. The last two are also featured in the old *Pottermore*'s exclusive content and publish news and reports on their areas as well as academic content.

According to the tabulation, there are 121 print magazine mentions in the analyzed corpus. They are relevant in two contexts that add up to 96 total: the first indicates that the magazines are a part of everyday life, present 61 times in the description of environment or scenery; the second indicates that news reports published by them become part of conversation, seen that they are mentioned 35 times in characters' speeches.

Journalists

Journalists, as characters, appear only in wizarding reality, despite there being television programs' hosts in muggle-centered scenes. Three muggle television reporters are named in the books—Ted, Jim McGuffin and Mary Dorkins, while others appear in the books as well as in the movies indicated only as program anchors.

In wizarding society, Rita Skeeter is the professional with the most appearances (148). The reporter works for the main print vehicles of the wizarding community: the *Daily Prophet* and the *Witch Weekly* magazine. Throughout her career, she also writes for *The Quibbler*. She is the only professional fulfilling the function of a journalist that works in all three platforms, being characterized by her unbeatable quest for fresh stories, scandal, and curiosity that can please the public and reverberate among wizards. She would be the journalist-villain: without scruples or any commitment to the truth, she manipulates facts to favor her story, is always seeking the mythical scoop, values the status that journalism grants her in society, and works for a company that cares only for their interests (profit and audience).

Xenophilius Lovegood appears 56 times among books, interactive story, and movies. He is the owner, editor, and reporter of *The Quibbler*, a publication that reflects his eccentricity. Lovegood chooses stories that are suitable to the magazine's profile, without concern for a particular public, profit, or popularity. He is neither seen as a villain nor achieves the status of a hero in his quest for the truth. His role becomes essential in the narrative after opening an interactive space for journalism in the magazine.

Ginny Potter, a member of the Weasley family and Harry's girlfriend, appears in books, movies, and interactive story as a young student of magic and wizardry at Hogwarts. It is only in the *Daily Prophet* section of the old *Pottermore* that she appears as an adult and a professional journalist. Ginny is the newspaper's sports correspondent and has sufficient experience to cover alone an event like the Quidditch World Cup. Since she is characterized as a journalist only in this section of *Pottermore*, we have opted not to categorize her along with the data collection instrument, which focused on the books, movies, and interactive story, where the character appears as a teenager.

There is also the figure of the *Daily Prophet* photographer. Firstly, he is not named, but, as he partners up with Skeeter, we discover that his name is

Bozo. He appears only in punctual moments in the books, as well as the movies, with 20 mentions total, and does not appear in the interactive story.

In the sixth volume of the series, in the movie as well as in the book, we have the first and only mention of Barnabas Cuffe, editor of the *Daily Prophet*, through the speech of another character. Generic reporters and photographers of the wizarding world, without identification of which vehicle they work for, appear in the movies in interview scenes with members of the Ministry of Magic. They appear taking pictures and asking questions, but their actions are not central to the plot. Only one of them asks a question that can be heard by the viewer, becoming a brief character in the movie.

Journalists appear in the corpus in three main contexts, which represent 216 out of 241 mentions. The first context is in the characters' speech, which demonstrates the interaction of journalists with the characters as well as the fact that the professionals become topic of conversation among them, who talk about news they have reported as well as their professional conduct. The second indicates the active role of journalists in the narrative, who appear as central characters in the scene, interacting with others and fulfilling their professional function. The third context is regarding their presence in the environment/scenery, but as supporting characters.

The professional ethos—to be a journalist and to work with journalism—permeates journalists' actions and behaviors in the series, encompassing the journalistic activity and creating the mythology around professionals and the journalistic field. The myth of the scoop, with a possibility of professional differentiation and the conquest of notoriety, appears not only as a merit to the journalist, but also to their communication vehicle, that can declare having exclusivity on the story. The myth of journalism as a big adventure and of the journalist as the responsible for the quest for the truth are also present in the series.

Specialis Revelio: *Social Function*

Journalism exists in a social context: by necessity, citizens and societies depend on accurate and reliable accounts of events (Kovach & Rosenstiel, 2014). In the transmedia narrative, journalism incorporates different social functions in muggle and wizarding realities, rooted in its legitimacy as a social institution capable of informing an audience and narrating everyday life events. The stories of fictional journalism are important not only to the characters, but also to the development of the narrative. The profession as depicted by Rowling takes information to its readers, spectators and fictional listeners, and has become essential for the construction of the characters' daily lives and for the unfolding of the narrative.

By analyzing of the presence of journalism in our *corpus*, we have mapped eleven functions attributed to the profession. These functions sometimes overlap and, at times, some of the roles credited to journalism become more relevant than others. Through all of them, however, the importance of the profession for the development of the society in which it is inserted can be perceived—whether in the real or fictional dimension.

The first function is *to inform*, as journalism exists because we need a vehicle specialized in the transmission of news (Miguel, 1999). Journalism is shaped by the role of informing the public—to seek the truth and to publish it, based on the reality of the facts and according to the social and collective interest.

In all the *corpus*, journalism corresponds to the characters' information needs, who seek the media to learn what is happening: "It's been all over the *Daily Prophet*, but I don't suppose you get that with the muggles" (Rowling, 1998, p. 107). Harry, for example, while isolated from the wizarding world and without a signature of the *Daily Prophet*, has no way of knowing the facts of magical reality.

The characters' concern for the lack of information when the media would stop publishing news on a subject also runs through the series. The difference that vehicles make when it comes to information can be noticed in characters' speech: "The Ministry's leaning heavy on the *Daily Prophet* not to report any of what they're calling Dumbledore's rumor-mongering, so most of the Wizarding community are completely unaware anything's happened […]" (Rowling, 2003, p. 9). It is only possible for the public to know of an event once it is disclosed in the media.

The second is to *contextualize, to interpret and explain reality*, as it is the means of communication that provide people with knowledge of the world, while the news helps them select, prioritize, understand and organize their daily life events. Journalism is expected not only to report the truth of events, but also to narrate them in a way that connects them to the public: contextualize and explain their meaning to the society in which it is embedded (Kovach & Rosenstiel, 2014).

The characters look at the news they have access to as accounts of reality and there is an expectation of reciprocity for this reliance on journalism. They follow the news believing they are an index of reality and that journalists will not cross the border between reality and fiction. More than being informed, the characters also seek the means of communication to understand the events around them.

To *motivate public debate* is the third and it relations to the ability of communication vehicles to set the topics people will talk about (Miguel, 1999) and allow an interaction between the characters, even those who were not previously known. In *Harry Potter*, what would be publicized in media is what people know about the subjects, which generates debate among wizards and muggles alike. Media provide the information necessary for the characters to give their opinions about events, discuss their perceptions, criticize, and reach agreements.

Monitoring powers is the fourth, as to speak of journalism is to speak of its ability to watch over other powers while delivering relevant information to the public according to their rights and needs. In the beginning of Rowling's series, when there are no conflicts of power within the wizarding society, media manage to efficiently fulfill their function of overseeing the government, represented in this case by the Ministry of Magic. The *Daily Prophet* reports on what was happening in the Ministry, mainly regarding its faults.

However, when conflicts arise, the government influences journalism. The pressures of the State on the media are clear throughout the story, and they prevent journalism from fulfilling its function of watching over the powers. The imperative of truth and public interest that governs journalism is abandoned when the government uses its resources to manage and to influence what communication vehicles reproduce.

If journalism should serve as an independent monitor of power (Kovach & Rosenstiel, 2014), the profession shows how clashes in society's power spheres can make it a complex function. The imperatives of truth and public interest should prevail over private interests, but this does not always happen, as Rowling's story rightly exemplifies.

The fifth function is to *form a social frame of reference*, considering that journalism is a discourse capable of representing and presenting a social frame of reference, which inserts us into the world. Media allow us to have a shared present; the present moment of different places and different people and their information become simultaneous—the lived world is shared (Karam, 2005).

In Rowling's story, journalism becomes the reference of reality and the profession allows everyone to have access to the same information, which links them together, bridging the muggle and the wizarding worlds. The social present of the wizards sometimes coincides with the muggles,' and sometimes it could not be further apart. Wizards, for the most part, show no interest in non-magical reality, and muggles are mostly ignorant of the existence of wizards. The conflict is present for wizards like Harry and Hermione, who live with non-magical families. Media become essential so that both can share the social presents to which they are linked.

To *guide how to live in the world* is the sixth social function, as journalism produces knowledge about the events of the world. The profession establishes rules for the normality or abnormality of a society through news stories (Motta, 2003). Journalism is an intrinsic part of Rowling's story, since the means of communication in Harry Potter's fictional universe become a way of explaining its logic, practices, and institutions; guiding the issues to be discussed, defining what is important to know in order to live with the other wizards.

Perceptions about Harry, for example, change with the different political contexts of society—from hero to liar, to hero again, then to fugitive and public enemy. The changes in Harry's image are a process that pervades the public mentality and suffers pressure by media. The vehicles are able to reinforce Harry's image at each moment, to make it consistent with the current opinion on the boy, one which media have also helped to form.

The seventh is to *organize the reader's (listener, spectator) time in everyday life*. We consider that journalism strengthens the desire for novelties and the insertion of the present in everyday life. It creates cultural and social habits with a temporal component, stimulating the interaction between people. In *Harry Potter*, in both muggle and wizarding societies, the means of communication become a way of building a periodic temporality in the private and public spheres, and monitoring media becomes a habit. At Hogwarts, for example, at breakfast, thousands of owls enter the Great Hall and distribute newspapers and magazines to the students, as well as letters that come from their homes with news.

Keeping society together is the eighth social function because of the way social life is organized and its demands for information. Journalism, within the wizarding society, is an aggregating element, a common reference for community integration. This present is fluid, sometimes conflicting, but it is capable of mobilizing public opinion.

In the fictional public sphere, the path traveled by the wizarding society depicts the aggregating capacity of journalism to oscillate, sometimes representing a voice that emerges from the State, sometimes a voice that starts from the general climate that permeates the population.

While the profession's capability to keep the society together seems undisputed, its aggregating potential, of creating a consonance in the wizarding community, is not always positive. Voldemort, who is in control of media for about a year, is able to change the public opinion about Harry, the Ministry's functions, and the mudbloods. His methods are grotesque, totalitarian, but he succeeds because media do not resist government pressure, and even those means operating on the margins of society fail to reach the public.

Journalism is able to establish pillars, principles, guidelines, and symbols that become consensual in the wizarding society. It establishes security, guarantees understanding and interprets everyday life. Of course, there will not be absolute unanimity, but as long as the majority is able to gather around these truths, the community will be stable.

The ninth social function is *to instruct and educate readers (listeners, spectators)* as "[...] journalism is, or should be, or should be expected to be, a factor of permanent education of the public" (Bucci, 2000, p. 49[2]). Journalistic information mediates the production of other sectors, transforms their events into facts of public interest that will be debated within the society (Karam, 2004), circulating knowledge from different fields and becoming a producer of knowledge.

In Rowling's narrative, the characters become aware of the facts as they are published in media. The profession broadens the conceptual and practical universe of individuals and society as a whole (Karam, 2005) and, from the news, the characters learn to deal with the events of their daily lives. Especially for those wizards who come from muggle families, journalism becomes a way of learning and internalizing the various elements that make up the wizarding reality—from the sport Quidditch to the course of political life in the Ministry of Magic.

To *add value to people, objects and institutions* is the tenth, considering that journalism gains power of speech in society, choosing themes, presenting relevant facts and assisting in setting values, as well as producing social credit by allowing some individuals to occupy positions of authority in certain fields (Miguel, 1999). By aggregating and disseminating information, journalism assumes a position of credibility and prestige.

Characters have in journalism a reference to establish what is important, good or trustworthy, believing what is said by media to formulate their opinions and make their choices. This is also related to more significant issues, such as the clash of information about the battle against Voldemort, and more trivial activities, such as choosing a broom to play Quidditch, for example.

The eleventh social function is *to entertain*. The means of communication play a role in occupying people's free time and leisure (Dejavite, 2007). Journalism can simultaneously deliver to the public content that provides a service, information and entertainment. There is also news with sellable subjects, light themes that instigate curiosity in both dimensions, wizarding and muggle.

Media publish the news because the public is interested in it and creates experiences of aesthetic satisfaction for those who accompany it, helping in the interpretation of their own lives (Schudson, 2010). In *Harry Potter*, the public cares about what concerns them—they want to participate and tell their own lives to themselves and to those who live with them. Information may not be considered serious, but it is still important for social cohesion, insofar as it incite our yearning, it allows us to vent our frustrations, and feed our imagination (Dejavite, 2007).

Legilimens: *Professional Ethos*

Information and journalism imply an ethical, moral and deontological reflection that systematically analyzes the relations between the media and its public. In this context, journalism ethos is a kind of profession awareness that shapes the values that guide professionals in the choices they face in their day-to-day lives at work.

We have mapped four professional profiles. At different moments in history, professionals can assume different profiles according to their personal and social context. While there are professional principles that permeate these profiles, the current investigation allowed us to realize that the ethos is not unique or immutable. In Rowling's narrative, the ethos is fluid and plural, so that different journalists represent diverse ways of practicing the profession.

The first profile is the *unscrupulous journalist*, incorporated by Rita Skeeter, who, to write her news, goes from spying on people in her *animagus*[3] form of a beetle to sensationalism or even inventing stories. Her profession and the communication vehicles for which she writes define her identity. Skeeter assumes that when working for a newspaper, she receives recognition before the wizarding community: "Hello. I'm Rita Skeeter. I write for the *Daily Prophet*. But of course you know that?" (Heyman & Newell, 2005).

Journalists operate a selection of events and a discursive reconstruction of these events that they select as news (Traquina, 2008). Guided by journalistic values, the news is an interpretation of the journalist, which is taken to the extreme by Skeeter: "[...] Reckon something's up? Think we should do a bit of digging? Disgraced Ex-Head of Magical Sports, Ludo Bagman ... snappy start to sentence, Bozo—we just need to find a story to fit it—" (Rowling, 2001, p. 391). The professional ethos is capable of driving the journalist to follow the ideal of the profession in their commitment to the truth and their duty to the public interest (BUCCI, 2000). However, when prestige and the possibility of visibility overlap with the professional's ethical ideology, the idea of disregarding the truth and harming the reputation of others seems acceptable to Skeeter. One of journalism's myths, getting the scoop, becomes central in the journalist's moral choices.

At the first possibility of a scoop, Skeeter did not care how she received the information or who was being harmed in the process. She gets her great story in finding out that Hagrid's mother was a giantess, beings known to be evil and rabid in the wizarding world. Hagrid, as a Hogwarts teacher, has notoriety, which makes the fact that he possesses blood from a hated and feared creature among the wizards even more shocking.

> DUMBLEDORE'S GIANT MISTAKE. [...] As if this were not enough, the *Daily Prophet* has now unearthed evidence that Hagrid is not—as he has always pre-

tended—a pure-blood wizard [...]. His mother, we can exclusively reveal, is none other than the giantess Fridwulfa [Rowling, 2001, pp. 380–382].

In the story, those who had met Hagrid know that, though his mother was the giantess Fridwulfa, he is a kind man and not vicious because of his heritage, as said by Skeeter. However, that does not matter to the journalist, since publishing an exclusive story gives her prestige and audience. The profession confers her legitimacy to inform, and until proven that she is, in fact, lying, the public, for the most part, continues to believe whatever her news stories say. Skeeter is a model of journalistic incompetence that, regardless of having the technical ability to investigate present and immediate reality, choose to reproduce incomplete and deformed information. Her personal interests surpass the public rights to information.

The *romantic journalist* is the second profile, identified by Xenophilius Lovegood, inserted into the narrative as Skeeter's antithesis. Ruled by his ethical and moral principles, Lovegood, although eccentric, defends the public interest and the duty of journalism to inform people about what they need to know. The character is known mainly through his daughter Luna's descriptions to her colleagues. Initially, as the owner of the magazine *The Quibbler*, the journalist is considered to be a reporter without credibility, but committed to opening a space for alternative features:

"*The Quibbler*'s rubbish, everyone knows that." "Excuse me," said Luna; [...] "My father's the editor" [Rowling, 2003, p. 192].

"He publishes important stories that he thinks the public needs to know. He doesn't care about making money" [Rowling, 2003, p. 568].

With a change of context in the magical world, the position of communication vehicles and journalists alters. Lovegood becomes a benchmark for journalists committed to the truth who struggle to keep the public informed. Loyalty to citizens is the most important possession an editor can have. It is what makes the content of their news reliable (Kovach & Rosenstiel, 2014). A journalist must not be influenced by politicians, advertisers or whatever external factors might affect his work. Lovegood, even under extreme government pressure to lie about Harry Potter, keeps his convictions despite being retaliated against.

The third profile is the *professional journalist*, incorporated by Ginny Potter, who appears as a journalist only in the old version of the website *Pottermore*. She is a reporter for the main wizarding community vehicle, the *Daily Prophet*, in the sports section. Faced with corporate and commercial pressures, her character is based on the ethical demands of the profession, bringing news that appeals to the public, but that is also accurate and respects the imperative of truth.

Ginny, when confronted with the possibility of seeing news published with incorrect facts, makes a point of correcting them, of fulfilling her duty to the public, of giving them truthful information. The journalist, for example, copiously corrects her colleague Skeeter throughout the coverage of the Quidditch World Cup final: "[…] my colleague, Ginny Potter, is approaching me, no doubt with another tedious correc…" (Rowling, 2014b, p. 8). Ginny's ideology is sustained by her professional duty to the truth (Cornu, 1994), perceiving information as a public right, managing, as proposed by Bucci (2000), to give more importance to the social function of her profession than to commercial one.

The *biased journalist* is the fourth profile, moldable and manipulated by the government; it does not appear through a specific character, but incorporates the narrative in the *Daily Prophet*. The journalists easily yield to the pressures of the government, which determines what will be published and how. Professionals, when presenting themselves as journalists, members of a communication vehicle, gain prestige and credibility before the public. They are, however, imbued with a responsibility in the interests of society. In posing as a reporter for the *Daily Prophet*, for example, the character already assumes a superiority towards the others, in the sense of being there representing an important vehicle that will be responsible for news read by thousands of people. But by submitting to the wishes of the Ministry of Magic, the journalists of the *Daily Prophet* betray their commitment to the public and fail to fulfill their function of monitoring the powers and motivating a full public debate.

Nox

The connection between the different social functions that journalism fulfills in a society is indissoluble, as all of them assume the profession is a social institution, endowed with the legitimacy and credibility to mediate reality and inform the public about what they need to know about their everyday lives. The ethos that pervades journalists implies how these functions are fulfilled—and whether they are, indeed, fulfilled.

The different profiles of journalists featured demonstrate that each professional is responsible for their journalistic work, and the way they choose to enter journalism determines their commitment to the social functions that the profession is capable of fulfilling. Through the universe built on different platforms, when a character searches for the news, they will want a truthful account, they will want to know what is happening in the world and will rely on journalism to provide them without distorting the facts. A relationship is formed between the public and the media, in which the former has the choice of renewing the link it forms with journalism.

There is fluidity in the spaces occupied by fictional journalism in Rowling's transmedia narrative, which shows that the profession is changeable, subject to the context in which it is inserted. The discussions of the public sphere guide journalism and vice versa—a circle is formed marked by the importance of information for the development of life in society. When the context of the magical world changes, the position of vehicles and journalists also change, as, according to Schudson (2010), journalism not only registers social changes, but also becomes part of them.

Notes

1. For the purpose of this work, we analyzed *Pottermore*'s old version, the *Daily Prophet* section and the interactive story available up to September 2015. We chose this version of the website because it truly transformed the *Harry Potter* series into a transmedia franchise, and prioritized an interactive version of the wizard's story. The current *Pottermore*, though still possessing new information regarding the story, is no longer centered on the plot—it now features current news regarding the franchise, quizzes, and lists.

2. Translated by the authors.

3. A witch or wizard who can morph him or herself into an animal.

References

Bardin, L. (2006). *Análise de conteúdo.* São Paulo: Edições 70.
Barthes, R. (1977). Introduction to the structural analysis of narratives. In *Image-music-text.* London: Fontana.
Bucci, E. (2000). *Sobre ética e imprensa.* São Paulo: Companhia das Letras.
Cornu, D. (1994). *Jornalismo e verdade.* Lisbon: Instituto Piaget.
Dejavite, F.A. (2015, October 20). A notícia light e o jornalismo de infotenimento. In *Congresso Brasileiro de Ciências da Comunicação, 30,* 2007, Santos. Anais.... Santos: Intercom, 2007. Retrieved from https://goo.gl/vUMZnk.
Ehrlich, M.C. (2004). *Journalism in the movies.* Urbana: University of Illinois Press.
Ehrlich, M.C. (2009). *Studying the journalist in popular culture.* [S.I.]. Retrieved from https://goo.gl/xAtNov.
Freeman, M. (2017). *Historicising transmedia storytelling: Early twentieth-century transmedia story worlds.* New York: Routledge.
Hazel, P. (2007). Narrative: An introduction. (Unpublished). Retrieved from http://www.paulhazel.com/blog/Introduction_To_Narrative.pdf.
Heyman, D. (Producer), & Columbus, C. (Director) (2001). *Harry Potter and the philosopher's Stone.* [Motion Picture] UK, USA: Warner Bros. Pictures.
Heyman, D. (Producer), & Columbus, C. (Director) (2002). *Harry Potter and the Chamber of Secrets.* [Motion Picture] UK, USA: Warner Bros. Pictures.
Heyman, D. (Producer), Columbus, C. (Producer), Radcliffe, M. (Producer), & Cuarón, A. (Director) (2004). *Harry Potter and the Prisoner of Azkaban.* [Motion Picture] UK, USA: Warner Bros. Pictures.
Heyman, D. (Producer), & Newell, M. (Director) (2005). *Harry Potter and the Goblet of Fire.* [Motion Picture] UK, USA: Warner Bros. Pictures.
Heyman, D. (Producer), Barron, D. (Producer), & Yates, D. (Director) (2007). *Harry Potter and the Order of the Phoenix.* [Motion Picture] UK, USA: Warner Bros. Pictures.
Heyman, D. (Producer), Barron, D. (Producer), & Yates, D. (Director) (2009). *Harry Potter and the Half-Blood Prince.* [Motion Picture] UK, USA: Warner Bros. Pictures.
Heyman, D. (Producer), Barron, D. (Producer), Rowling, J.K. (Producer), & Yates, D. (Director) (2010). *Harry Potter and the Deathly Hollows—Part 1.* [Motion Picture] UK, USA: Warner Bros. Pictures.
Heyman, D. (Producer), Barron, D. (Producer), Rowling, J.K. (Producer), & Yates, D. (Director) (2011). *Harry Potter and the Deathly Hollows—Part 2.* [Motion Picture] UK, USA: Warner Bros. Pictures.

Jenkins, H. (2009). *Cultura da convergência*. 2d ed. São Paulo: Aleph.
Karam, F.J.C. (2004). *A ética jornalística e o interesse público*. São Paulo: Summus.
Karam, F.J.C. (2005). O presente possível do jornalismo. *Estudos em Jornalismo e Mídia, Florianópolis, 2*(2), pp. 75–81. Retrieved from https://periodicos.ufsc.br/index.php/jornalismo/article/view/2217/3934
Kovach, B.; Rosenstiel, T. (2014). *The elements of journalism: What newspeople should know the public should expect*. New York: Crown.
Miguel, L.F. (1999). O jornalismo como sistema perito. *Tempo Social: Revista de Sociologia da USP, São Paulo, 11*(1), pp. 197–208. Retrieved from https://www.revistas.usp.br/ts/article/view/12301/14078
Motta, L.G. (2015, June 3). Sobre o trabalho simbólico da notícia. In: *Encontro Anual da Compos, 13*, 2003, Recife. Anais.... Recife: Compós, 2003. Retrieved from http://www.compos.org.br/data/biblioteca_921.pdf.
Pottermore. (2015, March 26). [Internet]. Retrieved from https://www.pottermore.com/en-us/.
Rowling, J.K. (1998). *Harry Potter and the philosopher's stone*. New York: Scholastic.
Rowling, J.K. (2000). *Harry Potter and the prisoner of Azkaban*. London: Bloomsbury.
Rowling, J.K. (2001). *Harry Potter and the goblet of fire*. London: Bloomsbury.
Rowling, J.K. (2003). *Harry Potter and the order of the phoenix*. New York: Scholastic.
Rowling, J.K. (2004). *Harry Potter and the chamber of secrets*. London: Bloomsbury.
Rowling, J.K. (2005). *Harry Potter and the half-blood prince*. New York: Scholastic.
Rowling, J.K. (2007). *Harry Potter and the deathly hallows*. London: Bloomsbury.
Rowling, J.K. (2015, March 24). Brazil versus Wales. *Pottermore* [Internet]. London, 2014a. Retrieved from https://goo.gl/a0tRFT
Rowling, J.K. (2015, March 24). Wales versus Germany. *Pottermore* [Internet]. London, 2014b. Retrieved from https://goo.gl/7u8LCW
Saltzman, J. (2005). *Analyzing the images of the journalist in popular culture: A unique method of studying the public's perception of its journalists and the news media*. [S.I.]. Retrieved from https://goo.gl/0CxGiF
Samoy, K.S. (2015). *How journalism ethics are portrayed in recent fictional television dramas*. 2015. 42 f. Conclusion paper (Undergraduate)—University of Arizona. Honors College, Journalism, Tucson (AZ).
Schudson, M. (2010). *Descobrindo a notícia: Uma história social dos jornais dos Estados Unidos*. Petrópolis (RJ): Vozes.
Scolari, C.A., Freeman, M., & Bertetti, P. (2014). *Transmedia archaeology: Storytelling in the borderlines of science fiction, comics and pulp magazines*. London: Palgrave Macmillan.
Traquina, N. (2008). *Teorias do jornalismo: A tribo jornalística—Uma comunidade interpretativa transnacional*. Vol. 2. Florianópolis: Insular.

Supplement or Supplant?
How Fan Editors Contribute to Fictional Universes

BRIAN P. BERNARD *and*
KIMBERLY D. MARTINEZ

The analysis provided in this essay follows from two primary assumptions. First, fans are not generally members of a single fan community. Being a Harry Potter fan does not preclude one from also being a Star Wars fan, for example. Second, contributing fans are generally multi-talented. A contributing member of a fan community could participate in cosplay or write fan fiction (or both). From these two assumptions, it follows that every piece of fan art has an opportunity cost, and each fan that chooses to produce a piece of art for that particular source material could have alternatively spent their time producing in a different artistic medium or creating for a different fan community.

Jenkins, Clinton, Purushotma, Robison & Weigel (2009) describe participatory culture as worthy of encouragement, and cite many new technological forms it can take, such as game modding and machinima, that are especially popular with young audiences. It may seem surprising then that one technological expression of fandom, fan editing (often "fanediting"), has not shown to be very popular among one of the largest fan populations, Harry Potter. This essay will analyze prototypical fan edited movies of major fictional movie franchises (Harry Potter, Star Wars, Star Trek, and Lord of the Rings) as well as some other forms of Harry Potter fan participation to consider possible motivations leading to such a difference in each franchise's level of participation in fan editing. The following analysis indicates that Harry Potter fandom focuses more on supplementing their fictional universe than other franchises which have significant portions of their fandom interested in supplanting their movies. This suggests that Harry Potter fans are satisfied with the film franchise as a whole and view it as an alternative (to the novels) canonical source that they are hesitant to change.

An Introduction to Fan Editing

The experience of viewing a fan edit can be described as re-watching a movie for the first time. Fan edits are full length movies that alter the original source material, but unlike a director's cut or officially released unrated version, fan edits are created by fans. Some are similar to feature length remix videos and they often appeal to the same media-literate creators and participatory audiences described in Booth (2012). This derivative art form also shares similarities with fan fiction, fan films, and machinima, but with one significant restriction. A fan editor does not typically create new original material, only edits existing, released content. In this way, it is more similar to vidding (setting clips from TV shows and movies to music, usually of similar duration to a music video). Middleton (2012) noted that the term "remix video" was insufficiently vague and failed to capture the vast differences between works that fit under such an umbrella term. Similarly, "fan edit" can also describe a wide variety of edited works.

Out of practicality, the edited films discussed in this essay are limited almost entirely to those listed in the *Internet Fanedit Database* (https://ifdb.fanedit.org/). Prior to listing any released edits in the database, IFDB requires editors to undergo a peer review process in which their edit is reviewed by an experienced editor, a member of the Fanedit.org Academy, who will provide them with detailed feedback. Only after this feedback has been fully addressed and all audio, visual, narrative or other flaws have been corrected will the editor be able to create a listing for their film. It should be noted though that this quality control does not resemble the checks against violation of canon as described by Mackey & McClay (2008) that is present in some online fan fiction communities. This central repository and peer review system are main reasons why fan edited films are the focus of this essay as opposed to shorter vids, which are largely uncatalogued and have much wider variation in quality, making comparisons between franchises difficult. As of August 2017, IFDB lists 272 approved editors, who have released a total of 1,189 fan edits that serve as the basis for discussion in this essay.

Compared to fan fiction, fan films, cosplay and a number of other forms of fan artwork, fan editing is a relatively new genre. It rose to popularity following the 2000 release of *Star Wars Episode I.I: The Phantom Edit* by The Phantom Editor [identified in Greenberg (2001) as Mike J. Nichols] a fan edit of *Star Wars Episode I: The Phantom Menace*. Along with the publicity given to this and other edits, this timeframe also reached a tipping point in cost and availability of editing hardware and software, which was previously only accessible to movie studios and editing professionals. By the mid–2000s, consumers had commercial editions of non-linear editing (NLE) software like Sony Vegas, Adobe Premier, and Apple's Final Cut that could be operated on personal computers, as well as peer-to-peer file sharing distribution methods like BitTorrent, which combined to eliminate the largest barriers to entry.

IFDB sorts fan edits into 8 different categories, the largest two of which are FanFix and FanMix. Similar to the description of fan art in Borojević (2016), both of these genres of fan edits arise from fan editors asking, "What if?" and then creating their new circumstances and releasing a revised movie to answer the question. FanFixes are generally collections of minor edits such as reordering scenes, removing lines of dialogue or performing color correction in order to polish the viewing experience. A classic example of a FanFix is the previously mentioned *The Phantom Edit*. Example changes made in this edit are the removal of most of Jar Jar Binks' physical comedy, as well as the removal of a lot of young Anakin Skywalker's dialogue. Jones (2006) describes Machinima as transformative play since its creators generate new media vastly different than anything intended by the game's original programmers. FanMixes are often similarly creative and transformative by merging multiple movies into a single film, significantly altering or removing a character, or changing the soundtrack of the original film. A successful example of a FanMix is *The Jigsaw Files* by Sunarep, which combines the backstory that is told in pieces as flashbacks throughout the first 6 Saw movies, into a standalone film. The similarity to mashups created by music fans are obvious and motivations and final products are often comparable between these art forms. There is an important motivational distinction between FanFixes and FanMixes. FanFixes are generally attempts to improve the original movie (by some measure) and to potentially serve as a replacement. FanMixes are generally attempts to change the original, often in such a transformative way that comparisons to the original such as better or worse do not even make sense.

There is quite a bit of loaded language in this discussion, especially "fix," "replace," "supplant," and similar descriptors for the motivation of some edited works. Though Mason (2008) portrays piracy as inevitable and an important source of innovation, his view of fan editors is that of a disgruntled fan. Jensen (1992) notes the common perception of fans as a *them*, not an *us*, and she would likely agree that modern fan editors would be similarly likely to be perceived as potential obsessed fanatics. Phillips (2012, p. 5.1) describes fan editors as using "the methods of content producers to subvert those very producers." He goes on to describe the unease and sometimes hostility that greet fan edits for changing canonical works. Similar to Wille (2014), and based on interactions with fan editors themselves on sites like Fanedit.org, we would reject this negative connotation of fan editing. Such a view by fan editors would be inherently self-defeating. Above all, fan editors are, by definition, fans, and editing is primarily a participatory and active part of fandom. Turk & Johnson (2012, p. 1.3) describe this duality as "while fan creators *are* audiences, they also *have* audiences," and Tryon (2012, p. 176) notes that the Emmy-Award-winning *Star Wars Uncut*, a fan film that is a shot for shot remake of *Star Wars Episode IV: A New Hope*, "gleefully displays its collaborative and amateur origins." Even fan edits that strive to "fix" an original film are often similar participatory acts of fandom and not necessarily a rejection of the original artists' efforts. Wille (2014, p. 5.1) recommends fan editors "be recognized primarily for their creative qualities" and their "contributions to an emerging culture of fluid media." So while this essay uses many loaded terms, in this context, "supplant" and others like it should not be misinterpreted as pejorative, but merely as an expedient (over?)simplification.

Famous authors each have their own opinion on copyright of their works with regard to fan fiction. George R.R. Martin (2010) has announced that he opposes fan fiction inspired by his novels for a variety of personal, legal, and other reasons. However, as reported by Waters (2004), J.K. Rowling has indicated (through her publishing company's spokesman) that she is pleased that so many of her fans participate in this avenue of fandom, though she does request that these works not be sold and that they remain appropriate for young readers by avoiding adult themes. Like fan fiction, fan editing's legality rests on whether or not it is protected by Fair Use. Like many sampling and mashup musical artists listed in a collected bibliography by Grobelny (2008) or the fan film makers described in Young (2008), it is possible that nearly all fan edits within the category of FanFix are not protected by Fair Use. CleanFlicks ran a business that removed objectionable content from movies like *Titanic* then rented and sold the edited versions. They lost their court case in 2006 and were forced to shut down, and a good description of the case can be found in Williams (2005). Lothian (2009) accurately identifies what is likely to be the primary issue for non-profit fan videos (and similarly fan edits) as the degree to which the derivative work is transformative. It is possible that some of the more creative FanMixes could meet this threshold; however, no fan editor has yet defended the copyright for their derivative artwork in court, so no specific precedent exists as to whether the law can distinguish between non-profit fan edits and for-profit companies like CleanFlicks.

Harry Potter Fan Edits

Of the 10 full-length fan edits of the Harry Potter franchise, 6 are listed in the IFDB database as FanFixes and 4 are categorized as Extended Editions, another category of fan edit with a primary purpose of re-inserting deleted scenes (included as bonus features on the commercially released Blu-ray or DVD releases) into the main feature to provide a single comprehensive viewing experience. Extended Editions typically contain only minor changes to the main movie besides reinserting these additional scenes.

Harry Potter and the Chamber of Secrets: Revisited (CoS-Revisited) by fan editor Q2 and *Harry Potter and the Half-Blood Prince—Fanedit* (HBP-Fanedit) by fan editor Threepkiller were both rated above 9.0/10.0 in IFDB. Viewers of the original films will note that SS and CoS were both directed by Chris Columbus, and the overall tone of the film series changed significantly when Alfonso Cuarón directed PoA. The listing for CoS-Revisited highlights new sound effects, music, and color, as well as storyline adjustments to add more of the grit present in the books and to better match the rest of the franchise. HBP-Fanedit similarly removes the green colored hue that accompanies many scenes in the original film and eliminates awkward, out of character dialogue and behavior. It also re-inserts several deleted scenes to be more loyal to the book's characters, as well as create a better fit for the movie in relation to the rest of the franchise. The common thread connecting these two edits is that their primary purpose isn't to objectively improve each film on their individual merits, but rather to make each film more closely match the narrative, visual and audio style of the other films in the franchise.

The next three full length Harry Potter fan edits were all reviewed with ratings below 9.0/10.0 in IFDB. Interestingly, these three fan edits all make more dramatic changes to the narrative than CoS:Revisited and HBP-Fanedit by removing more scenes and subplots. These fan edits are *Harry Potter and the Sorcerer's Stone: Revisited* (SS-Revisited) by fan editor Andreas, *Harry Potter and the Half-Blood Prince: Pure-Blood Edition* (HBP-Pure-Blood) by fan editor Shortround24, and *Harry Potter and the Deathly Hallows Part 1: The 90 Minute Wicked Edition* (DH1-Wicked) by fan editor AEmovieguy.

Similar to the previously described fan edits, SS-Revisited aims to match the visual style and tone of the later Harry Potter movies. However, its intention further states the goal to make the film better paced and more interesting to watch. One of many cuts made in this fan edit is removing the opening sequence of Dumbledore, McGonagall, and Hagrid delivering baby Harry to the Dursleys so that the audience discovers the existence of magic along with Harry as the story unfolds. Reviewers commented that some of these deviations from the book made the fan edit more difficult to watch. Shortround24's stated intention for HBP-Pure-Blood is to make it more enjoyable, not to make it closer to the book. HBP-Pure-Blood eliminates most love story elements present in the sixth film including most Cormac/Hermione interactions and some Ron/Lavender interactions, resulting in a more serious tone throughout the movie. Numerous scenes such as the waitress scene, and discussions with both Dumbledore and Hermione regarding Harry's love life were also removed.

The most polarizing Harry Potter fan edit is DH1-Wicked, which implemented extensive cuts, removing over a quarter of the original film to reach its final runtime. AEmovieguy removes "four inconsequential subplots" (Bathilda Bagshot, Godric's Hollow, Locket's Negative Properties, and Ron Leaving) and most of the camping scenes. The fan editor also claims to create a more exciting approach to the first part of *Deathly Hallows*. Multiple reviewers left extensive comments praising the cuts and explaining how they thought that each one improved the film or fixed a shortcoming in the original, and yet all also reached the same conclusion, that they enjoyed the edit, but still preferred the theatrical version.

There are no FanMix style fan edits currently listed in IFDB, but Roane and Bernard (2017) described a Harry Potter FanMix in-the-works that is worth mentioning here to demonstrate the creative potential of this artistic medium. *Harry Potter and the Boy Who Never Lived Part 1* (HP-BWNL) by RollWave anticipates a 2018 release and will mix scenes from a number of Harry Potter films as well as dialogue from the audiobooks in order to show a year at Hogwarts where the character Harry Potter is entirely absent. This will offer a radically different viewing experience by creating an alternate history in which Snape never alienated Lily, and therefore Harry Potter was never born. One released Harry Potter fan edit that could have been categorized as a FanMix and is one of the most highly praised Harry Potter fan edits (Winner of the Fanedit.org Favorite Edit of the Month in February 2016) makes many of the same changes as DH1:Wicked, and takes them even further. *Harry Potter and the Deathly Hallows* (DH-Q2) by fan editor Q2 removes nearly all scenes from DH1 and DH2 not directly related to Harry's quest to destroy the horcruxes (86 minutes cut in total) in order to combine DH1 and DH2 into a single 3-hour film. A simple psychological change in presentation made the difference to viewers. Changing DH1 alone was not enough to cause viewers to want to replace the theatrical version, but when DH2 was also changed, many fans were willing to accept the cuts as necessary in order to combine the two films into a runtime that is still watchable in a single sitting (not that Harry Potter fans aren't willing to sit through 5+ hour movie marathons). It should also be noted that all reviewers were impressed by the technical quality of the audio and visual editing of DH-Q2, and it is likely that this positively affected their ratings.

After examining the variations and cuts made to the Harry Potter fan edits, one notices that these changes are generally derived from some desire to do one or more of the following: insert deleted scenes to create a more complete volume, remove less significant subplots, rework aesthetic effects to better fit in relation to the rest of the franchise, or combine films to create a new viewing experience. Thus, fans choosing to edit the Harry Potter franchise have shown mixed tendencies in the question of supplement or supplant as a motivation. The next sections analyze the fan edits created for peer franchises and some stark differences are noted.

Harry Potter's Peer Franchises

The most direct comparison to the Harry Potter franchise is the Lord of the Rings (LOTR). Both franchises produced a series of big-budget fantasy films adapted from a successful series of novels and have enormous fan bases. Both the books and films were commercially successful and highly rated by audiences.

Star Trek also has a very large fan base, and some would argue that Star Trek is most responsible for popularizing the fan fiction genre of writing. Though not adapted from novels, or even strictly speaking adapted from the TV shows, the TV shows did create a certain level of expectation for the films that is in many ways comparable to the expectations a fan would have from a direct novel-to-movie adaptation. Another franchise with fandom that exceeds Harry Potter in many areas is Star Wars, and while the Star Wars films are all original screenplays, similar to Star Trek, Collins (1977) describes *Star Wars Episode IV: A New Hope* as visual literature, and in many ways the original trilogy did set a certain precedent that created a level of expectation for the prequel trilogy in the minds of fans that is comparable to a fan's expectations for an adapted screenplay. The re-released versions of the original trilogy could themselves be considered adaptations of the original releases several decades earlier.

IFDB lists 35 full length fan edits for the Lord of the Rings franchise, 27 FanFix and 8 FanMix. Star Trek has 25 full length fan edits listed, 19 FanFix, 1 FanMix, 3 Special Projects and 5 TV-to-Movie. The TV-to Movie categorization indicates that multiple episodes of the TV series were combined to create a single film-length, self-contained viewing experience. Star Wars has had over 10 times the number of fan edits as the Harry Potter series, with 131 full-length fan edits including 68 FanFixes, 24 FanMixes, 4 Extended Editions, 28 Preservations and Special Projects, and 7 TV-to Movie. The Preservations and Special Projects category here primarily encompasses preservation work in order to make available interviews, TV specials and other footage that was never commercially released.

Lord of the Rings Fan Edits

To more specifically assess the changes fan editors have made to the Lord of the Rings and Hobbit movies, it will help to further break down the editors' intentions beyond simply FanFix or FanMix. We have grouped these edits into 5 subcategories. The first 13 fan edits have the specific goal of editing the films in order to bring them closer to J.R.R. Tolkien's original novels. *The Lord of the Rings: Book 1—The Return of the Shadow* by Kerr is a popular example in this category. One specific change made is to remove the prologue and open with Bilbo's party just like the book.

Similar to DH1-Wicked, 8 LOTR fan edits attack the films' runtimes. Despite the success of the LOTR extended editions, a number of editors sought to instead shorten the length in order to create a leaner package, while retaining the most important plot points. Unlike the previously mentioned book edits, these fan edits don't necessarily try to more closely model the novels. *Hobbit: An Unexpected Journey—The Arkenstone Edition* by Kerr is an example fan edit in this category. The dwarf chase scene through Goblintown is a representative cut for this category of edit. While many viewers find the scene to be entertaining, this type of action sequence doesn't generally advance the plot and counterintuitively, removing these action sequences can actually make the fan edit seem more exciting since the story moves along so much faster.

The next 9 fan edits reduce the trilogies into only a single film, and in doing so, share many similarities with both previous LOTR categories as well as the Harry Potter fan edit DH-Q2. While these edits generally remove many scenes not included in the novels, and thereby become closer to the books, some editors specifically state that their intention is to create the best all-in-one movie they could, even if this includes portions not in the original novels. Nearly all side characters and subplots get removed from these fan edits and action sequences are generally shortened or removed. *The Hobbit: The Spence Edit* by Spence is an example edit in this category. One cut that Spence makes that is also cut in almost all Hobbit trilogy edits is removing the romance between elf Tauriel and dwarf Kili.

The last 5 Lord of the Rings and The Hobbit edits include 2 FanFixes that did not fit into any of the above categories and we would instead consider "general FanFixes" with miscellaneous reordering of scenes, rescoring portions, or minor edits to dialogue. The other 3 are more creative FanMixes, which specifically combine multiple films into a single movie, but with the goal of following only a single storyline. *Lord of the Rings: The Journey to Mordor* by samspider3 combines the last two Lord of the Rings movies into a single fan edit, but tells its story only from the perspective of Sam and Frodo, eliminating Aragorn, Legolas, Gimli, and others. Its companion piece,

Lord of the Rings: The Battle for Middle-Earth, also by samspider3, follows those two movies from the perspective of Aragorn's company of heroes, ignoring Sam and Frodo's journey.

Aside from samspider3's FanMixes, all other fan edits act to change or cut from the theatrical or extended edition versions. Many are explicitly intended to serve as replacement volumes. It is debatable as to whether the dramatic FanMix reorderings that serve to closely mirror the books would serve as a replacement for the movies as opposed to an additional version. However, as an overall trend, Lord of the Rings fan editors have fallen on the "supplant" side in their contribution to their community. It is proposed that this results from the original author being unable to participate in the creation of Peter Jackson's films which leads fans to not view them as protected canon in the same way as the Harry Potter films in which J.K. Rowling was heavily involved. This point will be revisited in the Star Wars and Conclusions sections.

Star Trek Fan Edits

Star Trek as a series has a virtual mountain of canonical tv episodes and movies to serve as a basis for fan art and Geraghty (2006) touches on a variety of these as well as the positive impact they have for Star Trek fans. Similar to several Harry Potter fan edits, *Star Trek: Reunion* by TM2YC is an attempt to more closely model the pacing, humor and emotion of the later films in the series. This was a popular fan edit with audiences, and it won the Favorite Edit of the Month competition at Fanedit.org in December 2014.

However most (13) of the Star Trek FanFixes would fit into the previously described "general FanFix" specific category where the editor's focus is on character development, overall narrative, poor dialogue, or other similar general critiques, which are unlike most edited Harry Potter films. For example, fan editor TM2YC created *Star Trek Vengeance*, which focuses on improving the movie's emotional impact. One fan edited movie, *Star Trek Nemesis—Recut*, by fan editor El Diablo Suizo, focuses primarily on the inconsistent central villain figure and redefines the motives behind the character.

There are several truly inspired Star Trek fan edits, and their contribution to fandom as new viewing experiences, as opposed to merely an altered experience, makes them worth discussing here. *Star Trek—Kirkless Generations* by CBB was awarded Fanedit.org's Favorite Edit of the Month in May 2006 and similar to HP-BWNL which removes Harry Potter, this fan edit achieved the ambitious goal of completely removing the character Captain Kirk from the original *Star Trek Generations* movie. Two other editors, Pauley79 and Merlin, each took a favorite Star Trek plotline, tribbles, and merged episodes from *The Original Series* and *Deep Space Nine* in order to create fan edits that follow the storyline of these creatures over 71-minute movies.

Besides these few unique attempts to tell a new story and several other efforts to turn multi-episode story arcs from the TV series into fan edited movies, the overwhelming majority of Star Trek fan edits fall on the "supplant" side of the discussion. That is, they attempt to fix or otherwise improve the original movies to potentially serve as replacement volumes. This should be expected since despite the popularity of Star Trek as a franchise, the movies have not received overwhelmingly positive reviews from audiences, with *Wrath of Khan*, arguably the best of the series, only being rated as 7.7/10 on IMDB.com, many of the films are rated between 6.0/10 and 7.0/10, and *The Final Frontier*, the lowest rated of the series, has user ratings of only 5.4/10. Only *Wrath of Khan* has a higher rating than the lowest IMDB rated Harry Potter film, Chamber of Secrets 7.4/10. Higher general satisfaction with the Harry Potter films would lead to a reduced interest in the fan base to improve them as compared to the Star Trek series.

Star Wars Fan Edits

Since there are 131 full length Star Wars fan edits, no simple categorization scheme will adequately describe all of them, however the three largest categories of fan edits are attempts to fix the prequel trilogy, attempts to restore the re-released versions of the original trilogy back toward their original versions, and attempts to create completely unique viewing experiences.

With the antics of Jar Jar Binks, "yippee!" coming from the mouth of the future Darth Vader, and all to in-your-face exposition like "what are midichlorians?" it's no surprise that *Star Wars Episode I: The Phantom Menace* was poorly received by die-hard fans, who McDermott (2006) observed responded with a variety of active modes of fandom, including fan editing. When choosing which projects to take on, Jenkins (1992) describes "potential" as a selection criteria fan artists use. Star Wars fans had decades to speculate on possible characters and storylines for the prequel trilogy, and this consensus of wasted potential has led to *The Phantom Menace* alone having 25 FanFixes listed in IFDB. This is the same total number of FanFixes for the entire Harry Potter and Star Trek series combined, and nearly as many as the entire Lord of the Rings and The Hobbit series. These FanFixes range from serious attempts to salvage the movie like *Star Wars—Episode I: Shadow of the Sith* by L8wrtr which improves pacing and removes most childish scenes and dialogue, to fan edits that essentially start from scratch. In *Star Wars: Episode 1—The Silent Menace*, fan editor Lukeburrage mutes all dialogue and tells his own story in an entirely subtitled version of the film.

The Star Wars original trilogy contains some of the most beloved films of all time. Yet, when they were digitally re-released several decades later, viewers had many complaints with changes that George Lucas made. *Star Wars—Episode IV: 2004 Special Edition Revisited* by Adywan is the most reviewed fan edit in the IFDB database, with a 9.9/10 rating. This fan edit purports to create the version of *A New Hope* that the special edition release should have been by meticulously re-compositing special effects, restoring and remastering scenes, and generally correcting most fan complaints with the re-released version.

Although there are a very large number of fan edits attempting to fix the movies, there are also a number of incredibly creative attempts to generate unique viewing experiences. *Pulp Empire* by NJVC is a fan edit that answers the question, "What would *Empire Strikes Back* have been like if it had been directed by Quentin Tarantino?" *War of the Stars* by The Man Behind the Mask presents a "grindhouse" version of *A New Hope* utilizing deleted scenes, alternate takes, and grainy special effects. *Star Wars—Episode 1: The Ridiculous Menace* by TV's Frink turns *The Phantom Menace* into a non-stop slapstick comedy similar to *Airplane* or *The Naked Gun* with overdubbed dialogue and a variety of other editing techniques. One other area that Star Wars fans have outdone fans of other franchises is in the area of preservations. There have been a large number of aired interviews, TV specials and other footage that was never released to the public in a commercially available format. There are a number of fan edits listed on IFDB that attempt to preserve this footage to make it available to fans who missed their original airings.

With an incredibly active fan editing community, Star Wars fans find themselves with a wide variety of edits that supplement or supplant the original films. Though when taking a closer look, the films being supplanted are rarely the original trilogy. Though a contentious issue, an argument can be made that once a canon work of fiction has been released, even the creator doesn't have the right to later change it. By editing the re-released original trilogy to more closely resemble the first release, the disappointed fans described in Goodman (2015) are taking action to oppose retroactive continuity. It will be interesting to see fan editors' responses to the Fantastic Beasts series of films. Will they be viewed similarly to the Hobbit films or Star Wars prequels and become popular targets of editing, or will there be a lower level of editor interest for many of the same reasons as the original Harry Potter films?

Gender and Fan Editing

Harry Potter isn't the only popular recent franchise with a low number of high-quality fan edits. IFDB lists 0 fan edits of the Twilight movies, and there are only 3 edits of The Hunger Games franchise. Searching through the comedy genre listings of IFDB shows a large number of edits of movies like *Army of Darkness* and other slapstick style comedies with an audience that is likely to skew male, but only a small number of edits of romantic comedies which typically appeal to primarily female audiences (some notable examples being *Love Actually: A DigitalMan's Bloated and Flatulent Extended Edition* and *13 to 30 Extraflirty* by CBB). The lack of romantic comedy fan edits can be contrasted against the "Western" and "War" film genres which combined have approximately 40 full length fan edits that are likely to have a larger appeal to male audiences. These counts seem to suggest that franchises and genres that stereotypically appeal to female audiences seem to receive far less attention by fan editors than franchises and genres that stereotypically appeal to male audiences.

While Kidday (2017) reports that approximately 17 percent of editors of major studio released films were female, the percent of female fan editors is suspected to be even lower. IFDB does not record this demographic information but personal communication with administrators of the site suggest that the percent of female fan editors in their database is likely to be less than 10 percent, and could even be as low as 1 percent. It is interesting that although the tools of the trade are the same, this fan editing population stands in sharp contrast to the vidding community, which Coppa (2008) describes as largely female. If it is accepted that fan editors would be most likely to spend their time on a film that interests them, then it may be expected that predominantly male fan editors would predominantly produce fan edits of films and franchises that appeal to male audiences. Does Harry Potter appeal to primarily female audiences, and does this explain the lack of attention paid by the primarily male fan editors?

Box office results do show that there was a slight bias towards female viewers (54 percent for DH2) (Kaufman 2011); however, this falls slightly closer to *Lord of the Rings: Return of the King* (50 percent female audience) (Day 2004) than *The Hunger Games: Mockingjay part 2* (60 percent female audience) (Young 2012). To look at more extreme examples, the opening weekend audience for *Star Wars: The Force Awakens* was only 42 percent female (Pallotta 2015), and *Twilight Breaking Dawn Part 2* was 79 percent female (McClintock 2012). Though the viewing audience is generally mixed or slightly skewed towards female, there are two other areas of Harry Potter fandom, garage bands and video games, which skew male and may discredit this explanation.

At the 2016 Game Developer's Conference, Electronic Entertainment Design and Research presented data suggesting that while over half of mobile gamers in North America are women, male players still comprise 60 percent and 64 percent majorities in console and PC gaming respectively ("Why Mobile Gamers," 2016). These percentages were likely higher a decade ago when two of the most successful Harry Potter video games, *Lego Harry Potter:*

Years 1–4 and *Lego Harry Potter: Years 5–7* were released in a variety of console and PC formats. These two games are stylistically similar to Lego games covering the Batman, Star Wars, Lord of the Rings, Marvel's Avengers, and Indiana Jones franchises. Since many of these franchises have majority male fandoms, and video game players generally skew male, Warner Bros and the game developer's decision to release this style of Harry Potter video game suggests that they anticipated a large enough audience to be profitable.

That terms like "all-girl bands" exist at all is evidence that participation in garage rock bands is another area of fandom that skews male (not dissimilar to "boy bands" which confusingly refer to pop singing groups, an area with much greater gender parity). One of the most interesting areas of Harry Potter fandom is the rise of Wizard Rock as a musical genre. Wrock is more of a topical musical genre as opposed to stylistic. Tatum (2009) argues that Wizard Rock does not classify as filk (which itself can be imprecisely described as science fiction or fantasy themed music, often taking place at fan conventions), however a comparison can certainly be made. Bands may sound like rock, metal, folk, pop, or a variety of other styles, but all attempt to either represent themselves as if they could be a band in the Harry Potter universe, or sing songs about the Harry Potter universe. Because garage rock bands are a predominantly male activity, it is not surprising that on Last.fm (https://www.last.fm/tag/wrock/artists), the top 7 Wrock bands sorted by number of listeners are all comprised entirely of males (Harry and the Potters, Ministry of Magic, Draco and the Malfoys, The Remus Lupins, The Marauders, The Whomping Willows, and Oliver Boyd and the Remembralls).

The number of male bands that dedicate countless hours towards Harry Potter themed music provides a direct parallel to the commitment required by fan editors. The release of Harry Potter video games marketed to the same audience as Batman, Star Wars, and Avengers games further demonstrates confidence in finding a male audience by companies with large amounts of money on the line. There does appear to be a correlation between most fan editors being male and most fan edits being released of films and genres that appeal to male audiences, with noticeably fewer edits of films and genres that have greater appeal to female audiences. However, based on these examples of males participating in other types of Harry Potter fandom, it does not seem like the Harry Potter franchise's fandom skews sufficiently female to negatively impact its appeal to male fan editors.

Harry Potter Fan Fiction

If there was any doubt that Harry Potter is not merely a consumption based "Read/Only" fandom as Lessig (2008) would describe, but rather a

"Read/Write" active audience, one need look no further than fan fiction. The total volume of Harry Potter fan fiction is staggering. Fanfiction.net lists approximately 773,000 uploaded works of fan fiction set in the Harry Potter universe. For comparison, this dwarfs the number of publications for Lord of the Rings (~56,000) and Star Wars (~45,000). Many of today's most prolific authors of fan fiction have built thriving online communities of beta readers described in Karpovich (2006). Due to this routine interaction between author and audience, publication often appears in short, regular contributions more comparable to a blog than a novel. A second website, HarryPotterFanfiction.com (HPFF), caters specifically to Harry Potter Fan fiction and lists nearly 400,000 stories and chapters in its database. In order to provide more direct comparisons to IFDB fan edits, this section specifically analyzes a small subset of these works, "completed" "novels" published at HPFF which are most comparable to the edited movies in previous sections in their scope and commitment required by the author. HPFF Lists 1,471 completed novels in their database.

In sharp contrast to fan editing, fan fiction authors have complete narrative freedom in their writing. Their choice of characters, settings, events, interactions and dialogue are not limited by released footage; rather, only by their imagination. However, when analyzing some of the completed Harry Potter fan fiction novels, similar trends appear in their creative choices. In trying to assess the motivation of fan authors, the clearest distinction can be drawn in the era in which these fanfics are set. The number of novels published in each of HPFF's 5 most popular timeframes are: 216 Marauders (when Sirius, Remus, etc., attended Hogwarts), 38 Pre-Hogwarts (any other pre–Harry Potter timeframe such as when Tom Riddle attended Hogwarts or when Harry was growing up with the Dursleys), 528 Hogwarts (during the main 7 year time frame of the novels), 255 Post-Hogwarts (in the 19 years between the Battle of Hogwarts and the Deathly Hallows epilogue), and 223 Next Generation (when the trio's kids attend Hogwarts).

Since the novels only hinted at most events outside the Hogwarts years, the 732 novels set in the Marauders, Pre-Hogwarts, Post-Hogwarts and Next Generation eras are clearly intended to supplement the main novels. These new works of creative fiction offer readers additional opportunities to visit the world of Harry Potter, generally without significantly changing canon events from the main series. These would most similarly resemble the Extended Edition variety of fan edit since they leave most existing canon scenes unchanged, and then add additional scenes and storylines.

The smaller number of novels set during the Hogwarts time frame represent a wide variety of interests that are difficult to qualify since so many fanfics fit into multiple categories. Some fan novels were written while the original series was still in progress, and thus were predictive in nature and so may have been supplements at the time, but a reader today may view them as alternative histories. Many others do specifically attempt to change characters or events in the original novels. Some examples of this are the 56 novels that list their main character interactions as Draco/Hermione, some (but not all) of which result in a romantic relationship between the two. Many of these novels also introduce their own characters, and interactions between canon characters and these new creations can lead to interesting new paths of character development, and would be comparable to a FanMix.

While some fan fiction novels change elements from Rowling's work, and some authors would even consider their revisions improvements, we were unable to find a single completed novel that appeared to be an attempt to rewrite one of the seven main novels in order to serve as a replacement volume, which would have been comparable to a FanFix.

Conclusions

Booth (2010) describes fan art as communal re-imagining of original works. By its very nature as derivative art, fan editing involves creating a new movie from one or more existing works, with two distinct common motivations. Some fan editors change the original films in order to fix them and create an improved final product that could serve as a replacement to supplant the original during future viewings. Alternatively, many fan editors change a film in such a way that the final product is a unique viewing experience, not intended to replace, but instead to supplement the original. All fan edits contribute to their universe by adding to the total number of options viewers have to enjoy their fandom.

The massive volume of fan fiction, along with video games, Wrock music, theme parks, fan conventions and a number of other participatory avenues for Harry Potter fandom clearly indicate that the fan base is large enough that Harry Potter could have a large volume of fanedits. It does appear that the overwhelmingly male population of fan editors are a primary reason for the lack of fanedits of Twilight and The Hunger Games, but based on other examples of male participatory fandom of Harry Potter, this does not adequately explain the low number of Harry Potter fanedits.

Instead, the explanation likely lies in one or two other areas. The first is based on the film creators. Peter Jackson's Lord of the Rings movies could themselves be viewed as very high budget fan films since Tolkien himself had no involvement in their creation. George Lucas's remastered versions of the original trilogy could be considered his personal fan edits of his own previous releases. These cases stand in sharp contrast to the Harry Potter movie adaptations for which J.K. Rowling was heavily involved, and which are generally considered to be an alternative (to the novels) canonical Harry Potter universe. We propose that fans would not have edited the Lord of the Rings films as much had they been directed by J.R.R. Tolkien, but they are perfectly happy to edit Peter Jackson's interpretation because his versions aren't canon, just like the remastered Star Wars releases aren't the canonical versions of the original trilogy in the eyes of fans. Thus, Peter Jackson's lack of authority over LOTR content may be the reason his films are so often edited, despite their very high ratings amongst viewers.

The second likely reason will catch exceptions that don't fit into the above explanation like Star Trek whose films are generally viewed as canonical, even though Gene Roddenberry wasn't directly involved in their production, and the Star Wars prequels which were written and directed by George Lucas himself. Fan editing often evokes a negative connotation. The language used in this essay like "fix" and "supplant" suggest a dissatisfaction with the original that may not always be justified. However, in the case of poorly reviewed Star Trek films and Star Wars prequels, we propose that fan dissatisfaction with the films failing to live up to their potential is a primary driver towards fan editing.

If fans view FanFix as an attack on the original instead of merely an alternative creative expression, then anyone satisfied with the original may not want to participate in this art form. This potential explanation for the low number of Harry Potter fan edits suggests that satisfaction with the movie adaptations may be even higher than their respectable viewer ratings on online ratings sites would suggest. While avoiding supplanting J.K. Rowling's films may be admirable, it is nonetheless unfortunate if a negative impression of fan editing has stifled supplementary FanMix edits. Who wouldn't want to watch Danny Trejo as the voice of Dobby in a Quentin Tarantino–styled Harry Potter fan edit?

References

Alexander, J. (2017, June 27). *Harry Potter's legacy will continue in the fan fiction culture it inspired*. Retrieved from https://www.polygon.com/2017/6/27/15876612/harry-potter-fanfiction-20th-anniversary

Booth, P. (2010). *Digital fandom: New media studies*. New York: Peter Lang.

Booth, P. (2012). Mashup as temporal amalgam: Time, taste, and textuality. In F. Coppa & J.L. Russo (Eds.), *Fan/Remix Video* [Special Issue], *Transformative Works and Cultures, 9*. doi:10.3983/twc.2012.0297

Borojević, J. (2016). Quenching the quill: How fan art builds meaning, creates bonds, and triggers information. In C.E. Bell (Ed.), *Wizards vs muggles: Essays on identity and the Harry Potter universe* (pp. 133–148). Jefferson, NC: McFarland.

Collins, R.G. (1977). Star Wars: The pastiche of myth and the yearning for a past future. *The Journal of Popular Culture, XI*(1), 1–10.

Coppa, F. (2008). Women, Star Trek, and the early development of fannish vidding. *Transformative Works and Cultures, 1*. doi:10.3983/twc.2008.0044

Day, P. (2004, February 1). 'Rings' films: Chick flicks? *Los Angeles Times*. Retrieved from http://articles.latimes.com/2004/feb/01/entertainment/ca-day1

Geraghty, L. (2006). A network of support: Coping with trauma through Star Trek fan letters. *The Journal of Popular Culture, 39*(6), 1002–1024. doi: 10.1111/j.1540-5931.2006.00331.x

Goodman, L. (2015). Disappointing fans: Fandom, fictional theory, and the death of the author. *The Journal of Popular Culture, 48*(4), 662–676. doi: 10.1111/jpcu.12223

Greenberg, D. (2001, September 7). Thumbs down? Re-edit the flick yourself. *The Washington Post.* Retrieved from https://www.washingtonpost.com/archive/business/2001/09/07/thumbs-down-re-edit-the-flick-yourself/52f04549-d8b9-41b1-8791-1ca271f9b5e6/?utm_term=.dd475ef652e7

Grobelny, J. (2008). Mashups, sampling, and authorship: A mashupsampliography. *Music Reference Services Quarterly, 11*(3–4). doi: 10.1080/10588160802570375

Jenkins, H. (1992). *Textual poachers: Television fans and participatory culture.* New York: Routledge.

Jenkins, H., Clinton, K., Purushotma, R., Robison, A.J., & Weigel, M. (2009). *Confronting the challenges of participatory culture: Media education for the 21st century.* Cambridge, MA: The MIT Press.

Jenson, J. (1992). Fandom as pathology: The consequences of characterization. In L. Lewis (Ed.), *The adoring audience: Fan culture and popular media.* New York: Routledge.

Jones, R. (2006). From shooting monsters to shooting movies: Machinima and the transformative play of video game fan culture. In K. Hellekson & K. Busse (Eds.), *Fan fiction and fan communities in the age of the internet* (pp. 261–280). Jefferson, NC: McFarland.

Karpovich, A.I. (2006). The audience as editor: The role of beta readers in online fan fiction communities. In K. Hellekson & K. Busse (Eds.), *Fan fiction and fan communities in the age of the internet* (pp. 171–188). Jefferson, NC: McFarland.

Kaufman, A. (2011, July 18). "Harry Potter" makes box-office magic. *Los Angeles Times.* Retrieved from http://articles.latimes.com/2011/jul/18/entertainment/la-et-0718-box-office-20110718

Kidday, G. (2017, January 01). Study: Female filmmakers lost ground in 2016. *Hollywood Reporter.* Retrieved from http://www.hollywoodreporter.com/news/women-filmmakers-2016-statistics-show-female-directors-declined-number-963729

Lessig, L. (2008). *Remix: Making art and commerce thrive in the hybrid economy.* New York: Penguin.

Lothian, A. (2009). Living in a den of thieves: Fan video and digital challenges to ownership. *Cinema Journal, 48*(4), 130–136. doi: 10.1353/cj.0.0152

Mackey, M. & McClay, J.K. (2008). Pirates and poachers: Fan fiction and the conventions of reading and writing. *English in Education, 42*(2), 131–147. doi:10.1111/j.1754-8845.2008.00011.x

Mason, M. (2008). *The pirate's dilemma: How youth culture is reinventing capitalism.* New York: Free Press.

Martin, G.R.R. (2010). Someone is angry on the internet [Blog post]. Retrieved from http://grrm.livejournal.com/151914.html

McClintock, P. (2012, November 18). Box office report: "Breaking Dawn—Part 2" bites off $340.9 million global opening. *The Hollywood Reporter.* Retrieved from http://www.hollywoodreporter.com/news/box-office-report-breaking-dawn-391789

McDermott, M. (2006). The menace of the fans to the franchise. In M.W. Kapell & J.S. Lawrence (Eds.), *Finding the force in the Star Wars franchise: Fans, merchandise, and critics* (pp. 243–263). New York: Peter Lang.

Middleton, K. 2012. Remix video and the crisis of the humanities. In F. Coppa & J.L. Russo (Eds.), *Fan/Remix Video* [Special Issue], *Transformative Works and Cultures, 9.* doi: 10.3983/twc.2012.0349

Pallotta, F. (2015, December 27). "Star Wars: The Force Awakens" by the numbers. *CNN.* Retrieved from http://money.cnn.com/2015/12/21/media/star-wars-the-force-awakens-box-office-numbers/index.html

Phillips, F. (2012). The Star Wars franchise, fan edits, and Lucasfilm. In F. Coppa & J.L. Russo (Eds.), *Fan/Remix Video* [Special Issue], *Transformative Works and Cultures, 9.* Doi: 10.3983/twc.2012.0385

Roane, A. & Bernard, B.P. (2017, February). *Character development in a Harry Potter digital fanedit*. Paper presented at the 39th Annual Southwest Popular/American Culture Association Conference, Albuquerque, NM.

Rogers, C. (2017, May 02). Are Star Wars fan edits a force for good? *Den of Geek*. http://www.denofgeek.com/us/movies/star-wars/264382/are-star-wars-fan-edits-a-force-for-good

Tatum, M.L. (2009). Identity and authenticity in the filk community. *Transformative Works and Cultures*, 3. doi: 10.3983/twc.2009.0139

Turk, T., & Johnson, J. (2012). Toward an ecology of vidding. In F. Coppa & J.L. Russo (Eds.), Fan/Remix Video [Special Issue], *Transformative Works and Cultures*, 9. doi:10.3983/twc.2012.0326

Tryon, C. (2012). Fan films, adaptations, and media literacy. In J. Telotte & G. Duchovnay (Eds.), *Science Fiction Film, Television, and Adaptation: Across the Screens* (pp. 176–189). New York: Routledge.

Waters, D. (2004). Rowling backs Potter fan fiction. *BBC News*. Retrieved from http://news.bbc.co.uk/2/hi/entertainment/3753001.stm

Wille, J. (2014). Fan edits and the legacy of The Phantom Edit. *Transformative Works and Cultures*, 17. doi: 10.3983/twc.2014.0575

Williams, D. (2005). Sanitizing the obscene: Fighting for the right to edit objectionable film content. *Jeffrey S. Moorad Sports Law Journal*, 12(1). 161–193.

Young, C. (2008). *Homemade Hollywood: Fans behind the camera*. New York: Bloomsbury Academic.

Young, J. (2012, March 25). Box office report: "The Hunger Games" posts third-best opening weekend ever with $155 mil. *Entertainment Weekly*. Retrieved from http://ew.com/article/2012/03/25/box-office-report-hunger-games/

Why mobile gamers are mainly women, while most PC and console gamers are male. (2016, April 8). Retrieved from http://www.scmp.com/lifestyle/arts-entertainment/article/1933985/why-mobile-gamers-are-mainly-women-while-most-pc-and MISSING TEXT

Harry Potter and the Development of Narrative and Media Literacies

ALISON HALSALL

"Dear Harry," writes 15-year-old Karen from the Philippines:

> Though our worlds are far apart (you in Britain and me in Asia), I think we have a connection.... You are a wizard—special, great, something to be amazed at. Well, I'm also a wizard, but I don't do magic. I'm a wizard in school, and I'm good in my academics.... I also get into mischief, and my teachers often get exasperated. Aside from that, I also have many friends. There are seven actually who are the closest to me. Like Ron and Hermione, they often get me into and out of trouble. Though we are tried and tested, we still stick close together [Adler, 2001, p. 11].

Bill Adler's compilation, *Kids' Letters to Harry Potter, from Around the World* (2001), highlights the extraordinary immersion of young readers in J.K. Rowling's magical world—their participation through flights of imagination or their creative interactions with this world through letters, or even fan fiction, blogging, or visits to the virtual website *Pottermore* to determine their school House. Why do these novels invite such participatory responses, on the parts of young readers, and what purpose(s) does this participation serve? As these letters show, Rowling's world interfaces with and even comments on personal challenges that young people experience in their own lives and particular socio-political contexts in a non-didactic fashion. As Karen's letter exemplifies, readers joyously draw parallels between their own and Harry Potter's world, slipping easily between make-believe and reality, delighting in the intricate details of this imaginary world, while remaining aware of the socio-cultural realities that shape Rowling's fantastical tales about class and racial prejudice, personal development, and power struggles between friends and enemies.

Karen continues:

> Oh, I almost forgot: You and I practically have the same school. No, I don't go to a wizarding school but Philippine Science High School is almost like Hogwarts. In a way it is. It's a special school for gifted students (and I'm one of them!). We have advanced classes and technology lessons. But when much is given, much is expected. It's definitely exhausting! I often stay up late just to finish homework. And besides, we also don't have all our parents around all the time. You're an orphan, right? I still have my both parents [sic] alive, but my father works abroad, and he comes home once a year. I really miss him terribly, especially during Christmas, and he misses me, too. But I know you miss your parents even more. Not even magic can bring them back [Adler, 2001, p. 12].

Karen's letter reflects a number of important responses young readers and writers make to Rowling's series. First, many of the letters draw parallels between Rowling's fantasy world and their own personal and sociocultural contexts. Second, as Karen's letter attests, the challenges Harry experiences as a youth can help young readers make sense of and even articulate the personal challenges they experience in their own lives (loneliness, a worry about performance and expectation, or the absence of a parent). In fact, so many of the letter writers in Adler's compilation find solace in knowing that Rowling's beloved characters experience their world in ways that are similar to their own.

Bill Adler's compilation includes letters that booksellers, bookstores, and teachers from around the world sent him, as well as interviews and summaries of interviews that he provided of some of the young letter writers. All of these letters are written by children, under the age of sixteen, from all around the world, including the United States, England, the Philippines, South Africa, Australia, Singapore, Estonia, and the Netherlands. They are all written to one of Rowling's young characters (Harry usually, sometimes Hermione and Ron), responding to and often expanding on her fantastical universe, and in the process demonstrating a number of different types of literacy (narrative, empathetic, sociocultural literacies, among others), as I will discuss below. Generally, many of these letter writers create a fictional identity for themselves when writing to Harry, and in the process display narrative literacy, when a reader is so deeply engaged in the source material that (s)he becomes a co-creator of the story (Mikkelsen, 2005). Rachel from Fairfax, Virginia, for example, scaffolds details taken from Rowling's stories into the identity she assumes in the writing of her letter: in signing her letter, she identifies herself as "Master Quidditch player and expert enchantress," begging Harry's pardon that she could not send her letter "by owl" (Adler, 2001, p. 6). Megan, from Winnetka, Illinois, signs her letter as "Expert Potions Master" (Adler, 2001, p. 182). Their personal immersion in the world, signaled by the fictional identities that they have woven for themselves, continues with particular spells that they invent that would help both Harry and themselves cope with personal challenges. Laura invents "Bottled Servant," for example, to put Draco Malfoy in his place: "First, add the skin of a boomslang, the hair of a unicorn, and bubotuber puss [sic]. Mix together well. Then add in Sleep Easy's Hair Potion and five dead spiders. Boil this with the other ingredients. This should do the trick!" (Adler, 2001, p. 76). Clearly, these young writers are deeply invested in the details and narrative intricacies of Rowling's stories, and model the content of their letters on Rowling's story structures, in the process apprenticing the craft of writing. As Ernie Bond and Nancy Michelson point out, "Reading is a constructivist process of meaning-making" (2003, p. 109). The literary investment that these young writers make in Rowling's series is evident in the particular details that they include in their personal responses and creations, details that in turn signal the different types of literacy that they are deepening in the process.

As Adler's compilation testifies in its responses from children around the world to *Harry Potter*, and as my own experiences of teaching Rowling's novels in the university classroom demonstrate, there is something transformative about Rowling's fantastical series, something that inspires a student's engagement with narrative that I see in the study of no other children's novel. Students, usually shy or reserved, unleash a torrent of knowledge and opinion. They have frequently read the series multiple times, watched all of the feature films, visited the website *Pottermore* or travelled to the Wizarding World of Harry Potter in Orlando. Invariably, they light up when I ask rhetorical questions about characters, thematics, and tropes. Unlike with other texts that we study in class, students have opinions about *Harry Potter*—often many of them—and are very excited to deepen their analysis. In every class, there are a few who have resisted the *Harry Potter* trend in the past, perhaps because they watched the films first or perhaps because they objected to the trend in the first place. Almost without exception, in reading the novel for class, students change their minds, devour it in a few sittings, and continue to read the series. Students refer to the comfort that these unusually long novels offer, their appreciation of the novels' suspense, mystery, and intrigue. Rowling's impressive depth of detail, as well as the careful balance she strikes between humor and seriousness, facilitates a young person's immersive experience. Reading the series to my six-year-old son, I have learned to appreciate even more the efficacy of Rowling's slapstick humor. The *Harry Potter* series also invites re-reading in a way that I have seen performed only rarely among students. This act of re-reading, in turn, signals a young reader's enjoyment of the text, the enhancement of her/his own reading abilities, and the proliferation of many types of literacy.

These letters in Adler's compilation demonstrate the "literary literacy" and "narrative literacy" of young people. Nina Mikkelsen defines "literary literacy" as the process by which young readers first uncover patterns of meaning in the structure, style, and subject of a text (2005, p. 4), in our case here, of Rowling's novel and series as a whole. "Narrative literacy," Mikkelsen goes on to define, is demonstrated by the stories that young readers in turn tell about one of the characters, often expanding on the author's story (Mikkelsen, 2005, p. 4). Ann, of Chula Vista, California, writes to Harry:

> My Muggle name is Ann, but in the wizarding world, my name is Arabella Arithmancy. I am an American 12-year-old. I am Muggle-born, like Hermione. In fact, I'm a lot like her. I am at the top of my classes, I dislike "fads" and the "popular" or "boy-crazy" girls, and I'm often misunderstood, even by those close to me. […] I was wondering: In your third year, you caught the animagus and you threatened to kill him if he transformed, but why didn't you just put him under the Full-Body Bind? If it wears off, you could have renewed it, and even if a strong wizard could break it, your adversary isn't exactly a strong wizard [Adler, 2001, p. 1].

This is the first letter Adler chooses to introduce in his collection and it certainly demonstrates various literacies (literary, narrative, critical) that Rowling's text inspires young readers to adopt and put into practice. Ann/Arabella, for instance, has immersed herself in the series: the fictional identity that she has invented for herself as her first point of entry speaks to the literary and narrative literacies she has developed in reading the first three novels of the series. Not only does she uncover patterns of meaning, in style and subject, in Rowling's stories, so typical of literary literacy, but Ann/Arabella walks about in the story as one of the characters, inhabiting the narrative itself while expanding the story by suggesting alternate responses Harry could have made to an enemy. Ann/Arabella is also able to perceive the thematic movement of the story, pointing out that "Friendship is a heavily stressed value in the books" (Adler, 2001, p. 2). Her analysis of Harry's response to the animagus Peter Pettigrew in the third book signals her critical literacy, her act of reading against the grain of the text to create changes in the work itself (Mikkelsen, 2005, p. 4). This letter—quite typical of the rest of the letters in Adler's compilation—speaks to the critical distance Ann/Arabella maintains that allows her the space to evaluate the writing more impartially, and even to suggest other choices that our protagonist could have made that would have had larger narrative implications.

As Ann/Arabella's letter suggests, J.K. Rowling's fantastical series is especially well suited for developing literary and narrative literacies among school-age and even post-secondary readers. It has a powerful ability to engage with literary tropes in ways that appeal to many a reluctant reader. Teachers and professors can use the series to discuss symbolism and character archetypes, morphemes (in the characters' names), and to encourage critical analysis of larger sociocultural realities through discussion of, say, Rowling's gender stereotyping or her exploration of class and racial prejudice. Indeed, *Harry*

Potter books are useful "cultural tools," in Lev Vygotsky's terms, "reference points that stimulate interaction and facilitate learning and cognitive development. The more familiar a cultural tool is to a child, the greater its potential benefit for learning" (Dempster et al., 2016, p. 270). A letter by Sigrid from Viljandi, Estonia signals the awareness of literary conventions that she has learned over the course of her reading experience, an awareness that she in turn redeploys in a letter to Harry:

> My name is Lily, and I am a beautiful 16-year-old enchantress with long silver hair and piercing gray eyes.... I go to the Quelynn School of Magic Arts, which is very far in the North. It is actually a beautiful ice castle on the endless snow fields, and our headmistress Lyana Van Heeusen is a true snow queen [Adler, 2001, pp. 91–92].

More specifically, Sigrid/Lily's letter displays literary and narrative literacies through her deep understanding of the literary and thematic elements of Rowling's first three *Harry Potter* novels, and through her development of an identity for herself within the parameters of the fantasy. Sigrid/Lily's letter speaks to a familiarity with fairy tale culture (referring as she does to Hans Christian Andersen's story, "The Snow Queen") and, even more to the point, the language and popular tropes of fantasy. In reading and inhabiting Rowling's narrative, young readers process narrative and thematic detail, deepening their perceptual, language and literary skills.

Importantly, Adler's compilation privileges the agency of the child reader and writer. Young people actively participate in the *Harry Potter* landscape, often finding their narrative voices and even personal identities in the process. My analysis of these letters takes a "reader response" approach that validates the many ways that readers make connections between past and present reading experiences and their individual interactions with a literary text, connections that, in turn, speak to the many levels of literacy that they acquire and hone in the process. "Meaning lies in that shared ground where the reader and text meet," Robert E. Probst reminds us; "it isn't resident within the text, to be extracted like a nut from its shell" (1994, p. 38). These remarkable letters demonstrate the dynamic process by which young readers interpret Rowling's pages and make them relevant to their own lived experiences. Critic Kathleen Malu writes that "reading is a transactional process between readers and text in which meaning is constructed each time readers read" (2003, p. 77). Reader response theory highlights the importance of particular, individual responses to what readers feel is the author's message. In turn, these readers bring multiple identities to their reading experiences, identities that are shaped by their gender, age, ethnicity, social class, sexual orientation, language use, religion, and personal and academic experiences (Malu, 2003, p. 78). Thus, Adler's compilation offers us unique insight into this dynamic process by which young readers interpret the words on Rowling's pages, and deepen their knowledge of genre and generic conventions, narrative structures, and the harnessing of tone and approach to suit the particular audiences for whom they write and create. Such a dynamic transaction proves James Ash's claim that "Children do not passively 'receive' messages, but interpret and use media in many different, creative and sometimes surprising ways—in other words, they are the co-producers of culture, and active participants in it" (2013, p. 222). Adler's compilation of letters effectively highlights this co-production of culture through the active participation that these young writers take in Rowling's world.

Rowling's *Harry Potter* series is obviously very important to these young readers in terms of language acquisition and language development, as well as "empathetic" and "aesthetic" literacies. Personal/empathetic literacy, according to Nina Mikkelsen (2005), occurs when a reader discovers something about a character that connects to her/his own life, and that draws her/him into a text more quickly. Aesthetic literacy can be seen when a young reader participates imaginatively in a work, which in turns leads to a deeper understanding of what it means to live in that story world (Mikkelsen, 2005). Michelle, from Capetown, South Africa writes to Harry:

> I'm just writing to say that I've been missing you very much. You wouldn't know me, because I'm just a nobody from the lowest grade in Hufflepuff. I've been watching you closely, but I'm not a mad killer who tracks you down everywhere. (I don't work for Vol-oops, You-Know-Who.) You see, ever since the holidays began, and we all went home (apart from you), I felt very sad because I wouldn't see you again until school (Hogwarts) started again. Well it's started again, so I'm not so sad anymore [Adler, 2001, p. 8].

Many of the letter writers included in this compilation direct similarly emotional responses to Rowling's protagonist, as though in writing to Harry, they are confiding in a diary. Letters like Michelle's frequently elide fantasy and reality (as Michelle does in collapsing the narrative distance between her summer holidays and the Hogwarts term), when these young people write out of worry that Harry will come to great harm in his encounters with Voldemort and his Death Eaters.

So many of the young writers included in Adler's compilation acknowledge that *Harry Potter* has benefited their reading, and that they have gained emotional payoffs, such as pride and self-confidence, in their reading abilities. Katie, from Chesterfield, Missouri, addresses the stimulation that Rowling's books have given to her literacy skills. In an interview, she acknowledges that the novels have expanded her vocabulary, and have trained her to look for deeper meanings in the stories themselves and in literature in general (Adler, 2001, p. 43). These emotional payoffs in turn motivate young readers to continue reading and trying more complex texts. In *Convergence Culture,* Henry Jenkins reminds us that the strength of a reader's connection with a brand is measured in terms of its emotional impact (2008, p. 69). Karen's letter (quoted at the beginning of this paper), and indeed all of these letters to Harry, are full of such emotional responses. This emotional connection is what solidifies the deep allegiances that young readers develop for Rowling's series, not to mention their critical investment in her lengthy serialized narrative and in narrative proper. Through the act of reading and even re-reading, young readers internalize story structures and conventions, in the process deepening their literacies and commitment to the story.

Characterization throughout the series, and the paralleling of story maturation with the maturation of its readers also helps to immerse young readers in the *Harry Potter* novels. Rowling's collective protagonist (Harry, Ron, and Hermione) is what endears so many readers to the series because it offers different characteristics that could appeal to different readers.[1] In effect, Rowling's progressive series about the Boy Who Lived grows up with its audience: the first two novels—*PS* and *CoS*—are geared towards a younger audience, while the remaining books gradually become more dark and serious, dealing with content that is more suitable for young adult (YA) readers. Harry's emotions become more complex in *PoA*, for example: as an adolescent, Harry is newly aware of Cho Chang, the Seeker on the Ravenclaw Quidditch team, and he registers Ginny Weasley's hero-worship of him after rescuing her from the clutches of Tom Riddle/Lord Voldemort in *CoS*. As a thirteen-year-old, Harry learns more sophisticated abilities at school: in Defense Against the Dark Arts class, he fights a Boggart, and learns to overcome his worst fear by conjuring a Patronus, or a special protective figure. Along with the increased sophistication of the school subjects that Harry must take comes the development of emotions that threaten to undo him in future books. In this third book, readers observe how Harry becomes more impulsive and impressionable, left to the mercy of his own violent emotions. There is much darkness in these later books, and this darkness is rooted in the psychological darkness that is associated with childhood and human development, feelings like anger, loss, death, grief, fear, and desire. Presumably, young readers become able to process complex emotions and events, as they grow with the series. In turn, as Jenkins writes, "Serialization rewards the competency and mastery of loyals" (2008, p. 78), as more character development in turn deepens readers' emotional allegiances to the characters.

Not surprisingly, Harry as protagonist is the principal figure towards whom young readers and writers direct the most emotion, according to the letters included in Adler's compilation. Indeed, Harry as an Everychild, vulnerable in his powerlessness, is what draws many of these writers to him, as their letters prove. Twelve-year-old Simrat, from New Delhi, India, is particularly impressed by Harry's continued survival despite Voldemort's repeated attempts on his life (Adler, 2001, p. 113). Many of these young writers speak of their admiration for Rowling's protagonist. Tamara, from Rangiora, New Zealand, says in an interview, "In a way I suppose, who Harry is, is the person I would like to be. Brave, kind, funny. Harry is a very, very cool guy" (Adler, 2001, p. 62). Kelly, from Sugarland, Texas, concurs, describing him as "bright, optimistic, precocious, a little awkward at times, shy, but always right there on the verge of greatness. Gosh ... I wish I had him for a boyfriend" (Adler, 2001, p. 29). Karen from the Philippines appreciates that Harry "has a mind of his own," that he stands up for what he believes is right, and that he is not perfect. In fact, it is these very imperfections that help her (and many of these writers, actually) to "relate to is [sic] character. I mean, sure he's a wizard and everything but he's also a kid like any of us—someone who has problems, emotions of happiness and sadness, feelings of love and hate. And I think that makes him very magical" (Adler, 2001, p. 13). Harry's seeming "normality" attracts these young writers.

Fascinatingly, some young letter writers identify particular aspects of Harry's character that speak to them personally. Sixteen-year-old Veronika, from Brooklyn, New York, argues that many readers can identify with Harry's orphan status, particularly "those whose parents are divorced" (Adler, 2001, p. 129). Katelyn, from Tulare, California, expresses a similar thought, but one again that speaks to her particular lived experience: she empathizes with Harry's loss of his parents because she lost her sister/brother who died before (s)he was born: "I heard that your mom and dad died," she writes to Harry. "I know how you feel—my mom had a baby, and it died in her stomach. Everyone is so sad" (Adler, 2001, p. 137). As these letters testify, Harry's combination of ordinary and extraordinary characteristics, his realistic youthful experiences and his role as the Chosen One in a magical world, allow young readers to see themselves in Rowling's character. When Jennifer, from Rockford, Illinois, writes that she wishes she were like Harry, and then thinks twice about this claim, she demonstrates another type of literacy that her reading of *Harry Potter* encourages her to develop: empathetic literacy or "the ability to become deeply involved with one of the story characters, usually the main one" (Mikkelsen, 2005, p. 18). "Oh, Harry, I wish I could be like you," she begins:

> Wait a minute, no, I don't. I guess the magic and everything would [sic] nice, but I don't think I would like Voldemort on my tail. Or to lose my parents. I would like to meet Dobby and Dumbledore, but I think I'd rather have my parents and sanity. Now look at me, all this time I've been sitting here envying the great and wonderful Harry Potter with all his magic and power, but not realizing the emotional baggage that came with that name (and scar) across your forehead. Yeah, the magic would be nice, but I would much rather be a Muggle than be Harry Potter [Adler, 2005, p. 46].

Jennifer's letter is particularly note-worthy in that she alludes to the pathos of Rowling's narrative, appreciating Harry's traumatic experiences of loss and abandonment, and in the process learns to think past herself. As Jennifer's letter suggests, Harry's vulnerability, imperfections, and isolation as a hero (at times) and a pariah (at others) speak to young readers; his personal empowerment in turn inspires them. Like them, he is complex and painfully human. Harry relies on his friends, though he still takes responsibility for his decisions and stands up for what he believes in. Although he has been victimized and tormented from an early age, he always displays great courage. Even more importantly, I would suggest, Harry is the polar opposite of the innocent Romantic child, a trope entrenched by Enlightenment theorists John Locke and Jean-Jacques Rousseau. Orphaned and scarred by the evil wizard Voldemort as a baby, Harry grows up with a lightning scar on his forehead that points to the burden that this horrific experience has left him with. Interestingly, in *PoA* and the later books, the wraithlike Dementors (guards of Azkaban prison and eventually the personal guards of Voldemort) affect Harry so deeply precisely because he is *not* innocent and because he has endured the terrible murders of his parents. The very presence of the Dementors forces Harry to relive this moment of traumatic loss in a physical and mental way time and time again. Harry's intimate knowledge of death speaks to the very real terrors that J.K. Rowling suggests young people *can* cope with, and it is Harry's courage in the face of terrible odds that inspires empathetic responses from many of the young readers and writers in Adler's compilation.

The immersion and personal investment that so many of these letters display in Rowling's narrative world in turn enhances a young reader's aesthetic and critical literacies. Critical literacy, according to Nina Mikkelsen, is "refusing to accept everything about a piece of literature, no questions asked; reading against the grain of the text to clarify what the reader feels and knows about the world and what the reader would do to create changes in the work" (2005, p. 4). Thirteen-year-old Chelsea, from Pleasonton, California, writes to Harry with some "new ideas for your upcoming books" (Adler, 2001, p. 49), thus eliding fiction and reality, and providing suggestions that in turn speak to her understanding of Rowling's story world and her critical engagement, as she offers not just individual details that she would change but also entire plot suggestions. Brian's letter includes some ideas on how Harry could "have made the Triwizard tasks a lot easier, quicker, and less nerve-racking" (Adler, 2001, p. 126). Brian's emotional investment in the fourth story in the series, *GoF*, his narrative competencies, and his narrative confidence are all strong at this point, so strong that when he proceeds through each task to advise Harry on how to perform it better, he structures his letter as he though he were writing a formal academic paper, complete with introduction, paragraphs of development for each task, and formal conclusion (Adler, 2001, p. 127). This sophisticated type of response, more typical of fan fiction than many of the letters included in Adler's compilation, shows how levels of literacy move readers past simply reading and making meaning, towards the act of creation.

"Children use stories to escape from or reaffirm aspects of their real lives" (2008, p. 182), Jenkins claims in *Convergence Culture*. Though, as Maria Nikolajeva argues, children's literature is a "unique art and communication form, deliberately created by those in power for the powerless" (2010, p. 8), these letters to Harry Potter from young people around the world are evidence of the subversive capabilities of children's literature, as these young people take control of and expand on the narratives that Rowling herself first imagined. In doing so, these letters are evidence of another type of literacy: participatory literacy. Participatory literacy, for Ernie Bond and Nancy Michelson, alludes to "the multiple ways readers take ownership of reading and writing to construct meanings situated within their own sociocultural characteristics" (2003, p. 119). Reading, writing, and fan art are "socioconstructivist processes" in which learners interact to create worlds of meaning that blend text, personal contexts, and prior knowledge (Bond and Michelson, 2003, p. 119). Amy, from Australia, tailors the narrative inventions she makes in her letter to Harry to her Australian setting, for example, in a letter that displays such participatory literacy. She writes to Harry about the New Defense Against the Dark Arts teacher, Professor Hufe, who is an Indigenous Australian: "(Pronunciation: Hyoof) He's really skinny. Every time you look at him you get this feeling that his bones are going to break any second. Hufe's an animagus, too; he turns into a kangaroo" (Adler, 2001, p. 186). As Amy's letter demonstrates, lived experiences inform a writer's inscription of self into the fiction she creates and then shares with readers. As Bond and Michelson argue, "Ways of seeing self and the world are co-constructed as people insert themselves and others into various storylines" (2003, p. 119).

This immersive, participatory response to Rowling's series is reflected by the spin-off creations—fan fiction, if you will—that some of these young writers have created, so inspired by Rowling's stories that they are impelled to create, textually adding to the wider *Potter* narrative. For example, Ciera, of Lamoni, Iowa, writes "Harry Potter and the Godfather," a creation in which Harry's godfather Sirius Black is finally cleared of all wrong-doing and Harry can live with him (Adler, 2001, p. 144). Participation, creativity, and production are central to the worlds of young people, James Ash claims (2013, p. 222). This immersive response to Rowling's stories is more deeply demonstrated in the detailed postings that fans enjoy in such fan forums and news sites on the Internet as *The Harry Potter Lexicon, The Leaky Cauldron, MuggleNet*, and *The Daily Prophet*, a web-based "school newspaper" for the fictional Hogwarts. Such sites on which young people post stories demonstrate their apprenticeship of the craft of writing and the various communities that they in turn develop with other young writers. Fan fiction allows writers to exploit gaps in the text, to invent "what if" scenarios, and to respond to a dissatisfaction with Rowling's narratives. Fan fiction writers participate in knowledge communities on these websites, looking for feedback, for their mistakes to be pointed out, encouraging beta readers (peer editors) to look for holes in the plot or to eliminate spelling or grammatical errors. For Kate McManus, fan fiction is a "place of speculation and imagination. Authors and readers are able to question and create possible futures in the wizarding world or construct what happened in the past. But perhaps most importantly, fanfiction creates a space in which readers and writers can analyze a text and place it firmly in the context of their own world" (McManus, 2015, p. 35). Many of the responses by young writers included in Adler's compilation thus approximate fan fiction, just not to the depth or sophistication that the Internet allows, since the compilation is a purely text-based medium. Creator of *The Daily Prophet*, 14-year-old Heather Lawver's description of the explicitly pedagogical goals that she intended to promote in the creation of her interactive and participatory website points to the participatory literacy that the exercise of fan fiction writing enhances. She writes:

> [an] exercise at the beginning of their tenure with the newspaper gave them a small, contained environment to start getting used to the idea of character development. Without even knowing it, they were writing their own development too. When writing for the *Daily Prophet*, a child could become the person they wanted to be, the best version of themselves. Choosing their best traits with their imaginations let loose, they created a new persona that, over time, with each successive article, without even realizing it, soon became reality in a way. Writing about the person they wanted to be gave them enough practice to help them become that best version of themselves [2017, September 19].

In this description, Lawver inadvertently addresses the literary and narrative literacies that these fictional creations would encourage young participants to hone in this new medium, not to mention the critical and aesthetic literacies that would deepen as they worked through their creations with beta readers.

Adler's compilation of letters to Harry Potter represents just one of the many ways that young readers and writers engage with Rowling's series and, in the process, deepen their literacies. Web sites (such as *The Daily Prophet*) function as sites for the development of young readers' active participation in the construction and circulation of textual meanings, and in the process, their narrative and media literacies. Young readers and writers learn their craft from the stories and images that are most familiar to them, and achieve an "intellectual mastery that comes only through active participation" (Jenkins, 2008, p. 185). This media literacy emphasizes critical thinking skills that are even more crucial in today's media culture and the contemporary moment's fascination with "fake news." In writing fan fiction, young readers and writers can develop and express independent judgments about media content, remaining aware of the impact of media on the individual and society, developing strategies to discuss and analyze media messages, and, perhaps most importantly, developing an ability to produce responsible and effective media messages. Thus, young readers deepen their literacies not simply by reading Rowling's seven novels, but also by engaging in discussions and other shared activities, such as reading and writing fan fiction, watching the films, and playing *Potter* playground and computer games (Dempster et al., 2016, p. 270). The urge to tell stories is common to all human cultures, and is "the primary means by which we structure, share, and make sense of our common experiences" (Jenkins, 2008, p. 121). With this in mind, these letters compiled by Bill Adler and *Harry Potter* blogs and fan fiction written by young people speak to a particularly participatory response that readers have to the series as a whole, which in turn becomes a shared form of media world building.

A recent United Nations Educational, Scientific, and Cultural Organization (UNESCO) report sums up the ever evolving definition of media education in the following way: "The emerging new paradigms consider youth as protagonists who are capable of making decisions, exercising choices, and more important, as individuals who are active agents in promoting democratic processes and civic engagement" (Strasburger et al., 2009, p. 523). As the letters in Adler's collection demonstrate, the narrative and media literacies gained in reading the *Harry Potter* novels teach young people about techniques and strategies that are typical of text-based media. Rowling's fantasy series requires no special training or even understanding of English literature, or even experience (since the first five novels of the series are relatively self-contained). Often these books—even though they are read in school, college, and university—do not feel like classical-C literature to students, and in fact seem very different from other books that they read in class, somehow more accessible and welcoming of readers. Jim Ford agrees: "Students learn without being aware of the fact, and what may seem like a break from serious college study is really a tremendous opportunity" (2012, p. 140). Students read for the sheer enjoyment of reading, which is, after all, the point. Ann/Arabella Arithmancy from California speaks of the sense of personal agency that Rowling's magical texts encouraged her to develop.

> Until I read the *Harry Potter* books, it was only reading. I read fantasy, that was it. After reading the books, though, I turned into an author—a writer, I imagine. Now I scrutinize and analyze books…. It's a different way of looking at things, and it has made me better appreciate what authors do and the works they create. I can now reread books and appreciate their value in sparking children's imaginations all the more [Adler, 2001, p. 2].

In his introduction to the letters, Adler encourages readers to reflect on "the force of children's curiosity and imagination" (2001, p. ix). As these letters to Harry Potter express, Rowling's series certainly "brings back the fun in reading" (Adler, 2001, p. 13), as one young writer puts it, but even more importantly, it tackles difficult topics honestly—like abuse, violence, murder—for readers, which in turn inspires young readers' participatory responses in various forums, thereby developing their narrative and media literacies, so important in our visual age.

NOTE

1. Rowling's third novel, *PoA*, juxtaposes two sets of collective protagonists to foreground the series' focus on family and to diversify character types that are on offer for young readers (Bell, 2011). The foursome—Sirius Black, Remus Lupin, Peter Pettigrew, and James Potter—are mirrored in the triad at the center of the Harry Potter series as whole (Williford, 2018). Years before Harry attends Hogwarts, these four supported each other by becoming Animagi to keep Lupin, the werewolf, company during the full moon. This deep friendship and loyalty are celebrated throughout the series and are attributes that in turn come to distinguish Harry, Ron, and Hermione's friendship. Loyalty and love are the two principal characteristics that distinguish "good" protagonists from "evil" in Rowling's series. While they are characteristics that are occasionally tested among our central protagonist—and with increased frequency as the series unfolds—it is this love and sense of familial loyalty that Rowling celebrates as the emotions that ultimately save Harry himself from Voldemort in the final novel, *The Deathly Hallows*.</NOTES>

REFERENCES

Adler, B. (Ed.). (2001). *Kids' letters to Harry Potter from around the world*. New York: Carroll & Graf.
Anatol, G.L. (Ed.). (2009). *Reading Harry Potter again: New critical essays*. Santa Barbara, CA: ABC CLIO.
Ash, J. (2013). New media and participatory cultures. In *Children and young people's cultural worlds* (pp. 219–267). Bristol: Policy.
Bell, C. (2011). Three is a magic number: The trinity archetype in Harry Potter. *Journal of Literature and Art Studies*, 1 (3), 209–218.
Bond, E, & Michelson, N. (2003). Writing Harry's world: Children coauthoring Hogwarts. In *Harry Potter's world: Multidisciplinary critical perspectives* (pp. 109–122). New York: RoutledgeFarmer.
Dempster, S, Oliver, A., Sunderland, J., & and Thistlethwaite, J. (2016). What has *Harry Potter* done for me? Children's reflections on their "*Potter* experience." *Children's Literature in Education*, 47, 267–282.
Driscoll, B. (2013). Using *Harry Potter* to teach literacy: Different approaches. *Cambridge Journal of Education*, 43 (2), 259–271.
Ford, J. (2012). Fantasy classics: Hobbits and Harry in interdisciplinary courses. In *Fantasy media in the classroom: Essays on teaching with film, television, literature, graphic novels and video games* (pp. 138–147). Jefferson, NC: McFarland.
Hallett, C.J., & and Huey, P.J. (Eds.). (2012). *J.K. Rowling, Harry Potter*. Houndmills, Basingstoke: Palgrave Macmillan.
Heilman, E.E. (Ed.). (2003). *Harry Potter's world: Multidisciplinary critical perspectives*. New York: RoutledgeFarmer.
Heilman, E.E. (Ed.). (2009). *Critical perspectives on Harry Potter* (2nd ed.). New York: Routledge.
Jenkins, H. (2008). *Convergence culture: Where old and new media collide*. New York: New York UP.

Konchar Farr, C. (Ed.). (2015). *A wizard of their age: Critical essays from the Harry Potter generation*. Albany, NY: SUNY Press.
Lawver, H. (2017, September 19). Daily Prophet. Retrieved, September 18, 2017, from http://www.heathershow.com/dailyprophet/
Malu, K.F. (2003). Ways of reading Harry Potter: Multiple stories for multiple reader identities. In *Harry Potter's world: Multidisciplinary critical perspectives* (pp. 75–95). New York: RoutledgeFarmer.
McManus, K. (2015). Loading the canon: Harry Potter and fanfiction. In *A wizard of their age: Critical essays from the Harry Potter generation* (pp. 35–47). Albany, NY: SUNY Press.
Mikkelsen, N. (2005). *Powerful magic: Learning from children's responses to fantasy literature*. New York: Teachers College Columbia University.
Nikolajeva, M (2010). *Power, voice and subjectivity in literature for young readers*. New York: Routledge.
Probst, R.E. (1994). Reader-response theory and the English curriculum. *The English Journal*, 83, 3, 37–44.
Strasburger, V.C., Wilson, B.J., & Jordan, A.B. (2009). *Children, adolescents, and the media* (2nd ed.). Los Angeles, CA: Sage.
Sunderland, J., Dempster, S., & and Thistlethwaite, J. (2016). *Children's literacy practices and preferences: Harry Potter and beyond*. New York: Routledge.
Williford, M.S. (2018). What is a hero? An analysis of legacy symbolism. In *Inside the world of Harry Potter: Essays exploring the potterverse* (pp. 263–287). Jefferson, NC: McFarland.

Harry Potter and the Transmediality of Artistic Expression

Caitlin Boyle

> "Ah music," he said, wiping his eyes, "a magic beyond all we do here."
> —Dumbledore, *Harry Potter and the Sorcerer's Stone* (1998)

With regard to *Harry Potter*, there is almost no limit to the types of responses fans have made to represent their interpretation and interest in the books and story. Currently, most academic conversations about and responses to the *Harry Potter* series are overrun with discussions of fan fiction. Though this type of response contributes positively to fan communities, an argument can be made that musical interpretations add connections to the original story and create a unique experience for its audience due to its multimodal production and its contribution to the transmedia canon of the books. In what ways are unauthorized fan artistic productions based on *Harry Potter* examples of transmedia? What kinds of unique interpretations and contributions do they make to the original text?

Very little investigation has been made to explore these fan made productions, even while many musical adaptations are being created for other works, including *Matilda*, *Tuck Everlasting*, and *Charlie and the Chocolate Factory*. These authorized adaptations of their respective books have been very successful and have spurred a continued interest in musical adaptations of children's literature. My own personal interest and love of the *Harry Potter* series has further encouraged this line of inquiry, and has included following many of the works that have been produced in response to the series. The investment in the series has broadened my range of knowledge in the series and the massive amount of additional content and commentary surrounding the *Harry Potter* canon and its phenomenon. This inquiry is guided and structured by a theoretical framework that includes reader response theory, media studies, and more specifically, transmedia.

Reader Response

Louise Rosenblatt, a leading authority of reader response, describes reading and its interpretation as a reader centered process: that a story is just words on a page and that "text is just ink on a page until a reader comes along and gives it life" (1995). This active participation in reading, according to Rosenblatt, can be just as important as the text itself and promotes and encourages readers to engage in the text through responding to it in whatever way allows the reader to gain the most understanding of the text. I argue that this expanded view of reader response can include multimodal responses, including art, writing, and even music. This theoretical frame will lead my examination of unauthorized productions, since readers of *Harry Potter* most commonly create these types of responses to the literature. Transforming a book into a theatrical production provides an alternate format in which audiences can "read" the text. Vincent Murphy, author of *Page to Stage* (2013), finds that, "the pleasure of adapting into another medium, like the pleasure of reading itself, is in the permission you have to engage your own imagination and experience with the art at hand, in making manifest those personal discoveries" (p. 18). The examples of fan responses that will be reviewed later in this discussion reflect this type of production process and reading response.

In their article "Bringing Literature to Life for Urban Adolescents: Artistic, Dramatic Instruction and Live Performance," Certo and Brinda (2011) analyze how students respond to portrayals of assigned books on the stage and in live performances of the text. Presenting a novel to students with a live performance enhances their engagement in the text, while also assisting with their comprehension and providing them with a deeper understanding of the emotions of the characters, thus blending efferent and aesthetic reading to the reader (2011, p. 24). In creating visual representations of the books, whether on stage or online, the creators of these productions allow people of all ages to experience a text. Many productions involving an original text require the producers to read the text in order to create content that represents the story. However, these producers are not necessarily inspired by the text, which cannot be said of many unauthorized productions. These fan-made productions seem to be created through a passion for the books, especially those examined in this inquiry, involving unique musical responses to *Harry Potter*.

Indeed, an element of the series' success is the emotional involvement of the consumers and fans (Gunelius, 2008). Perhaps it is the emotional connection to the series—to its consistent and reliable plot structure, its invitation to readers to share the experiences of the characters, and the main story arc—that keeps readers enthralled "until the very end" (Rowling, 2007), which is essential to the creation of these productions. Notable children's literature researcher and theorist Perry Nodelman says, "what distinguishes the most important literature is its ability to engender new interpretations" (Bixler, 1994, p. 101). In addition to these responses being created by readers of the books, they can also be considered extensions of the original text and broaden the scope of the wizarding world and its characters into a variety of different mediums and platforms.

Transmedia

Henry Jenkins, whose work includes convergence culture, fan culture, and media, states that:

> Transmedia storytelling represents a process where integral elements of a fiction get dispersed systematically across multiple delivery channels for the purpose of creating a unified and coordinated entertainment experience. Ideally each medium makes its own unique contribution to the unfolding of the story [Transmedia Storytelling 101, 2007].

He argues that a successful production of transmedia storytelling involves filling the gaps of the narrative and focusing on specific characters and plotlines. This type of storytelling appears to reflect a reader's interpretation of the story using a medium that best suits them, an idea that seems to reflect the key ideas of reader response. Adaptation theorist Linda Hutcheon supports fan created productions, stating that, "fan culture has taken imaginative possession of the fate of its favorite stories" (2012, p. xix). Though artistic responses to Harry Potter have been identified primarily as examples of cross-mediality, or the expansion of one story into different mediums, I'd argue that the musical representations of *Harry Potter* can be categorized under transmedia. These productions do more than just retell the story; they add content and include reinterpretations of the story, particularly by using parody and humor to amplify certain traits and events. These productions also tend to pull content from across mediums, including fan fiction and popular culture, which essentially creates intertextual connections between all works within the wizarding world. Robyn McCallum (2016) suggests that "the study of adaptation is not simply a matter of comparing a book and a film, since there will be a whole range of diverse texts, discourses and media which mediate and intersect with books and films" (p. 199). Indeed, where *Harry Potter* is concerned, fans and producers must look beyond just the books in order to correctly portray the story and wizarding world as a whole.

With these additions in mind, I'd recommend extending Jenkins' definition of transmedia, changing it into an action—"transmediality" or the process of using transmedia content in new transmedia productions. Extended discussions and content have been incorporated into the musical productions produced based on *Harry Potter* and expand the story and character motivations, as Jenkins states transmedia storytelling must do. Artistic and musical interpretations of the *Harry Potter* books explore and respond to the text in unique ways, and I argue that these ways can be classified as transmedia. Jenkins' concept of participatory culture, in which a community of people interested in the same text come together and participate in discussions, debates, and general interest in that content (2006, p. 3), is clearly a part of how these responses are shared and encouraged, especially with *A Very Potter Musical*, which was seen primarily via YouTube. Jenkins also discusses the idea of "co-creation" or the production of content that allows the user (in this case, the reader) to become both the producer and consumer (2006, p. 105). This "co-creation" is most evident online, through blogs and fan sites, but can now be seen in the production of these musical representations of the books. Co-creation and the transmediality of these artistic and musical productions will become evident as I share several examples, all of which contribute to the ongoing responses to the *Harry Potter* books: Wizard Rock, *Potter Puppets Pals*, *A Very Potter Musical* and *Puffs: Seven Increasingly Eventful Years at a Certain School of Magic and Magic*.

Wizard Rock

Along with his work with fan culture, Jenkins identifies a unique fan created content known as filking, or creating songs or lyrics that reflect on a fan text or story, and is inspired by folk culture and storytelling. He says that may be "a vehicle for building or commenting on pre-existing media texts, a way of pulling to the surface marginalized characters and subplots" (1992, p. 257). Filking by *Harry Potter* fans has been renamed Wizard Rock. In 2002, Wizard Rock began with the creation of the band Harry and the Potters, who were quickly joined by many other bands, including Draco and the Malfoys, Ministry of Magic, and many more. These producers explore characters and their motivations, events and plotlines through original songs, which also reflect their own interpretations of the text and even advance other readers' understanding of text. The platform used to create these musical interpretations of the series provides its listeners with a closer connection to the narrator or voice of the song and provides a bit more insight into the meaning and emotions of the character being portrayed. In order to be successful and create strong connections to the characters, these "performances need to be faithful representations in sound of the composer's conception" (Leech-Wilkinson, 2013, p. 3) or interpretation of the text. I will provide a few examples of how these songwriters have developed their own interpretations of the books and its characters, and how their songs enhance these responses.

The band Ministry of Magic decided to respond to "The Snape Debate," as it is called in many conversations in online forums, through their song "Snape vs. Snape" (Ministry of Magic, 2010). This debate questions whether Snape has redeemed himself and become a good character by the end of the series, or if "no one stops being a death eater" (Heyman & Newell, 2005). The band has turned a character's dual identity into a song that relates the conflict in the character's own voice. Ministry of Magic is not the only band to create songs that use a character voices, inner thoughts, and explore relationships in the books. Another example is the band Moaning Myrtles, whose songs are written from the perspective of the ghost that haunts the girls' bathroom in Hogwarts, Moaning Myrtle. As this character is a minor one within the scope of the series, this band has extended its audiences' knowledge of the character by exploring the character's emotions and motivations. This idea is reflective of Jenkins' parameters for transmedia storytelling and of filking, both of which expand the wizarding world as a whole.

Potter Puppet Pals

A creative way a group of fans responded to the series was through puppets in their YouTube series, *Potter Puppet Pals*. This is certainly less directly connected to the books, as is clear in Wizard Rock songs, but these fans have found an alternative medium in which to extend the story. Transmediality is clearly evident in their performances and connection to the *Harry Potter* canon. One of their more popular videos is called "The Mysterious Ticking Noise," and involves hand puppets of characters from the series, including the main Trio, Harry, Hermione, and Ron, as well as Snape, Dumbledore, and Lord Voldemort. The creator has each puppet sing a short line of song consisting of the character's name, which eventually results in a musical canon with all the characters singing together, all to the rhythm of the ticking noise. Though there is not much substance where content and relationship to the book are concerned, the way that the puppets sing their parts actually reflects aspects of their characters' personality and role within the series.

A Very Potter Musical

I further examined fan responses with the theatrical, fan-made musical production, *A Very Potter Musical*. It was created and performed at the University of Michigan in 2009, and has since appeared on YouTube and has had over 13 million views to date (StarKid, 2009). Though the creators chose to not stick closely with the timeline of the books, this production does retell parts of the story, adding humor to their representation of books, while also including popular culture references and content from fan fiction, creating a parody version of the original story. For example, in this musical, the producers portray Dumbledore as gay, a character element that author J.K. Rowling shared on social media while the films were being released. These performers also play off a popular fan fiction story that suggests that Draco Malfoy is in love with Hermione Granger, which is not the case in the books. In addition to these transmedial character traits and relationships, the musical also explores the relationship between Lord Voldemort and Professor Quirrell, which is rarely mentioned in the first book. Quirrell has the odd situation of having Voldemort sharing his body, and the musical plays up the hilarity of this predicament and lays out the possible friendship that might have arisen from this situation. These altered representations, though more meaningful when viewed than what I can describe here, exemplify the extraordinary way a book can be transformed and portrayed by its readers.

In the opening number, the musical's creators chose to take a humorous approach and incorporate parody elements into their show. Harry, for example, is playing up his celebrity status, stating that, "everybody thinks I'm cool" (StarKid, 2009). They also add humor in the way they represent magical elements of the story, like floo powder, and accentuate the personalities of Ron and Hermione. And though not strictly aligned with the book's original interpretation, it seems to be nevertheless entertaining and enjoyable to its audience. And, though the songs aren't necessarily up to the standard of most official musicals, they are catchy and fit within the context of the production. The popularity of the first musical led the group to create additional productions, including *A Very Potter Sequel* and *A Very Potter Senior Year*. The producers took some liberty with their portrayal of the books, but in doing so, created a musical and theatrical response that created a unique entertainment experience for the performers and their audience, the type of experience that Jenkins defines as a successful form of transmedia storytelling.

Puffs

The last production I will explore and examine is the Off Broadway show *Puffs: Seven Increasingly Eventful Years at a Certain School of Magic and Magic*. As an Off Broadway show, this parody of the *Harry Potter* series has managed to continue to build a following and has become steadily more successful. Essentially, this play looks at the events that unfold over the course of the series from the Hufflepuffs' perspective. The play follows three Hufflepuffs, affectionately known as Puffs, who seem to have some blatant similarities to the primary three characters in the series. This Puffs trio must deal with not only life in the magical world, but with all of the horrific and terrifying things that happen while Harry Potter is at Hogwarts. With tons of humor, connections to events that take place in the books, and with numerous intertextual references, this fan-created adaptation and parody seems to embrace transmediality in its entirety. Creator Matt Cox admits that he's added content from new installments of the wizarding world and is surprised at how much die-hard fans love the parody. When asked why he chose to use the Hufflepuffs' perspective, he said, "Since we got (the story) from the heroes side, and we got to spend a lot of time with the brave, courageous people ... what it's like from the people who everyone else thinks less of. Plus, there (sp) the people we know the least amount of information about in the books, so it was fun to use them" (Sblendorio, 2016). Cox also wanted to set *Puffs* apart from other *Harry Potter* parodies out there: "It's not just about what happens in the books, but its about how the events in the books are seen from another perspective, and I don't think that's something that we see a lot in other shows like that" (2016). Unlike *A Very Potter Musical*, *Puffs* aimed to stick closely to the books, while adding the humor and content needed when telling the story from the loveable underdogs, the Hufflepuffs.

Fan-Created Productions

The explorations shared throughout this essay should confirm that these musical and theatrical interpretations enhance and expand the *Harry Potter* story and suggest that they should be considered a valuable type of transmedia storytelling. These types of productions add to the reading responses to *Harry Potter* in profoundly unique ways, such as incorporating parody, character voices, popular culture, and other fan fiction. In doing so, they encourage their audiences to produce unique responses to these productions, a response that may differ due to the multimodality of this type of expression. Transmediality, as described in earlier discussion, is displayed in these productions adding both value and distinctive elements to their representations of the books. It seems curious that, though these productions incorporate content from outside the scope of the books, they have continued to receive such a positive reception from even the most devoted fans of the series. While I normally value adaptations and representations of books that to remain as close to the original source as possible, I find these adaptations provide more enjoyment for me, as I have gained a wealth of knowledge that extends beyond the books and that allows these productions to feed my extended knowledge and enthusiasm for everything *Harry Potter*.

Throughout this exploration, several questions came up concerning fan created content and its unofficial capacity, as well as how much these productions can stray from the original canon, a few which I will reflect on briefly. The first of these questions is, in what ways do parody elements and popular culture references add to or detract from the original story? As I shared earlier, these intertextual references seem to actually enhance the enjoyment of the parody, as a surprised Matt Cox of *Puffs* shared when interviewed. Most fans claim to be disappointed if an adaptation doesn't stick closely to the original text. Indeed, Chris Columbus, who directed the first two *Potter* films, shared his concerns about this saying, "people would have crucified me if I hadn't been faithful to the books" (Hutcheon, 2012, p. 123). That being said, how far away can these theatrical responses get from the original timeline and story before they either aren't reminiscent of the original or aren't entertaining to its audience? The answer remains unclear, although I'd imagine that there is a point-of-no-return where adaptation changes are concerned.

The next of my lingering questions pertains to how these unauthorized musical productions are able to provide stronger emotional connections to the books than responses in other formats. When looking at emotional connections, it becomes a bit of a challenge to come up with a concrete answer that applies to every consumer. Researcher Matthew Reason attributes the "liveness" of theatrical productions as one explanation for why the emotional connection might be stronger compared to other mediums (2016, p. 240). In his study on liveness, he found that students felt "more a part" of the production and the story when attending a live theatrical performance (p. 230). And though only one of the four interpretations consists of attending a live performance, it is one attribute of these productions that encourages a stronger emotional connection to the performance and the original story. In regard to music, many studies have been done concerning the emotional nature of music. Lucy Okikawa (2006), who studied how musical adaptations of literature strengthened the comprehension of visually impaired youth, suggests that music and songs immediately "set the tone of a character's feelings," (p. 372) which allow for a deeper understanding of character motivations and emotions. In establishing these contributing factors, there may be a firmer basis for the claim that music and live performance are more enticing and engaging for audiences, especially where fan responses are concerned. There may also be the element of camaraderie when theatrical performances are concerned, as the audiences are able to react more closely with the show and with the other viewers around them. A more thorough investigation is still needed to understand this idea fully, but these elements certainly hold some ground in confirming the claim.

Conclusion

My final thought that was not discussed in this exploration is while "franchised film adaptations of classic and popular literary texts for young people have attracted large budgets, mass audiences and critical attention," (McCallum, 2016, p. 198) why haven't fans been discouraged from continuing to create their own responses to the *Potter* series? I'm in no way insinuating that these fan-created productions should hold any lower ground to "authorized" productions, but it would be interesting to determine what drives these fans to continue producing these performances. Additionally, with all of the productions across mediums of the series, where do these producers go for inspiration? Do they look solely at the original books or do they explore all extensions of the story? *Puffs'* Matt Cox has added content to his play as new productions of the series have emerged. These extended stories of the wizarding world include the play and printed screenplay *Harry Potter and the Cursed Child* and the projected five-movie saga, *Fantastic Beasts and Where to Find Them*, both wildly popular, and in turn, broadening the world and story's fan base. A recent development within fan-created content is the recent authorization and approval by Warner Bros. for a fan created film about Lord Voldemort's early life to be produced and hopefully released in some monetary capacity. This is a huge shift from Warner Bros. previous reactions to fan-created productions, which have been very possessive and controlling in regard to the *Harry Potter* franchise. This promotion of fan-produced material must bring hope for those currently creating responses to the books, that if they work hard enough and produce something of consequence, then they can have their work supported by the franchise also. If we look at these fan productions as adaptations, Hutcheon suggests that "if we cannot talk about the creative process, we cannot fully understand the urge to adapt and therefore perhaps the very process of adaptation" (2012, p. 107). The process enters undefined territory and the motivations of fans and producers to create their responses and performances will vary immensely, although all reasons stem from their love of the literature and the story.

These fan-created musical and artistic expressions offer unique contributions to the continuing responses and representations of the *Harry Potter* books, allowing for new and multiple mediums to be used by these producers, resulting in meaningful creations. I intend to continue to explore *Harry Potter* musical productions as examples of transmedia, and intend to discover how the parody elements influence the success of representations of the books. I also plan to implement a close reading of these productions and responses as they compare to the original text, making a determination on whether they can be truly considered part of the canon. Musical and theatrical productions allow for a variety of interpretations using different modes and expand the ever-growing world and narrative of *Harry Potter*. Further investigation of these ideas could be valuable in understanding the true nature of these productions' successes, but we are left in little doubt that more artistic responses to the *Harry Potter* series are yet to come.

REFERENCES

Bixler, P. (1994). The secret garden "misread": The broadway musical as creative interpretation. *Literature 33*, pp. 101–123.
Certo & Brinda (2011). Bringing literature to life for urban adolescents: Artistic, dramatic instruction and live performance. *The Journal of Aesthetic Education 45*(3), pp. 22–37.
Gunelius, Susan (2008). *Harry potter: The story of a global business phenomenon*. New York: Palgrave Macmillan.
Heyman, D. (Producer), & Newell, M. (Director) (2005). *Harry Potter and the Goblet of Fire*. [Motion Picture] UK, USA: Warner Bros. Pictures.
Hutcheon, L. (2006). *A theory of adaptation*. Taylor and Francis Publishing.
Jenkins, H. (1992). *Textual poachers*. New York: Routledge.
Jenkins, H. (2006). *Convergence culture*. New York: New York University Press.
Jenkins, H. (2007). *Transmedia storytelling 101*. Retrieved from http://henryjenkins.org/2007/03/transmedia_storytelling_101.html.
Leech-Wilkinson, D. (2013). The emotional power of musical performance. *Oxford Scholarship Online*.
McCallum, R. (2016). Palimpsestuous intertextualities. *International Research in Children's Literature*, 9.2, 197–214.
Murphy, V. (2013). *Page to stage*. Ann Arbor: University of Michigan Press.
Rosenblatt, L. (1995). *Literature as exploration*. New York: Modern Language Association of America.
Rowling, J.K. (1998). *Harry potter and the sorcerer's stone*. New York: Random House.
Rowling, J.K. (2007). *Harry potter and the deathly hallows*. New York: Random House.
Sblendorio, M. (2016). BWW interview: Meet Matt Cox, the writer behind the magical puffs. *Broadway world: Off-Broadway*. Retrieved from https://www.broadwayworld.com/off-broadway/article/BWW-Interview-Meet-Matt-Cox-the-Writer-Behind-the-Magical-PUFFS-20161010
YouTube (2009). *A very potter musical*. StarKid Productions. Retrieved from https://www.youtube.com/playlist?list=PLC76BE906C9D83A3A
YouTube (2010). *Snape vs. snape*. Ministry of Magic. Retrieved from https://www.youtube.com/watch?v=su1BqbNex4E

Harry Potter Fandom and Narratives of Inequality in the United States Presidential Election of 2016

SERGEY MEDVEDEV *and* ELENA PRONKINA

The narrative of inequality has always played a prominent role in the way the *Harry Potter* fandom reflects on the issues of the actual world. This essay explores how *Harry Potter* fans negotiated the 2016 United States presidential race and made sense of their own political participation by using representations of inequality from the *Harry Potter* storyworld. We argue that the Harry Potter universe has effectively transcended the realm of pure fantasy and become a site of political re-imagining, engagement and activism. We begin with conceptualizing inequality to see what types of inequality are present in J.K. Rowling's story about "the boy who lived."

The Narrative of Inequality and the Harry Potter *Storyworld*

In their article *Equality: putting the theory into action*, Baker et al. (2006, p. 3) distinguish two major types of inequality among others, i.e., material inequality and what they call "the inequality of respect and recognition." The latter refers to the injustices of social statuses, prejudices and various sorts of non-economic discrimination. With respect to material inequality, Karl Marx's model of class struggles suggests that inequality emerges as a result of the malicious will of power holders turned against the oppressed class (Marx & Engels, 1848, p. 14). Inequality thus is neither natural, nor fair. Liberal, or libertarian, perspectives on economic inequality suggests that inequality is inevitable because people are not equal in the choices they make and the efforts they exercise to achieve the individual good. Therefore, the only possible equality is the equality of everyone before the law, while the equality of opportunity may be achieved only with a "magic wand," in Robert Nozick's words (2013, p. 235).

Another type of inequality, according to Baker, is the inequality of respect and recognition. It also can be referred to as cultural inequality since it pertains to the processes occurring in the Marxian "superstructure," rather than in the economic "basis." The theoretical considerations on this type of inequality are well-developed by Cultural Studies and Critical Theory of the Frankfurt School. The key point here is that culture as a superstructure is an extension of economy and the cultural domination in the form of mass culture reproduction is the way the privileged prolong their economic dominance. The focus on culture allowed the researchers of the Marxian tradition to proceed from the analysis of inequalities with respect to economic classes to the inequality and discrimination of various social groups based on gender, race and so on.

Structural inequality in the *Harry Potter* universe is evident in both cultural and economic dimensions. Cultural inequality or discriminatory perception of individuals based on their origins is central to the structure of the *HP* storyworld. First, in the *Harry Potter* universe, people are divided into wizards and muggles. Muggles are ordinary people who have no magical lineage and hold no powers to cast spells. Notably, muggles are defined in the universe through their lack of "wizardness," especially when called "No-Majs," as in *Fantastic Beasts and Where to Find Them*. Following Bourdieu, naming is a symbolic power that is used to construct social reality in the process of symbolization (Bourdieu, 1985, p. 741). It also can be used in a discriminatory fashion as exemplified by the way no-wizards are named, No-Majs. Thus, symbolic power has a role in creating and dividing social groups.

The division between No-Majs and wizards is not the only example of structural inequality with respect to the inequality of respect and recognition in the *Harry Potter* universe. The society of wizards is not homogeneous. "Wizardness" as an identity depends on the "purity of blood." Pure-bloods are those whose parents are wizards. They represent the most ancient and noble families. Half-bloods are born in the families with one of the parents being a muggle. Finally, a mudblood is the wizard who is born in a muggle family and has no kinship ties with wizards. The word "mudblood" obviously has a strong negative connotation and is associated with prejudices, bullying and even violence. Hermione Granger, who is one of the central characters of the story, is described as a "mudblood."

Along with the cultural inequality, within the world of wizards there is also the economic inequality that affects its structuration. Some families, even the pureblood ones like the Weasleys, are relatively poor, while the other ones like the Malfoys belong to the wealthy aristocracy.

It is interesting that with regard to those two types of inequalities the *Harry Potter* fictional world may operate under the same rules of social structuration as the actual one. For instance, the head of the Weasley family, Arthur Weasley, exemplifies what Bourdieu called the *homology* of position between groups belonging to different classes. Homology describes a resonance or affinity between two different groups of people arising from a similarly shaped social position (Bourdieu, 1985, p. 737). For instance, intellectuals as a group dominated on the level of cultural production can be in a homological relations with workers as a group dominated in economic sphere—because of the similarity of their situation. Despite belonging to the culturally "privileged" group of wizards, even pureblood wizards, the Weasleys as economic have-nots sympathize with No-Majs dominated on a cultural, symbolic level. The same homology (or alliance of position) between those treated unfairly in a cultural sphere and those oppressed with relation to the economy can be seen in Hermione Granger's fight to liberate elves. The social position the elves occupy in the *Harry Potter* universe is close to that of slaves. Unlike the Weasleys, Hermione Granger does not suffer economically, but she belongs to the culturally discriminated group of "mudbloods," which allows her to identify and empathize with the economically oppressed elves.

The above exemplifies how the issue of inequality was exposed in the *Harry Potter* story through the conflicts inside its universe. Although one can certainly see parallels with the processes occurring around us, those conflicts are grounded completely in the plot of the fictional world and do not require any references to the events of the actual world. The other way to represent inequalities in an imaginary world—instead of portraying a conflict inside the fictional world—is to incorporate the elements which will be decoded by viewers/users/players as "statements" with regard to the events of the actual world and its injustices. In *Fantastic Beasts and Where to Find Them* movie, for instance, the president of the Magical Congress of the United States is portrayed as a black woman. That is a big statement about equality in the wizarding world, especially with comparison to the actual world of 1926, where the movie is set. It is hardly possible to imagine a person of color or a woman (not to mention both) to be the elected leader of any of the Western countries in that period. Incidentally, the movie was released on November 10, 2016, only two days after the U.S. presidential election of 2016, in which the Democratic hopeful Hillary Clinton tried to become the first woman to win the presidency. Of course, none of that was said in the movie, but this intertextual relation between fantasy and current affairs could be read by viewers. As a result, the case found its way to become a part of the real-life narrative of inequality.

Another instance of referencing to the inequalities of the actual world in the *Harry Potter* universe is the case of "black Hermione." In December 2015, it was announced that the role of Hermione Granger in the new *Harry Potter and the Cursed Child* stage play would be performed by the black actress Noma Dumezweni. The news provoked a buzz as some users found the choice inconsistent with the canon, while others (including J.K. Rowling) blamed the reaction on racism and prejudices. As in the story about the president of the Magical Congress being a black woman, Hermione's skin color in the stage play was of no importance to its plot—definitely the play was not a story about a black magician being discriminated against—but it became a statement in conjunction with the reaction of the public. It served as a positive provocation. Deliberately or not, the stage play invited the audience to a conversation about race equality.

Hillary Clinton, Bernie Sanders and Harry Potter Fandom

Harry Potter fandom activities demonstrate how, on the left side of the political aisle in this election, the narrative of cultural equality came into collision with the narrative of economic equality—not the narratives themselves but those representing them in the politics. The narrative of cultural diversity, and the fight against misogyny in particular, was centered around Hillary Clinton campaign, while Bernie Sanders, a self-proclaimed social democrat, had a strong message of material equality. The two messages constitute a logical whole as the basis and the superstructure of the Marxian theory of society. But in this election, they were torn between the two candidates. Let's explore this point in detail.

The Harry Potter Alliance is an online community that engages thousands of *Harry Potter* fans through work for equality, human rights and literacy. The Alliance uses the wizarding universe to interpret and address the issues of the actual world. As its website reads, "We are changing the world by making activism accessible through the power of story" ("What We Do," n.d.). In 2016, the fandom engaged in the United States presidential election with the #ReadyForHermione campaign. First it was declared to be a campaign for promoting literacy around the globe, but it eventually turned into a political campaign that coincided with the election. In an imaginary election, the all-witch (read as all-women) ticket of Hermione Granger and Luna Lovegood ran on a platform focused on education access for all, cooperation between magical and non-magical communities, environmental justice, and ending institutionalized discrimination against transgender and non-binary people. The official campaign slogan "I'm with Herm" referred to Hillary

Clinton's "I'm with Her." As a campaign press release put it, "the two candidates solidified their feminist base and made headlines with their progressive policy proposals." The Granger campaign said she wanted to show that "politics can serve a greater purpose beyond just the cultivation of political careers and consolidation of power among the well-monied and influential few" (Granger/Lovegood, 2016). Plus, it was revealed in *Harry Potter and the Cursed Child* play that Hermione Granger grew up to become the Minister of Magic. The campaign "Nerds for Her" also drew parallels between Hillary Clinton and Hermione Granger. Hermione Granger is a perfect political candidate due to her personal characteristics and commitment to fight for the rights of the oppressed. Therefore, the allegory provided Hillary Clinton with additional symbolic capital ("Nerds for Her," n.d.).

The character of Hillary Clinton fell in line with the desire of many Americans to expand the boundaries of equality, to finally break that glass ceiling and elect the first female president of the U.S. But along with this asset, the Democratic frontrunner had a liability of her background as a wealthy career politician, who receives large donations from Wall Street and belongs to the establishment. It became especially clear in comparison with her opponent in the primaries, Bernie Sanders. His anti-establishment and economically left rhetoric resonated with the younger generation. In the Pennsylvania primary, for instance, Bernie Sanders won 83 percent of the votes of those aged under 30 ("Young vs. Old Votes," 2016). As Hillary Clinton infamously said in a private conversation, Bernie's fans are those who "live in their parents' basement." She acknowledged the appeal of Bernie's message on economy to the younger people saying "If you're feeling like you're consigned to being a barista, or some other job that doesn't pay a lot, and doesn't have some other ladder of opportunity attached to it, then the idea that maybe, just maybe, you could be part of a political revolution is pretty appealing" (Moore, 2016).

Importantly, the demographic group of Bernie Sanders' supporters—not Hillary's—corresponds to the demographics of *Harry Potter* fandom. On the *Harry Potter* forum dedicated to American presidential race of 2016 on potterforums.com, 49 percent of users responded "Bernie Sanders" when asked, "Which of the top candidates most impresses you?" ("American Presidential Race," 2015). This electronic poll hardly is representative, but even this poll tells a lot if one compares Bernie's almost 50 percent to Hillary's modest 14 percent. As one of the *Harry Potter* fans commented on the forum:

> I'd rather have Hillary as the current president than Trump, that's sure. But what about the future? Bernie has to become president, because otherwise, there will again be stagnation and degeneration. If Clinton gets president, then the next one will most likely be another clone of her. Really, the world's only hope in that case is Bernie [Sugar quill, 2015].

But unfortunately for Bernie Sanders, he is a white male who does not represent *personally* the narrative of inequality of respect and recognition at all. Thus, in this election, *Harry Potter* fans may have been torn between the narrative of cultural inequality pushed by the new texts by J.K. Rowling and the Harry Potter Alliance on the one hand, and their real-life concerns about their economic well-being on the other.

At this point, it can be concluded that the fandom's treatment of the presidential election represents the problem common to the Democratic vote in this election in general. It is the narratives of cultural and economic equalities being split between the two democratic candidates, and Hillary Clinton seen as unfit to represent the economic component of the narrative of equality.

Donald Trump and Harry Potter *Fandom*

Along with the "civil war" on the Democratic side of the aisle evident in the context of *Harry Potter* fandom, another notable theme within the fandom was the Republican hopeful Donald Trump. Central to the HP storyworld and its fandom, the principle of equality came into collision with the substance and rhetoric of the unorthodox campaign the real estate mogul ran. While for the Trump's base his campaign could mean the triumph of common sense over political correctness, for many it turned to a symbol of bigotry and intolerance.

We suggest that the narrative of inequality played a major role in how the Harry Potter fandom reacted to the presidential campaign of Donald Trump. Over the course of the 2016 presidential race, there was a number of statements Trump made that could be perceived as contradicting the idea of cultural equality. Trump's call for "a total and complete shutdown of Muslims entering the United States until our country's representatives can figure out what is going on" is one of the most prominent examples (Donald J. Trump for President, 2015). The statement was made in a campaign press release on December 7, 2015, following the terrorist attack in San Bernardino, California, on December 2, 2015. By many the statement was interpreted as a manifestation of intolerance and prejudices towards people based on their religious affiliation. When announcing his presidential bid on June 16, 2015, Donald Trump made a statement about illegal immigrants from Mexico as follows: "They're bringing drugs. They're bringing crime. They're rapists, and some, I assume, are good people" (Trump, 2015). The words were widely interpreted as a deeply offensive and unacceptable attempt to demonize Mexican people in general. On October 7, 2016, the so-called "*Access Hollywood* tape" was released by the *Washington Post*. The tape, dated back to 2005, had Trump talking about "kissing, groping and trying to have sex with women" in a private conversation (Fahrenthold, 2016). Consequently, Trump was accused of lacking respect for women and misogyny. Among other notable controversies were Trump ridiculing the appearance of a disabled *NYT* reporter ("Did Trump," 2016) and inciting violence against protesters at his rallies (Sullivan, 2016).

All of these scandals—among many others—contributed to constructing the image of Donald Trump as a perfect villain of the presidential election of 2016, in the opinion of many in the U.S. and beyond. Although the younger generation—which *HP* readers certainly belong to—traditionally tends to support Democratic presidential candidates regardless of their personalities, some also argue that Donald Trump was a special case for many *HP* readers. The study that was retweeted by J.K. Rowling herself concludes that "each *Harry Potter* book read lowered respondents' evaluations of Donald Trump by roughly 2–3 points on a 100 point scale ... but for someone who has read all seven books, the total impact could lower their estimation of Trump by 18 points out of 100" ("New Study," 2016). Although the overall impact on readers was not dramatic, Diana Mutz found the general adherence of the HP readers and viewers to the three cross-cutting themes in the story of Harry Potter: "1) the value of tolerance and respect for difference; 2) opposition to violence and punitiveness; and 3) the dangers of authoritarianism" (Mutz, 723). The figure of Voldemort as the main villain of the *Harry Potter* books who embodies those themes became the symbol of the Trump campaign for the *Harry Potter* fandom.

Following Trump's call for a "Muslim ban," J.K. Rowling drew a parallel between the Republican hopeful and the main villain of the *Harry Potter* book series, the Dark Lord Voldemort. With this regard she famously tweeted: "How horrible. Voldemort was nowhere near as bad" (Rowling, 2015). At the 2016 PEN Literary Awards Gala, the *HP* author called objectionable "almost everything that Mr. Trump says" and accused him of being "offensive and bigoted" (Kreps, 2016). In her essay *On Monsters, Villains and the EU Referendum*, she branded Trump a "fascist in all but name" (Rowling, 2016). Later in 2016, she admitted that the plot of the *Fantastic Beasts and Where to Find Them* movie grew out of world events and was "inspired by the newfound popularity of leaders like Trump" (Begley, 2016).

In the same manner as to an author, it is natural to readers to draw analogies between fictional events and the actual politics, compare fictional characters to the politicians of today. In Rebecca Nicholson's retrospective analysis, "every generation has its go-to pop-culture political analogy" with *Star Wars* playing this role in the 80s, for example (Nicholson, 2017). This is not necessarily the case in the over-mediatized world of today when there are too many successful franchises to ascribe a leading role to one of them.

As Emily Nussbaum speculates, *Game of Thrones* also was used by its fans as an allegorical text for the 2016 presidential race to highlight the parallels between Bernie Sanders and the High Sparrow, or Hillary Clinton and Daenerys (or even villainous Cersei) (Nussbaum, 2016).

When it comes to *Harry Potter* fan art, one of the themes chosen to connect Donald Trump to Voldemort was the theme of horcruxes. According to one version, Donald Trump's five horcruxes were Obama's birth certificate, Trump's wig-like hairstyle, Ivanka Trump, The 6th hole at the Turnberry golf course and Unknown object in the Oval Office, Washington, D.C. (Barrell, 2015). Another source identified seven horcruxes of Donald Trump as Donald Trump's Twitter account, the private server of Hillary Clinton, Donald Trump's hair, the birth certificate of President Barack Obama, the head of the University of Pennsylvania mascot, the original chair from Donald Trump's show "The Apprentice" and the mini Mercedes of Barron Trump (McDonald, 2017).

It can be better understood through the social theory of vilification, how the Trump-Voldemort allegory served to meet the needs of *Harry Potter* fandom as a social group. According to Orrin E. Klapp, the author of *Heroes, Villains and Fools, as Agents of Social Control*, vilification is "a kind of symbol-making that groups engage in under certain conditions in order to repair and defend the social structure and to build consensus and morale for certain kinds of social actions" (1959, p. 71). The act of vilification is "a collective and moral process of imputing a villain concept to somebody and treating him accordingly" (Klapp, 1959, p. 71). As Pillar suggests, "the need for a villain is a matter of public psychology and, because of that, also a matter of politics" (Pillar, 2013, p. 218). Orrin Klapp highlights the social structural need for villains who are "fundamental social symbol naturally created by the group as part of its organization" (Klapp, 1959, p. 71). For a fandom as a social group which uses shared value code expressed through common symbolic system to make social change, the process of assigning someone with a villain status is a "natural" mechanism to extrapolate hero-villain symbolic system of a fictional universe on the actual world. As a mechanism, it is morally neutral in a certain sense. While some particular case of vilification could be an example of scapegoating, in some other cases, the object of vilification can be "as bad as the villain concept with which he is impute" indeed (Klapp, 1959, p. 72).

Then how does vilification work? First, the *Harry Potter* story, its events and characters, become symbols when seen as an allegory for the real-life opposition to race, gender and other prejudices in the eyes of the reader. The meaning is transferred from the actual world into the novel by the author and then the public, so that the perception of the text is expected to change, enriched with the cultural layers the author and readers learned from their life experience. For instance, the concept of bigotry that is derived from the real life is applied to Voldemort and makes the Dark Lord its symbol. That is what Klapp called "long run phase of vilification." In that phase, "the stock of images of types of evildoers [is] contributed to by artists and writers as well as all the processes that form folklore, such as storytelling, rumor and gossip" (Klapp, 1959, p. 72).

The process of an opposite direction can be called "short run phase of vilification." It implies "dramatic imputation of images to specific parties in appropriate situations and the formation of consensus concerning their evil character—that is, 'making' or defining villain" (Klapp, 1959, p. 72). The process occurs when the symbol, a culturally-reinterpreted story, is extrapolated back upon the events or personalities of the actual world to make sense of them. It was not Trump who made Voldemort the symbol of bigotry; it was Voldemort as a symbol of bigotry who was used to define the persona of Donald Trump. With this transition, the negative emotional appeal to Voldemort is conferred to the politician. In Klapp's taxonomy of villains, Trump was assigned with the features of "the Persecutor" type, "a powerful figure of evil who oppresses the weak" (Klapp, 1954, p. 58).

The Internet, and social media specifically, create a perfect environment for such practices because of their non-hierarchical structure. Online sphere implies "no single instant at which [a person] becomes a villain" (Klapp, 1959, p. 72). That is of importance because—as a rule—a person is not branded a villain at a specific time and specific place by someone's individual decision. Instead, vilification usually takes on a form of public "talks": gossip, agitation, name calling and "other forms of symbolic interaction over a period of time" (Klapp, 1959, p. 72). On the Internet, this process may take the form of users creating and sharing photo memes, posting hashtags on Twitter, and so on. The cascade of these small individual actions creates a general picture, which was the case with Donald Trump repeatedly and enthusiastically portrayed as Voldemort in memes or the #Trumpdemort hashtag.

In the #ReadyForHermione campaign by the Harry Potter Alliance, the Trump campaign was portrayed through the ticket of Vincent Crabbe and Gregory Goyle, with slogans like "Make Hogwarts Great Again" and a pledge to build a wall around Hogsmeade to ensure our last purely wizarding village remains muggle-free. According to the press release, "Vincent Crabbe and Gregory Goyle have captured the attention of the magical community's remaining Voldemort apologists and blood purists" (Granger/Lovegood, 2016).

Vilification is a rational process and is invoked by a social group as a mechanism of self-regulation. First, it fosters group cohesion and solidarity in the face of a well-defined enemy and reinforces group values against the opposite values of the villain (Klapp, 1954, p. 62). In Klapp's words, vilification "can serve stability by defining troublemakers" (Klapp, 1959, p. 71). Second, vilification helps to understand the complicated external world through simplification when "multiple, confusing or unknown factors are simplified, and complex issues are personified as conflicts between champions and villains" (Klapp, 1954, p. 61). Third, vilification encourages action and facilitates change "by supplying targets of action for revolutionaries and reformers" (Klapp, 1959, p. 71). With this regard, Mueller & Sutherland (2010) also concluded that the number of heroes and villains in discourse corresponds to the level of fan involvement. In case of Voldemort, the vilification of Donald Trump could also give the sense of psychological relief to fans, since the fandom knew the villain was defeated at the end of the story.

Although Donald Trump became a perfect villain indeed, the story required a hero. However, the hero-villain opposition did not work well with Hillary Clinton and Donald Trump both being the most distrusted presidential candidates in the history of the U.S. politics (Collins, 2016). Although Hillary Clinton was widely compared to Hermione Granger within the fandom, she also was portrayed as Dolores Umbridge, another villainous character of the *HP* books, in a series of memes. Also, the fact that the *HP* fans were split between Bernie Sanders and Hillary Clinton made the image of the main hero in the basic hero-villain opposition uncertain. Nevertheless, the character of Donald Trump as a personified evil in the story encouraged participation within *Harry Potter* fandom.

Harry Potter *Fandom and Activism*

In the final part of the essay, we will discuss general aspects of *Harry Potter* fan participation and activism in the 2016 presidential election in the U.S. Henry Jenkins defines fan activism as a "form of civic engagement and political participation that emerge from within fan culture itself, often in response to the shared interests of fans, often conducted through the infrastructure of existing fan practices and relationships, and often framed through metaphors drawn from popular and participatory culture" (Jenkins, 2012). He also explains this phenomenon by the common feeling of solidarity and shared resistance (Jenkins, 2012).

Bould and Vint suggest that fantastic social structures facilitate "a critique of our own taken-for-granted social structures and relationships" (2012, p. 103). Apparently, this mechanism works on a group level as well. According to Ernest Bormann's Symbolic convergence theory, stories or what one could call "fantastic social structures" create common cultural field for their consumers (Olufowote, 2006). Henry Jenkins notes that convergence culture "inspires civic participation by mapping content worlds onto real-world problems" (Jenkins 2012). In their book *Harry Potter and International Relations*,

Nexon and Neumann outline the four roles popular culture can take in the context of political issues: popular culture and politics, popular culture as mirror, popular culture as data and popular culture as constitutive (2006, p. 9). In the context of the "popular culture and politics" role, popular culture is both the beginning and the end of politics. Taking stock of popular-culture-as-mirror function allows researchers to think about the parallels between real and fictional worlds. Popular-culture-as-data approach discusses social norms and beliefs within cultural texts. Popular-culture-as-constitutive role of popular culture reveals its constructivist nature that creates social norms and beliefs (Nexon & Neumann, 2006, p. 10). Thus, the *Harry Potter* universe can both represent some social processes and provoke their emergence.

Participation as a mechanism to change social reality, personal responsibility for standing against injustices and the importance of an individual choice are central to the *Harry Potter* storyworld (Barratt, 2012, p. 2). In the series of the *Harry Potter* books, some advocates of the blood purity were not pure-blood wizards (Voldemort and Dolores Umbridge, for instance). Dumbledore once characterized Tom Riddle, who eventually became Voldemort, as "a boy who made all the wrong choices" (Heyman, Barron & Yates, 2009). On the other hand, it was Harry Potter's choice not to be sorted to Slytherin, "the faculty of wicked wizards." He chose a different path despite being—as the Sorting Hat advised him—"better suited" to study there. In both cases, personal choices of the wizards let them ignore their origins. In this context, the friendship of Harry, Ron and Hermione has a symbolic meaning. Their friendship is one of the main counter-arguments against a racist logic because they all are of different origins. They chose to be friends based on the shared intolerance to the injustices, prejudices and inequalities of the wizarding world. Thus, despite the social structures outlined in the *Harry Potter* storyworld, the choice between right and wrong crosses the borders of social groups, so that there is no "good class" and "wicked class." The structure-agency problem is resolved by J.K. Rowling in favor of an individual freedom to transcend social roles and make choices independently of personal position in the structure. People are seen by the writer not as the victims of their circumstances, but the products of their choices.

Beyond highlighting the importance of an *individual choice,* the story created by J.K. Rowling encourages participation in social processes as a *collective action.* The idea of Dumbledore's Army is the symbol of youth activism. Hermione Granger's bid for the liberation of Elves is another example of social activism in the *Harry Potter* story. In the U.S. presidential election of 2016, *Harry Potter* fans put that theory into practice. As an example, the Wizard Rock the Vote 2016 campaign was backed with donations from 1,500 online users and raised $52,000 for its get-out-and-vote effort ("Wizard Rock," n.d.). The Granger Leadership Academy hosted one hundred and fifty Potter fans in October 2016 to teach them how to be leaders in fan activism.

The most common questions for *Harry Potter* Studies are what makes the *HP* fandom go offline, how the political identity of the *HP* fans is formed through civic activism and how fictional narratives are used in this process (Hinck, 2012). The analysis of the Harry Potter Alliance, which is one of the most prominent examples of fan activism in the context of the *HP* universe, can shed the light on those aspects. The group defines its goals as follows: "We are changing the world by making activism accessible through the power of story. Since 2005, we've engaged millions of fans through our work for equality, human rights, and literacy" ("What we do," n.d.). Among the values the Alliance highlights on its website is the power to make change.

There are a lot of examples of the communal power in the *Harry Potter* storyworld. In the *HP* book series, the main struggles unfold with the involvement of wizards organized in groups, such as Dumbledore's Army, Death Eaters and Order of the Phoenix. The *HP* books pay much attention to the problem of group participation so that one should not be surprised that the *HP* universe can inspire young people to cooperate and take an active part in social life. A shared interest in a certain fictional universe allows people to come together for the purposes of discussing the fiction and participating in civic life. As a result, a well-organized fandom can become a subject of social and political processes.

The Harry Potter Alliance underlines the importance of connection. The list of its values includes the idea to revise old boundaries and the principles of demarcation in general. In particular, the HP Alliance points out the need for building bridges between online and offline activities. The Internet creates new opportunities for cooperation and changes everyday practices. So, the line between online and offline spheres becomes nominal, and online campaigns become a part of offline politics. Also, the revision of boundaries is reflected on by the Alliance in the idea to incorporate fantasy into social communication. As the Alliance formulates it on its website: "We know that fantasy is not only an escape from our world, but an invitation to delve into it" ("What We Do," n.d.).

The concept of "cultural acupuncture" as the way of engaging young people into civic activism was proposed by Andrew Slack, the founder of the HP Alliance. By "cultural acupuncture," Jenkins understands "mapping the fictional content world onto real-world concerns" (2012). The approach also highlights the importance to connect real and fiction practices. It means that fictional characters, events, and stories can be used to interpret the issues of the actual world. The concept can also be applied to interpret fan participation (Jenkins, 2012).

Some researchers claim that young people are not interested in politics and demonstrate passive attitudes to civic activism (Buckingham, 2000). The probable reason is a discursive gap between generations. In this context, "cultural acupuncture" becomes a mechanism to reshape the sociopolitical discourse and an effective instrument to involve young people in civic activism. This approach is based on a free imagination play, acceptance of diversity, and eliminating the boundaries between different parts of human experience. With regard to this new paradigm of civic activism, Andrew Slack said: "What we do not have is the luxury of keeping the issues we cover seemingly boring, technocratic, and inaccessible. With cultural acupuncture, we will usher in an era of activism that is fun, imaginative, and sexy, yet truly effective" (2011).

The Wizard Rock the Vote 2016 campaign launched by the HP Alliance followed the pattern of transforming an ordinary fan into a hero. In accordance with this, the campaign proclaims that fans "have the power to make substantial impact on important issues and challenges facing our world" and can protect the ideals of democracy ("Wizard Rock," n.d.). The campaign was meant to engage fans in the voting process and highlighted the transformative function of activism. In fact, the Wizard Rock the Vote 2016 campaign is not just a chance to make social change; it also gives fans the opportunity to transform themselves. The campaign puts it as follows:

> our leadership development programs continue to equip young adults with the essential skills and confidence they need to excel as leaders in their communities. As 85% of our core members are women and nearly half identify as LGBTQIA+, our programs are helping to shatter barriers that hold back certain people from advancing in their chosen careers, academic institutions, and anywhere else that traditional gender and orientation barriers exist ["Wizard Rock," n.d.].

#Nevillefightsback is another noteworthy example of the activist campaign organized by the HP Alliance in the scope of the 2016 presidential race. In 2016, the campaign worked to swing the Electoral College vote after Donald Trump's victory and now is centered around protecting the Affordable Care Act, aka Obamacare (Neville Fights Back, n.d.). As Jhaveri suggests, Neville represents Bernie Sanders and his supporters (2016). The campaign summary on the HP Alliance website begins with Neville Longbottom saying: "The thing is, it helps when people stand up to them, it gives everyone hope. I used to notice that when you did it, Harry" (Neville Fights Back, n.d.). The statement highlights the real meaning of activism, which does not necessarily relate to the sphere of practical use. Actually, it may be even more consequential just to encourage people to act and make them believe in the importance of their actions. One hero or the group of heroes may not make a significant change, but can give other people hope, the feeling that can consolidate the fandom. At the same time, this campaign reminds of a small contribution one person can make in promoting social change at large.

Despite Harry Potter being the main character of the story, it was obviously Neville Longbottom who became the key figure of this campaign. One of the reasons may be that in the story he is portrayed as an ordinary person who takes responsibility in a crucial moment. He is not the chosen one but one of many who fight the evil. Because of that, the Harry Potter fans can easily relate themselves to this character. It is also important that Neville is a Dumbledore's Army member. So we can see the parallel between the *HP* fandom and the fictional army. The character reveals the idea about personal responsibility for changing this world. Although Harry Potter remains Voldemort's main antagonist, he could not defeat the enemy without his friends' support.

The story of Harry Potter can be interpreted as a story about a hero passing through various stages of initiation on the way toward a new status. This narrative structure is common to cultural texts (Campbell, 2008). On his way to the new status, the hero departs from the former status and goes into an intermediate state, often associated with immersion into the other world or death. Then the hero finds a way back and gains the new status. As a rule, this initiating process requires defeating a monster. Harry Potter represents such type of hero, but the hero-monster opposition in J.K. Rowling's world is more complicated. The evil in the *HP* universe is decentralized and originates from the nature of the social relationships established in the magical community. While Voldemort personifies the evil, he is not its only embodiment, the only "monster." After all, the evil comes from the social relationships that take different personified forms. That is why there cannot be only one hero in this story as well.

The duty of killing a decentralized monster is partially delegated to Harry Potter's companion, Neville Longbottom. In fact, he largely follows the path of the protagonist and also passes through transformation and initiation rite. But if Neville Longbottom can walk the path of an archetypical hero, then the fans can do the same engaging in civic activism. #Nevillefightsback campaign illustrates the need for a hero. In the context of the 2016 presidential election, Neville Longbottom becomes a hero. But in accordance with the HP Alliance's message, the figure also represents the collective image of *Harry Potter* fans.

The way *Harry Potter* fandom reflected on the 2016 presidential election in the U.S. illustrates the blurring between popular culture and politics. It demonstrates that fantasy is not just a site of mollification and entertainment. It can also be a site of political re-imagining, engagement and activism. In convergence culture, fans are not merely enthusiastic consumers of stories. They are also creators and citizens who participate in social campaigns on the border between fan and political activism.

References

American Presidential Race. (2015). *PotterForums*. Retrieved from https://www.potterforums.com/viewtopic.php?f=42&t=57573.
Baker, J., Lynch, K., Cantillon, S., & Walsh, J. (2006). Equality: putting the theory into action. *Res Publica, 12*(4), 411–433.
Barrell, R. (2015, December 8). Donald Trump's five horcruxes found. *Huffington Post UK*. Retrieved from http://www.huffingtonpost.co.uk.
Begley, S. (2016, November 17). Why Donald Trump's election makes J.K. Rowling's Fantastic Beasts even more timely. *Time*. Retrieved from www.time.com.
Bethany, B. (2012). *The politics of Harry Potter*, New York: Palgrave Macmillan.
Bould, M., & Vint, S. (2012). Political readings of the fantastic. In E. James & F. Mendlesohn (Eds.), *Cambridge companion to fantasy literature* (pp. 102–112). Cambridge: Cambridge University Press.
Bourdieu, P. (1985). The social space and the genesis of groups. *Theory and Society, 14*(6), 723–744.
Buckingham, D. (2000). *The making of citizens: Young people, news and politics*. London: Routledge.
Campbell, J. (1990). *The hero with a thousand faces*. Princeton, NJ: Princeton University Press.
Collins, E. (2016, August 31). Poll: Clinton, Trump most unfavorable candidates ever. *USA Today*. Retrieved from https://www.usatoday.com.
Did Trump really mock reporter's disability? Videos could back him up. (2016, September 14). *Fox News*. Retrieved from https://www.foxnews.com.
Donald J. Trump for President. (2015, December 7). *Donald J. Trump statement on preventing Muslim immigration* [Press release]. Retrieved from https://web.archive.org/web/20170130001335/https://www.donaldjtrump.com/press-releases/donald-j.-trump-statement-on-preventing-muslim-immigration.
Fahrenthold, D.A. (2016, October 8). Trump recorded having extremely lewd conversation about women in 2005. *The Washington Post*. Retrieved from https://www.washingtonpost.com.
Granger/Lovegood facing fierce challenge from Crabbe/Goyle. (2016, March 31). *The Harry Potter Alliance*. Retrieved from https://d3n8a8pro7vhmx.cloudfront.net/hpalliance/pages/649/attachments/original/1459440180/hpa-pr-3-31-16.pdf.
Heyman, D. (Producer), Barron, D. (Producer), & Yates, D. (Director) (2009) *Harry Potter and the Half-Blood Prince*. [Motion Picture] UK, USA: Warner Bros. Pictures.
Hinck, A. (2012). Theorizing a public engagement keystone: Seeing fandom's integral connection to civic engagement through the case of the Harry Potter Alliance. *Transformative Works and Cultures, 10*. doi:10.3983/twc.2012.0311.
Jenkins, H. (2012). "Cultural acupuncture": Fan activism and the Harry Potter Alliance. *Transformative Works and Cultures, 10*. doi:10.3983/twc.2012.0305.
Jhaveri, H. (2016, July 25). DNC speaker compares Bernie Sanders to Neville Longbottom. *USA Today Sports*. Retrieved from http://ftw.usatoday.com.
Klapp, O.E. (1954). Heroes, villains and fools, as agents of social control. *American Sociological Review, 19*(1), 56–62.
Klapp, O.E. (1959). Notes toward the study of vilification as a social process. *The Pacific Sociological Review, 2*(2), 71–76. doi:10.2307/1388372.
Kreps, D. (2016, May 17). J.K. Rowling: "I find almost everything that Donald Trump says objectionable." *Rolling Stone*. Retrieved from http://www.rollingstone.com.
Marx, K., & Engels, F. (1848). *Manifesto of the Communist Party*. Retrieved from https://www.marxists.org.
McDonald, A. (2017, January 13). We've identified the 7 horcruxes needed to vanquish Donald Trump. *Huffington Post*. Retrieved from http://www.huffingtonpost.com.
Mueller, T.S., & Sutherland, J.C. (2010). Heroes and villains: Increasing fan involvement in pursuit of "the elusive fan." *The Journal of Sport Administration & Supervision, 2*(1), 20–30.

Moore, J. (2016, October 1). Here's what Hillary Clinton actually said about Millennials. *GQ*. Retrieved from http://www.gq.com

Mutz, D.C. (2016). Harry Potter and the deathly Donald. *PS: Political Science & Politics, 49*(5), 722–729. doi:10.1017/S1049096516001633

Nerds For Her. (n.d.). Retrieved September 30, 2017, from Nerds for Her website http://www.nerdsforher.com

Neville Fights Back. (n.d.). Retrieved September 27, 2017, from The Harry Potter Alliance website, http://www.thehpalliance.org/nevillefightsback

New study shows reading Harry Potter lowers Americans' opinions of Donald Trump. (2016, July 20). *Annenberg School for Communication at the University of Pennsylvania*. Retrieved from https://www.asc.upenn.edu

Nexon, D.H., & Neumann, I.B. (2006). *Harry Potter and international relations*, Lanham, MD: Rowman & Littlefield.

Nicholson, R. (2017, March 13). He who must not be named: How Harry Potter helps make sense of Trump's world. *The Guardian*. Retrieved from https://www.theguardian.com

Nozick, R. (2013). *Anarchy, state, and utopia*, New York: Basic Books.

Nussbaum, E. (2016, July 4). The Westeros wing. *New Yorker*. Retrieved from https://www.newyorker.com

Olufowote, J.O. (2006). Rousing and redirecting a sleeping giant: Symbolic convergence theory and complexities in the communicative constitution of collective action. *Management Communication Quarterly, 19*(3), 451–492.

Pillar, R.P. (2013). The role of villain: Iran and U.S. foreign policy. *Political Science Quarterly. 128*(2), 211–231. doi:10.1002/polq.12040

Rowling, J.K. (2016, June 13). On monsters, villains and the EU referendum. *J.K. Rowling's website*. Retrieved from https://www.jkrowling.com

Rowling, J.K. [jk_rowling]. (2015, December 8). How horrible. Voldemort was nowhere near as bad. [Tweet]. Retrieved from https://twitter.com/jk_rowling/status/674196610683940864

Slack, A. (2011, May 25). Cultural acupuncture and a future of social change. *Huffington Post*. Retrieved from http://www.huffingtonpost.com

Sugar quill. (2015, May 5). I do not prefer having Trump as president [Web log comment]. Retrieved from https://www.potterforums.com/viewtopic.php?f=42&t=57573&p=2022741&hilit=BERNIE+HAS#p2022741

Sullivan, A. (2016, March 20). Trump refuses to condemn violence at his U.S. presidential rallies. *Reuters*. Retrieved from https://www.reuters.com

Trump, D. (2015, June 16). *Donald Trump presidential campaign announcement full speech (C-SPAN)* [Video file]. Retrieved from https://youtu.be/apjNfkysjbM?t=3m27s

Young vs. old votes for Bernie and Hillary in the 2016 primaries. (2016, April 27). *The Economist*. Retrieved from http://www.economist.com

What we do. (n.d.). Retrieved September 30, 2017, from The Harry Potter Alliance website http://www.thehpalliance.org/what_we_do

Wizard Rock the Vote 2016. (n.d.). Retrieved September 30, 2017, from https://www.indiegogo.com/projects/wizard-rock-the-vote-2016

The Magic of Translation
An Analysis of the Brazilian Portuguese Version of Harry Potter and the Philosopher's Stone

BÁRBARA CARDOSO DE SOUZA

A Brief Explanation to Clarify Some Thoughts

The *Harry Potter* books were translated into 68 languages and distributed over 200 territories, according to the Scholastic website ("Meet author J.K. Rowling," n.d.). It is a huge phenomenon and has reached many people around the world. Many of these were a generation that has grown with *Harry Potter* and followed the story since they were young. Also, many of these probably had their first contact with the series through a translated version of the books. The translation was a valuable tool in which the books and the story could get in touch with people from a variety of cultures and places, and which transported the story to another location through language. Translation can face some challenges when the source material has particular terms or information that belong to a certain place, and sometimes words are even created to the specific use of that universe. This is the case of the *Harry Potter* series. The challenging work of translation deals with it. In Brazil, the translated books of the series have sold over three million copies, according to the website Veja ("*Curiosidades númericas da saga*," 2010). In this essay, I will discuss some of the challenges of the translation of *Harry Potter* into Brazilian Portuguese, the process, and the final product of the translation of the first book, *PS*. In the first section, there is a brief explanation about translation, which will help understand the process of the Brazilian translation made by

Lia Wyler. Then there will be two analysis sections. Every time the Brazilian Portuguese is referenced, it will be mentioned as PT BR.

The Translation

Each culture has its particularities and characteristics. It is something that will vary from place to place, wherein one may find particular beliefs and traditions, and in another something different. Not only the culture, but language—which is part of the culture—will also vary. It changes in the matter of vocabulary, accents, and language itself. When we think about the practice of translation, having a text in a specific language and the task of putting it into another one is not easy. Even though the same language is spoken in many countries, there will be some differences from place to place; this is the importance of translation: it is the translator's job to make the content make sense in another language. The translation demands work and dedication. It is not a gift; it is the product of constant work to improve it. Silveira comments, adding some elements for a good translation:

> The Art [of translation], as it deals with a subject that, in addition to technique, study, practice and other relevant requirements, requires and demands a great deal of general culture, not only literary, but also psychological, historical and, of course, artistic—or it would not be Art. Without forgetting creativity, and last but not least, Ethics [Silveira, 2004, p. 8].

Translation needs ability and cultural knowledge. It is necessary to understand the phenomenon between the languages, using it to find a way to translate one language into another, making the non-speakers of the first language understand without the necessity of speaking the original language. Observing this task, Ottoni (2005) raises the discussion about the deconstruction of the translation practice. The deconstruction is a concept used by Ottoni as a reflection, where he comments that translation and deconstruction come together and combine to reveal the mystery of meaning, and taking it to the extreme, we can make one the synonym of the other. This concept is based on an analysis of the process: it starts observing and interpreting the source language, and from this try to interpret (by the meaning) through the target language. It is a deconstruction because we are no longer using the same terms, and same words, but other terms, and other words from the target language, that will give the same meaning as was intended in the source language. This concept leads to another thought, often discussed in the translation area: untranslatability. Knowing a language goes further than only speaking it, because when we talk about translation, we seek semantics and semiotics, not only the words' meaning. We need to know both languages from a linguistics aspect, but also from a cultural perspective. Ottoni comments that "the practice of the difference is only effective in translation if we think not only of the multiplicity of languages but also of what this multiplicity enacts: reciprocal translation in the production and infinite transformation of meanings" (Ottoni, 2005, p. 19). Back to the concept of deconstruction, we visualize untranslatability during the practice of translation: terms that will not find an equivalent word in the target language, but which is possible to be expressed through the sense or intention. It is important to consider both languages' environment, cultural traditions, and activities. Knowing both languages will help the translator to find a form of translating that delivers the initial intention of the text or information. Ottoni shows that in relation to the fidelity to the text, it is no longer a critical aspect to be considered, as "the intertwining of languages reveals that the question of fidelity to the text now becomes a philosophical question," especially considering that the translation word by word or meaning by meaning might not reach the reader with the primary intention of the original (Ottoni, p. 13). Ottoni comments about the work of Lori Chamberlain (as cited in Ottoni, 2005, p. 13) where she discusses the sense of fidelity: "the meaning of this word, in the context of production, changes according to the purpose to which translation must serve in a wider aesthetic and cultural context." This way, the first step is to understand the intent of the translated work and also the circumstances of the environment to which the translation is intended so that we can find the choices regarding the way in which the text will fit. However, Johnson sets some basic principles related to the classical notions of philosophy and translation:

> The separability of style and thought, and the priority of meaning over the signifier, whose only legitimate role is to create order and sequence. Faithfulness to the text means fidelity to the semantic content, with as little interference as possible to the restrictions of the vehicle. Translation, in other words, has always been the translation of meaning [Johnson, 2005, pp. 31–32].

The fidelity the author comments about is not related to translating word by word, but by making it comprehensible to the reader of the target language, with the essence of the source language. Sometimes fidelity will appear correlated with its opposite, a betrayal in the text. It is important to notice that there are many styles of documents, such as literary texts, essays, or technical books, among others, and there is no pattern to translate; so, in other words, each one will have its kind of translation method. Even though texts may come from the same language, they can be about different subjects, fields, and publics. The translation cannot be faced as a math operation, or as something uniform, with a pattern. Pagano et al. comments about this notion of "betrayal" in the text:

The idea of "betrayal" presupposed, among other things, is another still widespread belief, which translates into a temporal and cultural vacuum, in which an idea formulated in one language can be automatically transposed into another language as if it were a mathematical operation dictionary-mediated equivalence of words. This assumption led to the belief that there would be an ideal and unique transposition that would then be the perfect translation. Because translations often differed or did not meet the specific requirements of an evaluator, the result was labeled treason, imperfection, inaccuracy [Pagano, et al., 2013, pp. 14–15].

Not meaning the same thing as it is in the source language does not mean that it is a bad or wrong translation. It may mean that to reach the public in the target language, some changes or even adaptations are necessary.

The Translator

The person responsible for translating also needs to commit to the text. Ottoni cites "the translator inevitably gets involved and commits himself to the language he translates. Translation is in the language, and the translator is responsible for 'showing' the language" (Ottoni, p. 12). This work will carry a load of responsibility, especially if we consider that the translator will be developing a job that needs to satisfy the expectations of the readers. Several aspects surround the process involving the two languages, as well as the strategies, which can vary according to the type of text to be worked. The use of criteria, taking into consideration the environment, the target audience, and the future use of the text (literary, academic, or journalistic) will compose the texture of the text, the reconstruction of it. These criteria can be seen as macro- and micro-linguistic aspects. The macro-linguistic perspective will analyze the languages as a whole, evaluating them concerning the societies that use them, while the micro-linguistic aspect will explore the words, their forms, influenced by society. When we work with the text, it is necessary to perceive them, and once they are identified, one can begin the process of practice. Besides these, we find some fundamental skills utilized in the translator's work. Pagano et al. explains this:

> A feature of the experienced translator is first and foremost a proficient reader and text analyst. Related to this ability are several strategies of lexical analysis, the authors supposed intention of the text, the effect of lexical choices on the reader of the original text, all oriented to the production of a suitable translated text that can attract attention of the reader in the new culture in which the text is being inserted through translation [Pagano et al., p. 22].

The author elicits that the translator is also a reader, and because of it, there is a remarkable sensibility to the text. The person not only translates, but also reads, and comprehends other translated texts. The analysis of the lexical is also relevant, because it will be the interpretation of the characters present in the source text, and from this analysis comes the observation of the intention of the author. The choice of words, terms, or sentences shows the author's intention, and studying these options, we can give the opportunity of understanding what will be translated. These aspects are to be faced and incorporated by the translator, and through them, define the traces of the text. To reach a translation that will be understood with the initial intention, for a variety of readers, it is necessary to go beyond semantics, because superficial knowledge will harm the text. Talking about cultural knowledge and the translator, Silveira comments:

> The best translations are almost always done by translators who know the work, the environment and the literary personality of the author, as reflected in his books. They are made by translators who know the history, literature and literary, social, economic and philosophical tendencies of the time and country in which the author lived [Silveira, 2004, p. 25].

The translator does not need to be an expert about the author's story or the text itself, but it is important to get to know it. This research helps the translator to expand the knowledge about the work. When translating, the translator has the freedom to read the original text and interpret it. Through this interpretation, the translator works on the content, having in mind the original language and its culture, and the target language as well.

Analysis

For the development of this analysis, I use the book *Harry Potter and the Philosopher's Stone* (1997), by J.K. Rowling, and the translated Brazilian Portuguese version, *Harry Potter e a Pedra Filosofal* (2000), translated by Lia Wyler. All terms and information concerning *Harry Potter* used in this essay, either in English or Portuguese, were taken from these two books.

Even though the wizarding society is a fictional community, it has all the traits a real community would have, especially when it comes to the communication area. For example, one of the most important activities related to magic, the spells, are related to the language itself.

For this reason, I am going to analyze three important aspects of the language present in the first book: (a) the translation of words and expressions, (b) the linguistic aspects of Hagrid's speech; and (c) the influence of the translator's choices in the Portuguese version of the book. For the linguistic analysis of the accent, it is necessary to consider that the *Harry Potter* saga contains a variety of characters who come from many parts of the United Kingdom, therefore different origins, so it is possible to assume that they may have different accents, which we assume as part of the characters' personality. The character chosen to be analyzed is Rubeus Hagrid.

Rubeus Hagrid/Rúbeo Hagrid Speech

Rubeus Hagrid is a charismatic, humble and friendly character. He is a half-giant, who is the Keeper of the Keys and Grounds of Hogwarts, where he works and lives. Hagrid is a wizard, but he had his wand confiscated because of an incident that happened when he was at Hogwarts as a student, and he ended up not finishing school. The function of taking Harry out of the ruins of his house after the attack on him and his parents by the villain Voldemort was delegated to Hagrid. His first important appearance in the book is in Chapter Four, The Keeper of the Keys (1997, p. 39—PT BR: *O Guardião das Chaves*; 2000, p. 46). One of his first phrases in the book brings the following sentence, on page 40.–"Anyway—Harry (…) a very happy birthday to **yeh**. Got **summat fer yeh** here–I **mighta** sat on it at some point, but it'll taste all right."

Through this short sentence, it is possible to notice Hagrid's strong and different accent—even so, it is not feasible to establish where he came from. Throughout Hagrid's appearances in the book, it becomes possible to receive more information regarding his speech, and it is easier to track his accent origins, as in the example in this sentence: "Suppose the **myst'ry** is why You-Know-Who never tried to get 'em on his side before… probably knew they were too close **ter** Dumbledore **ter** want **anythin' ter** do with the Dark Side" (Rowling, 1997, p. 45). Most of the time, the character's speech has the presence of the West-Country accent, also affirmed by the author, J.K. Rowling. Santika stated the origin of the accent, in the publication about the dialect present in Hagrid's speech:

> It is strengthened by Rowling's statement that the dialect used by Hagrid is West Country one. Rowling was interviewed in March 2001 on BBC Radio. When she was asked about Hagrid's language variation, she answered that he belongs to the West Country where she comes from [Santika, 2014, p. 9].

The western region, where the accent is used, is comprised of the areas of Cornwall, Devon, Somerset, Dorset and parts of Wiltshire and Gloucestershire, yet the division of the west and south regions are hard to define. The West-Country accent origins are a bit confusing, but there are great clues that the accent has its roots in the language used by the Western Saxons. The west of England concentrates the rural part of the country, and this accent is often associated as a non-sophisticated accent, used by countryside people, and lower classes, and far from the English language standard. It is important to emphasize that these regional varieties are defined as dialects because they are used in particular areas, and not all around the country. Also, from the point of view of the sociolinguistics, when dealing with spoken language, there are no rights or wrongs. Some of Hagrid's sentences taken from the English and the Brazilian Portuguese version of the first book will be analyzed side by side, showing the main differences between these versions. The changes in the standard version will be indicated by the words in bold in Table 1.

Table 1. Hagrid's quotes: first in the original English, and then in PT BR.

Quotes in English	Quotes in PT BR
"'Sorry?'—barked Hagrid, turning at the Dursleys, who shrank back into the shadows. 'It's them as should be sorry! I knew **yeh** weren't **gettin' yer** letters but I never thought **yeh** wouldn't even know **abou'** Hogwarts, for **cryin'** out **loud!**" (1997, p. 41)	"Sente muito?—vociferou Hagrid, virando-se para encarar os Dursleys, que tinham recuado para as sombras—Eles é que deviam sentir muito! Eu sabia que você não estava recebendo as cartas, mas nunca pensei que nem ao menos sabia da existência de Hogwarts, para apelar!" (2000, p. 41)
"'**Dunno,**' said Hagrid casually, 'he **wouldn't** take his cloak off.' (...) 'It's not that unusual, **yeh** get a lot o' funny folk in the **Hog's** Head— **that's** one of the pubs down in the village. **Mighta bin** a dragon dealer, **mightn' he?**" (1997, p. 193)	"Não lembro—respondeu Hagrid com displicência –, ele não quis tirar a capa... (...) Não é nada demais, tem muita gente esquisita no Cabeça de Javali, o pub do povoado. Podia ser um vendedor de dragões, não podia?" (2000, p. 192)
"Sent owls off **ter** all yer parents' old school friends, **askin' fer** photos.... Knew **yeh didn'** have any.... **D'yeh** like it?" (1997, p. 220)	"Mandei corujas para todos os velhos amigos de escola de seu pai e sua mãe, pedindo fotos.... Eu sabia que você não tinha nenhuma.... Gostou?" (2000, p. 119)

Note: All quotes sourced from Harry Potter and the Philosopher's Stone/Harry Potter e a Pedra Filosofal.

Surely, when reading the English version of the book, it is easy to notice the dialectic marks presented on the character's speech, and some divergence between the Standard English. To make it easier to notice the main differences, a group of sentences from many parts of the book were selected, and the analysis is made through the following sentences:

(a) "**G'night**, Professor McGonagall"—p. 17
(b) "True, I haven't introduced **meself.**"—p. 40
(c) "I'd not say no **ter summat** stronger if **yeh've** got it, mind"— p. 40
(d) "**Yer** a wizard, Harry"—p. 42
(e) "Not **s'pposed ter** use magic now I've got **yeh.**"—p. 51

(f) "Like I said, **yeh'd** be mad **ter** try **an'** rob it"—p. 57
(g) "**Dunno**—he **wouldn'** take his cloak off"—p. 193
(h) "**Yeh** could've died! All **fer** a dragon egg!"—p. 219

I start this analysis using the pronouns. The change in the pronouns is something very common in the West Country accent, as pointed by Santika (2014, p. 7), "another prominent feature attributed to West Country dialect is the exchange of the pronoun. Marshall (as cited in Santika, 2014, p. 7) pointed out that a variant changing of pronoun exists in the dialect." In sentences c, e, f, and h, there is the change of the pronoun "you" (PT BR: *você*) for "yeh." The pronoun "you" is pronounced using [ju]; however, Hagrid, when using this pronoun, pronounces it as [jə]. The same happens in sentence d, when the character addresses Harry Potter, informing him that he is a wizard: contracting the pronoun "you" plus the auxiliary verb "are" (you're), the character uses "yer," pronouncing it as [jə]. In the sentences c, e, f, and h, there is also a change in the pronunciation form, recurring in the use of the prepositions "to" (PT BR: *para*) and "for" (PT BR: *para*). The pronunciation, observing the pattern in English of "to" would be [tuː], but the character pronounces it differently, as [tə]. Also, with the preposition "for," the same happens. "For" [fɔː] becomes [fə]. On sentence b, the reflexive pronoun "myself"—[maɪˈsɛlf] changes to "meself"—[məsɛlf].

The sentences studied were taken for the recurrent use of the contraction form and are analyzed individually. In sentence a, we have "g'night"—[gˈnʌɪt], which is a contraction of "good night"—[gʊd naɪt] (PT BR: *boa noite*). In sentence b, "somewhat"—[ˈsʌmwɒt] (PT BR: *um pouco, ligeiramente*) becomes "summat" [sʌmət]. In sentence e, we have the contraction of "supposed"—[səˈpəʊzd] (PT BR: *suposto, presumível*), where the omission of the letter "-o" happens, and the character then pronounces it "s'pposed" [spəʊzd]. In sentence g, we find two contractions: "dunno" and "wouldn." The first one is frequently used in other varieties and English dialects, being more common in related to its use. "Dunno" is the contraction of "don't know" (PT BR: *não sei*). The pronunciation of the contraction is very close to the original: in "dunno" we have [dəˈnəʊ], and in "don't know" we have [dəʊnt nəʊ]. The second contraction of sentence g deals with the omission, in the pronunciation, of the last letter. Hagrid pronounces "wouldn"—[wʊdn] when using "wouldn't"—[wʊdnt], omitting the final letter "-t." So, in sentence f, we have "yeh'd," resulting in the combination of the pronoun "you" plus the modal verb "would." Not only here the modal verb is contracted (in this case, a very common option among the speakers of English Language), but also the use of the pronoun is modified, using [jɛ]. Finally, in sentence f, we have the omission of the letter "-d" in the conjunction "and" (PT BR: *e*). Hagrid omits the final letter, pronouncing "an"—[ən], instead of "and" [ænd].

It is known that accents are aspects that culturally characterize a region or community, exposing its origins, customs, and history. Carvalho explains about the identity tied to the language, which leads us to different accents:

> The identity becomes perceptible in the attitudes and reorganization of the thoughts and knowledge that we acquire throughout our lives. Allied to language, which can be one of the biggest factors to identify the individual, is the culture and attitude that is assumed concerning that language [Carvalho, 2013, p. 30].

There is a connection between language and its origins because it is through it that someone can be characterized, and its identity as well. As a consequence, it is through accents that people's personalities are highlighted. With the character Hagrid, it is through language and the way he communicates that we have hints not only of his formation (birth place) but also his personality itself. Yet, in the translated version, there is no record of the accent; dialectic marks and regional expressions were taken away or re-written, according to the translator's choice. Through the Brazilian blog "Da Penseira," a channel of *Harry Potter* content in Brazil, the translator was asked about her choice of not translating the accent, after which Lia Wyler answered:

> Hagrid's speech was not translated by the translators and publisher's decision. The reason? What speech should Hagrid use? The one from Rio de Janeiro, the one from São Paulo or from Minas Gerais, or the one from Nordeste? This would be a distortion of the character that instead of being a "rustic" English, [the accent] would enter into an existential crisis and would speak a random speech, strange to its environment ["Lia Wyler e a tradução," 2010].

The option of not translating the accent, therefore, is an option of the translator and the Brazilian publisher, Rocco. The effort of bringing Hagrid's accent to the PT BR would result in the mischaracterization of the character, and it could make the reader have a mistaken interpretation of the accent. Considering that in Brazil the book is classified as literature for young people (children and teenagers), the readers of this age group would hardly know the origins of the West Country accent, used in England. Also, considering how big Brazil is, and that there are many different accents, each reader would interpret the accent differently, resulting in many forms of interpretation of the accent, mischaracterizing Hagrid himself.

Terms—Lexical Analysis

Many of the Brazilian readers of the *Harry Potter* books read the books firstly or only in the PT BR version, and had their first experiences with the translated version of the books. However, with the movie adaptations of the books, many of those readers started to notice some differences in some terms and some proper names. Some of these terms were selected because of the substantial changes and variations that occurred. There are records of the translator related to some of her choices. It is important to point out that many of the translations were made considering a cultural adaptation into PT BR to make sense or be better understood by the readers. To analyze the names and terms, I use a comparative parameter, using some quotes of the British version of *PS*, and the PT BR version translated by Lia Wyler, *Harry Potter e a Pedra Filosofal*. To analyze and compare properly, there are three main subjects: (1) the Houses of Hogwarts; (2) some of the proper names and literal translations; and (3) adaptations.

The Houses of Hogwarts

In the next two tables, the Houses of Hogwarts are analyzed. The four houses are an important object of the *Harry Potter* series, because it is through them that Hogwarts students are separated. Also, it is part of the mystic of the story. In the story, the Hogwarts School of Witchcraft and Wizardry was created by four founders, and their students were divided by their characteristics, which were similar to those attributed to the founders. The four houses, respectively, received the founders' last name. Through a magic object called the Sorting Hat, the students are selected into their houses. It is also by the Sorting Hat that the new students understand the logistics of the school and its internal organization. The characteristics used in the descriptions are made among the founders' characteristics, which had themselves the same features. During the process of translation, the translator chose to translate the names of the Houses, but she did not translate the founders' last names—from which the houses derived from—as it is possible to see in Table 2:

Table 2. The Houses of Hogwarts and the Founders

Founders	*Houses in English*	*Houses in PT BR*
Rowena Ravenclaw	RAVENCLAW	CORVINAL
Salazar Slytherin	SLYTHERIN	SONSERINA
Helga Hufflepuff	HUFFLEPUFF	LUFA-LUFA
Godric Gryffindor	GRYFFINDOR	GRIFINÓRIA

Note: Sourced from Harry Potter and the Philosopher's Stone/Harry Potter e a Pedra Filosofal.

The first and last name of the founders were kept in English, while the Houses received versions in PT BR. In some of the houses, it is possible to observe a similarity in the sound, like in Gryffindor and Hufflepuff, that in PT BR become respectively *Grifinória* and *Lufa-lufa*. Yet, with Slytherin and Ravenclaw, this similarity does not occur. The house of Ravenclaw, in PT BR becomes *Corvinal*, and it is possible to observe a semantic similarity here: the word "raven," which refers to the animal with the same name, would be *corvo* in PT BR. It is possible to assume that to create the House *Corvinal* (PT BR), the translator possibly chose this word because the raven is often thought of as the symbol of the house, in Brazil. In relation to Slytherin, the word "sly" is an adjective usually attributed to people who deceive others in order to get what they want, and the translation of it in PT BR would be something similar, translated as *dissimulado, sonso*. It seems that the translator may have used this close meaning to create this house. Leite comments about the translator's option, and possible results of her choices:

> The translator had chosen to translate only when the name had relation to the houses, but when it was talking about the founders, the names—in this case, the last names—were kept as in the original. This can be understood as a mythological deletion, because when there is the translation, both the reference to the founders as the characteristics of personality—initially thought by them—can be lost [Leite, 2017, p. 58].

Yet the names of the founders have a relationship with the houses; when the translator created new names in PT BR to describe the houses, she opted to facilitate to the readers of the target language. The names of the Houses in English may give the reader some hints about the characteristics of the house and its folklore, however, in PT BR, especially for a reader that is not familiarized with the English language, the names would not make sense. It is necessary also to emphasize that English language and Brazilian Portuguese language do not have the same phonemes, and many of the sounds are pronounced differently; consequently, it would not be possible for the reader of the target language to pronounce the names assertively. As the name of the houses are seen more frequently than the founders' names, the translator possibly has chosen to translate only the houses' names, facilitating articulation of the words, reading and comprehension, and as the founders' last names are not so frequently, and probably because they are last names, the translator may have chosen to keep them in English.

The Translation of Proper Names and Proper Nouns

When facing the translation of some of the terms and expressions created in another language, it is possible to find some difficulties when trying to translate it in some way that the readers can comprehend the sense and the purpose used by the author in the text. Many of the objects and creatures used by J.K. Rowling were taken from the reality: through mythology, ancient history and experiences of the author, but so many others as well, were invented by the author. In the following pages, I analyze how the translation of such things were made, just as the names of the characters, creatures, objects, and nouns.

Proper names. Many of the names used by the author have derivatives of the Roman language. Of these names, we can observe that there is a pattern in the translation: names ending in "-us" frequently replace these final letters for "-o," according to the Table 3:

Table 3. Proper Names with Derivatives of Roman Language

Name in English	Name in PT BR
Al*bus* Dumbledore	Al*vo* Dumbledore
Rube*us* Hagrid	R*ú*be*o* Hagrid
Arg*us* Filch	Arg*o* Filch

Note: Sourced from Harry Potter and the Philosopher's Stone/Harry Potter e a Pedra Filosofal.

Besides these changes, some other modifications were made in these names: the name of the principal of Hogwarts, Dumbledore, not only had his first name changed at the end ("-us" to "-o") but also had the letter "-d" replaced by "-v," where Albus became Alvo; Hagrid also received another adjustment, receiving an acute accent in the first syllable of his name, an accent which in PT BR is very common. The changes at the end of some names and words derived from the Roman language are very common, in accordance with the work of Leite (2017, p. 4), thus being this the probable reason for the translator's choice in the translation of these names.

In Table 4, it is possible to see some of the names translated by Lia Wyler, in which the translator possibly used literality and a vocabulary closer to the PT BR.

Table 4. Translations Close to the Literality

What is it?	In English	In PT BR
A place	Diagon Alley	Beco Diagonal
	Leaky Cauldron	Caldeirão Furado
A creature	Scabbers	Perebas
	Bane	Agouro
	Fang	Canino
	Peeves	Pirraça
An object	The Mirror of Erised	O Espelho de Ojesed

Note: Sourced from Harry Potter and the Philosopher's Stone/Harry Potter e a Pedra Filosofal.

The two places on the table above refer to places visited and used by wizards in the books. In the translation of both places, it is possible to affirm that the translator used equivalents in PT BR to the terms. The word "diagon," when translated into PT BR, refers to the adjective diagonal, in PT BR *diagonal* as well, and the adjective "alley," when translated, refers to *beco, ruela*. To create the place, the translator used the translation of both words, making Diagon Alley become, literally, *Beco Diagonal*.[1] The same thing happens to the famous wizarding bar, the Leaky Cauldron: the word "leaky" can be translated as *vazante*. "Cauldron" can be translated as *caldeirão*. However, in the spoken language, the term *vazante* is not so used in PT BR, so the translator looked for the word with the closest meaning, and used more often which is the male noun *furo*, turning it into an adjective, and creating the term *Caldeirão furado*.

In relation to the creatures, their definition according to the Cambridge Dictionary ("Cambridge dictionary online," 2015), and their translation can be seen below, in Table 5.

Table 5. Translations of Creatures

Fang—noun → a long, sharp tooth/PT BR: *dente canino, presa*

Scabbers comes from the adjective "scabby" → covered in scabs or scab/PT BR: *Coberto por crostas ou feridas*

Bane—noun → a cause of continuous trouble or unhappiness/PT BR: *Causa de problemas contínuos ou infelicidades*

Peeves comes from the verb "to peeve" → to annoy someone/PT BR: *irritar alguém*

Note: Sourced from Harry Potter and the Philosopher's Stone/Harry Potter e a Pedra Filosofal.

From the meaning of each one of these creatures, it is possible to observe that the translator used the meanings themselves, and their equivalents into PT BR, to organize them, adapting them from the translation of their meanings. So, the dog Fang receives a name with the equivalent into PT BR, *Canino*, since both words in both languages refer to the sharp tooth.

"Scabbers" becomes *Perebas*, which, if we consider the concept of the word in English, and the word in PT BR, the translated version reminds us the original one. The centaur Bane receives the name of *Agouro*. Both words are nouns that indicate a situation of unhappiness and tragedy, thus the name of the character in both languages means the same. The poltergeist of the castle, Peeves, becomes *Pirraça*. The verb "to peeve" is used when someone is annoyed by someone else. In this translation, a verb is also used in PT BR, which is *pirraçar*, which in Brazilian Portuguese reminds us of being stubborn, or making tricks or pranks. Having in mind that the poltergeist is known for practicing all these acts, his name becomes *Pirraça*, derived from the verb *pirraçar*.

The last one is an object. This is found in the twelfth chapter, called "The Mirror of Erised" (p. 143), PT BR: *O Espelho de Ojesed* (p. 142). The translator's choice here was very simple: "the mirror" translated into PT BR becomes *O espelho*, literal translation; however, the last word, "erised" is actually the word "desire," written backwards. "Desire" translated into PT BR is *desejo*. Therefore, the translator translated the words, and used the same "formula" with the equivalent word in PT BR, writing *desejo* backwards, ojesed, creating *O Espelho de Ojesed*, the equivalent of "The Mirror of Erised."

In the last table, some translations are not literal. Some of the proper names were translated or rewritten with equivalents into the PT BR language, considering a cultural adaption into it.

Adaptations

Some of the names and objects below were adapted into PT BR, starting with the adapted names, as shown in the Table 6.

Table 6. Adapted Names

What is it?	In English	In PT BR
	Lily Potter	Lílian Potter
	James Potter	Tiago Potter
Character	Vernon Dursley	Válter Dursley
	Dudley Dursley	Duda Dursley
	Charlie Weasley	Carlinhos Weasley
	(William) Bill Weasley	(Guilherme) Gui Weasley

Note: Sourced from Harry Potter and the Philosopher's Stone/Harry Potter e a Pedra Filosofal.

The names of the characters in the chart above received adaptations with their closest version in PT BR, starting with Lily Potter, that becomes Lilian Potter. A prevalent example and traditional in the translating activities in Brazil is the translation of William or Bill to respectively Guilherme or Gui, and James to Tiago. Charlie Weasley becomes Carlinhos Weasley. Except for Vernon to Válter, and Dudley to Duda, which are not common in PT BR, all the other names, even considered "foreign names," are largely known in PT BR; the translation of these names is not necessary.

About the place of boarding of the Hogwarts Express, the train that takes the students to the school, there was a modification. In English, the name of the platform is "nine and three-quarters," literally translated as *nove e três quartos*. However, in the translated version, the term becomes *nove e meia*, which means "nine and a half." A math matter does not apply here, considering that this is the name of the platform, not a real math issue. In the blog "Da Penseira," the translator was once more interviewed in 2010, and was asked about the translation of this term, which Lia Wyler answered:

> The obvious intention here [the translation of nine and three quarters to nine and a half] was to number an intermediate platform that only exists for a wizard, and can only be fully understood if we think of a child of 9–12 years for whom the book is. From 9 to 12 years old a child has not yet crystallized the knowledge of fractions, nor

does they use "quarter" in the sense that is understood and used by the English child. It was, therefore, a cultural translation ["Lia Wyler *e a tradução,*" 2010].

Then, we have a term that was entirely created by the author. "Quidditch" is the term used by the author to describe the sport played by young wizards. There are four balls in this game, which probably helped the translator to come up with the term *quadribol,* joining the word *quadri* (Latin origin) which gives the idea of "four," plus *-bol,* a suffix frequently used in the name of sports in PT BR like *futebol* (soccer), and *voleibol* (volleyball). Adding the idea of the use of four balls plus the suffix, the translator created the term *quadribol.*

The last term is one of the most polemic among the readers that read both versions of the book. The term "muggle," according to the Cambridge Dictionary, is "a person who does not have a particular type of skill or knowledge."

The term in English describes the non-wizards perfectly, because they do not have the same abilities or magical knowledge as a wizard would have. In PT BR, the translator chose the word *trouxa,* which often brings the idea of someone who is inferior, not smart, or is frequently cheated, but in a deprecatory way. It is understood that the objective of the translator was not to depreciate the non-wizards, but to make clear their lack of abilities and knowledge. At the same time, in the book it is possible to observe that the wizard society needs to hide themselves from the non-wizards and often bewitch the non-wizards to cover up an event or information. Considering this perspective, the term *trouxa* reminds us of someone who is frequently foolish, highlighting the aspect of the term in the translation.

During the process of translation, it is possible to notice that the translator observed the entire work of the book itself, and tried to bring the story closer to the public. In many parts of the book the translator used literality in an attempt to make the terms clear to the Brazilian readers, but keeping some relation to their original in English. Also, it is important to highlight that some objects and things in the story were adapted into a reality to make the Brazilian reader comprehend and understand the original idea in the story. Considering that in Brazil, the book is classified as youth literature, the translator's choices were probably chosen to help the reader during the reading.

Conclusion

Translation is indeed a meticulous work: it is necessary to observe the details and understand that sometimes keeping the original will not be an assertive choice. Some choices may be problematic, but the important thing is to keep what is substantial to the story, even though it means looking for another resource in the target language to describe it. During the process of translating, the translator Lia Wyler faced significant challenges; for example, the choice of translating Hagrid's speech or not. When she opted for not giving him slang in PT BR, she understood that it would be impossible to establish a pattern of slang in the language, which would mischaracterize the character. Also, thinking about many terms used by J.K. Rowling, many of them created by her, the translator had to find mediator terms in order to translate them, creating, in another language, new terms to define what the author intended, but also trying to reach the public of the target language.

It is essential to emphasize that the process of translations leads to adaptation (considering that both languages, the source, and the target one, are different) and that the literality will not always be a synonym of quality. We can notice by Lia Wyler's work that she tried to make the British book comprehensible to the Brazilian audience. Likewise, the choices of the translator reflect in all the translated books, and through it, the translated books can provide clear notions of the universe of *Harry Potter*. Even though this work uses only the first book of the series, it is interesting to mention that Lia Wyler translated all the seven books of the series in Brazil. Such a story and its universe can provide a wide scenario for linguistics, textual analysis, and naturally, for the studies of translation, but the common cliché applies: this is a subject for further research and other possibilities.

NOTE

1. In PT BR, the noun comes first.

REFERENCES

Carvalho, E.M.S. (2013). Uma abordagem sociolinguística da identidade estrangeira. *PLURAIS-Revista Multidisciplinar, 1*(3).
Curiosidades numéricas da saga Harry Potter. (2010, November 22). Retrieved from http://veja.abril.com.br/entretenimento/curiosidades-numericas-da-saga-harry-potter/
Cambridge dictionary online. (2015). Cambridge University Press.
Johnson, B. (2005). A fidelidade considerada filosoficamente. In P. Ottoni (Ed.), *Tradução: A prática da diferença*. Campinas: Editora da Unicamp.
Leite, I.A.N. (2017). A tradução dos nomes em Harry Potter. *Rónai–Revista de Estudos Clássicos e Tradutórios, 5*(1).
Lia Wyler e a tradução de Harry Potter. (2010, July 6). Retrieved from http://dapenseira.blogspot.com.br/2010/07/lia-wyler-e-traducao-de-harry-potter.html
Meet author J.K. Rowling. (n.d.). Retrieved from http://harrypotter.scholastic.com/jk_rowling/
Ottoni, P. (2005). *Tradução a prática da diferença*. Campinas: Editora da Unicamp.
Pagano, A., Magalhães, C., & Alves, F. (2013). *Traduzir com autonomia: Estratégias para o tradutor em formação* (fourth ed.). São Paulo: Contexto.
Rowling, J.K. (1997). *Harry Potter and the philosopher's stone* (first ed.). London: Bloomsbury.

Rowling, J.K. (2000). *Harry Potter e a pedra filosofal* (first ed.). Rio de Janeiro: Rocco. (Translated by Lia Wyler)
Santika, R. (2014). An analysis of west country dialect used by Hagrid in J.K. Rowling's Harry Potter. NOBEL: *Journal of Literature and Language Teaching*, 7(1).
Silveira, B. (2004). *A arte de traduzir* (first ed.). São Paulo: Melhoramentos, Editora Unesp.

Transmediated Weasleys
A Tale of Two Ginnys
CHRISTOPHER E. BELL *and* CELINA SMITH[1]

Of all of the characters to undergo the transmediated transition from novel to screen to a myriad of attendant merchandise, games, and the like, perhaps none has suffered as much in the process as Ginevra Weasley. The youngest of the seven Weasley children, and the only girl, Ginny occupies an interesting space in the narrative arc. Who is Ginny Weasley? Red hair, incredible skill, and clever wit are all accurate characteristics. Ask a fan of the *Harry Potter* films, and s/he will likely respond that Ginny is Harry's girlfriend and Ron's little sister; maybe s/he will mention that Ginny is the one Voldemort lured into the Chamber of Secrets in the second film. But ask a book fan, and it's much more likely that s/he will engage in a discussion of Ginny's strength, fiery wit, and incredible skill. Ginny is a Quidditch captain, a fearsome witch, one of the prettiest girls in school, and every bit the equal of the others in the Core Six of Dumbledore's Army. Ginny Weasley's role and character development were clearly diminished when the *Harry Potter* books were translated (transmediated) to the films and consubstantial merchandise, which lessens her ability to be a positive role model for young girls and does the character a tremendous amount of injustice.

Adaptation as Transmediation

At its most basic, transmediation is "the process of translating meanings from one sign system (such as language) into another (such as pictoral representation)" (Seigel, 1995, p. 456). Within the realm of media, this has come to be understood as narratives that "unfold across multiple media platforms, with each new text making a distinct and valuable contribution to the whole"

(Jenkins, 2006, p. 95). Traditionally, there has been a distinction made between transmediatied texts and adapted texts. Adaptation can be understood as both "a product (as extensive, particular transcoding) and as a process (as creative reinterpretation and palimpsestic intertextuality)" (Hutcheon, 2006, p. 22)—"palimpsestuous" meaning, "directly and openly connected to recognizable other works, and that connection is part of [the adapted work's] formal identity" (Hutcheon, p. 21). Adaptation, therefore, involves texts that share constituent elements, but in specific, ranked order.[2] The original text is necessarily primary, and the adapted text is necessarily secondary (Hutcheon, 2006).

Harry Potter is nearly unique in that its adaptation is, in fact, a transmediated experience—as Marie-Laure Ryan categorizes, a "snowball effect": "a certain story enjoys so much popularity or becomes so prominent culturally that it spontaneously generates a variety of either same-medium or cross-media prequels, sequels, fan fiction, and adaptations" (Ryan, 2013, p. 363). That is to say, *Harry Potter* was so popular as novels that films, video games, and other merchandise were natural avenues of expansion of the narrative. Jenkins refers to this as "entertainment for the age of media convergence, integrating multiple texts to create a narrative so large that it cannot be contained within a single medium" (Jenkins, p. 95). *Harry Potter* is a perfect example of this "snowball effect" transmediation, because, as Jenkins points out:

> In the ideal form of transmedia storytelling, each medium does what it does best—so that a story might be introduced in a film, expanded through television, novels, and comics, and its world might be explored and experienced through game play. Each franchise entry needs to be self-contained enough to enable autonomous consumption. That is, you don't need to have seen the film to enjoy the game and vice-versa [Jenkins, pp. 95–96].

For *Harry Potter* consumption, one does not need to have read the novels to enjoy the films, nor does one need to have seen the films to enjoy the novels, or to play the video games or board games, or to participate in the live experiences of *The Wizarding World of Harry Potter*. Each entry into the transmediated experience of *Harry Potter* can stand on its own and "enable[s] autonomous consumption." However, like other forms of transmediation that spring from a single-authored primary source, "we inevitably fill in any gaps in the adaptation with information from the adapted text" (Hutcheon, p. 121). That is, if the adaptation leaves something vital out of the narrative, we use the collective experience of transmediation to retroactively add the vital piece back in. This is often referred to as a "deep media" experience. The more elements of transmediation one has consumed, the larger pool of knowledge one has to draw upon to fill in missing pieces:

[Deep media] takes the form of an inverted pyramid. At the top are the hundreds of millions of people who've seen a couple of the movies and know [*Harry Potter*] as a cultural icon. Just below them are the hundreds of millions of people who respond to the story in different media—gamers who play the games, readers who love the books, collectors who obsess over the toys. And at the point of the pyramid are the *otaku*—the hundreds of thousands of superfans who are most deeply connected to the saga [Rose, 2011, p. 74].

The *Harry Potter* "*otaku*"[3] are able to take the collective knowledge of many different iterations of the text and fill in narrative gaps in any one of the franchise entries. However, because, as Jenkins points out, a good transmediated text does not require, as necessity, the consumption of multiple iterations of the text, there will be some consumers that have relatively little or no pool of knowledge from which to draw. Those consumers—as Rose demonstrated, hundreds of millions of consumers—only know the text through the single iteration they have consumed. In a real sense, the only Ginny Weasley many fans have ever experienced is the Bonnie Wright filmic version of the character. *Potter otaku* know that Ginny is a complex, fascinating character because they can fill in the missing information from other sources. For those single-iteration film consumers, "movie Ginny" *is* Ginny Weasley, and that's problematic for a variety of reasons.

A Chronology of the Two Ginnys

Ginny Weasley is first introduced in *SS*, accompanying her brothers to Platform 9¾ on the first day of school. In *SS*, Ginny is ten years old, and therefore not yet eligible to attend Hogwarts. We get nothing by way of character development of Ginny in the first novel, other than a brief idea that she is star-struck at the idea of meeting Harry Potter. She is a non-entity, a simple filler to enhance the idea that the Weasley family is very large.

In *CoS*, we begin to establish Ginny Weasley as an actual character, with history, personality, and agency. It also cannot be overstated that, although the Trio are, of course, the main focus and protagonists of the story, Ginny is *the* central engine of the narrative in *CoS* (which we will return to in a moment). At the beginning of the book, Harry shows up to The Burrow and startles the youngest Weasley, who "appeared in the kitchen, gave a small squeal, and ran out again"(*CoS* p. 35). Ron tells Harry that she has been talking about him all summer, and this is the first we hear of her crush on Harry. Ginny spends most of that visit from Harry either hiding from him or embarrassing herself in front of him in small ways, like spilling her porridge (*CoS*, p. 43) or putting her elbow in the butter dish (*CoS*, p. 44). It should be noted that, even in these early stages of Ginny's introduction, these behaviors are completely out of character for her, as Ron remarks: "You don't know how weird it is for her to be this shy. She never shuts up normally –" (*CoS*, p. 40).

In Flourish and Blotts, as everyone else presses forward to meet and greet Gilderoy Lockhart, Ginny is found "out of the limelight [on] the edge of the room" (*CoS*, p. 61). Here, she encounters Draco Malfoy. Keep in mind that Ginny is 11 years old, and has not yet spent a single day at Hogwarts. Yet, despite this, she openly confronts Malfoy, glaring at him and demanding that he leave Harry alone. It is during this exchange that Arthur Weasley and Lucius Malfoy get into a fist fight, which leads to the elder Malfoy having access to Ginny's books, into which he slips Tom Riddle's diary.

Ginny's inheritance, so to speak, of Riddle's diary is the most important narrative driver of the story. The diary is in her custody for the majority of the school year, up until February, when she makes the conscious decision to attempt to destroy it by flushing it down Moaning Myrtle's toilet. Pause and step back for a moment—at this point in the narrative, Tom Riddle has been speaking to Ginny Weasley through the diary for months. He is slowly taking possession of her—he has already forced her to kill Hagrid's roosters, and to write "THE CHAMBER OF SECRETS HAS BEEN OPENED. ENEMIES OF THE HEIR, BEWARE" on the hallway wall (*CoS*, p. 138). We are (much later) told that Voldemort is the most powerful legilimens in the world. At 11 years old, Ginny Weasley is able to shake off enough of his possession of her mind and body to attempt to fight back, summoning the fortitude to throw the diary away. Ginny is not some weak sister (pun intended) in this tale; she is already a formidable opponent to even the first and strongest of Voldemort's horcruxes. Also keep in mind that the diary is only possessing Ginny to work its way toward Harry Potter. Once it accomplishes that goal, and is finally in the hands of Harry, Ginny is still able to subsequently pilfer it from Harry's room, much against its wishes. Ginny *wants* to ask for help, but is prevented from doing so by Percy, because he self-importantly believes she is going to rat him out for dating Penelope Clearwater (although why this would be a source of embarrassment for him is unclear). Because she cannot ask for assistance, Ginny is forced to fight Voldemort's most powerful horcrux alone, and nearly manages to do so for almost an entire year.

So much of Ginny's story is excised from the film version of *CoS* that she becomes a bit player in her own narrative. In a very real way, Ginny is reduced in the Columbus text to a glorified MacGuffin.[4] The power of Ginny's fight against Riddle's horcrux is largely absent from the film, and Harry's rescue of her in the Chamber reads very much like a damsel in distress moment, rather than the extraction of a fellow soldier, as it is presented in the novel.

PoA sees Ginny's role scaled back even further, although this is not the fault of the films; Rowling herself all but removes Ginny from the narrative. While Ginny is present as, essentially, a background extra in several key scenes (such as Harry's first encounter with the dementors), she has no real role in the story. The film diminishes that role even further; in total, Ginny speaks exactly six words on screen. Similarly, *GoF* is mostly Ginny-free, both in the book and in the film; she does attend the Quidditch World Cup with her family, and is present for the Death Eater attack on the World Cup village, but we do not really see her much for the rest of the book. She attends the Yule Ball with Neville Longbottom, and we later learn that there, she has met Michael Corner—Corner will become Ginny's boyfriend briefly.

That this storyline of Ginny and Michael Corner is removed from the film is an important development in the way filmic Ginny is portrayed. Over the course of *GoF, OotP,* and *HBP,* Ginny's feelings for Harry are barely addressed, but we find out that she has moved on and started dating other boys. Hermione tells Harry and Ron, "Ginny *used* to fancy Harry, but she gave up on him months ago. Not that she doesn't *like* [Harry], of course" (*OotP,* p. 348). By moving on, Ginny makes it possible for a friendship to blossom between she and Harry, and—more importantly—it demonstrates that she made the decision not to allow her life to revolve around one boy not liking her back. This is a powerful message for young readers everywhere, especially girls, and one that the films do not convey.

Beginning with *OotP,* Ginny begins to occupy a much larger role in the narrative. It is Ginny (not Hermione, as played in the film) who introduces Harry to Luna Lovegood on the Hogwarts Express. It is also Ginny (not Hermione, as played in the film) who decides the secret group of 28 students that initially meets to practice Defense Against the Dark Arts should be called "Dumbledore's Army." When Fred and George Weasley and Harry Potter are all banned by Dolores Umbridge from playing Quidditch, it is Ginny who takes over as the Gryffindor seeker—when her brothers express surprise at her skill level, Hermione informs them, "She's been breaking into your broom shed in the garden since the age of six and taking each of your brooms out in turn when you weren't looking" (*OotP,* p. 574). After Harry (intentionally) overhears Mad Eye Moody speculate that Harry could be possessed by Voldemort, and chooses to hide from his friends rather than talk about it, Ginny is the one who reproaches him with, "That was a bit stupid of you … seeing as you don't know anyone but me who's been possessed by You-Know-Who, and I can tell you how it feels" (*OotP,* p. 499).

None of these events take place in the filmic version of *OotP,* once again reducing Ginny to minor side character at best. Although Ginny is present during many key scenes early in the film, she has few lines and almost no action. For example, at 00:48:20, Ginny snatches the potions book from Harry, opens it, and asks, "Who's the Half-Blood Prince?" (Yates, 2009); she fails to bring up her own possession or connect the potions book (or Harry) to Voldemort in any way. It isn't until the end of the story where the book at the film begin to dovetail, in terms of Ginny's character, and even then, the filmic version of Ginny is much less agentic than the book version. In both iterations, Ginny is one of only three members of Dumbledore's Army to show up and accompany the Trio to the Department of Mysteries, for what they believe is a rescue of Sirius Black. Ginny and Luna are sent to create diversions while the Trio sneaks into Umbridge's office, but all six members of Dumbledore's Army are caught. Umbridge takes Harry and Hermione into the Forbidden Forest to retrieve a "secret weapon," but escape when Umbridge is abducted by centaurs. Upon their return to the castle, they meet up with Ginny, Ron, Luna, and Neville, who have also escaped. In the film, they escape because Ron feeds them Puking Pastils. However, in the book, Ron clearly attributes their escape to Ginny: "Ginny was best, she got Malfoy—Bat Bogey Hex—it was superb, his whole face was covered in the great flapping things" (*OotP*, p. 760). Also in the novel, during the eventual fight against the Death Eaters in the Department of Mysteries, Ginny is the first to be threatened with torture, but she stands her ground. She does break her ankle in the melee, but attempts to refuse assistance: "It's only my ankle, I can do it myself!" (*OotP*, p. 796). In the film, Ginny's major contribution is casting the spell that collapses the entire prophecy room—while useful for their retreat, it is an action that results in what appears to be hundreds of thousands of lost prophesies.[5]

Also important here is Ginny's mention of having broken up with Michael Corner over a Quidditch match, and her announcement that she is currently dating Dean Thomas. She makes this announcement in passing, matter-of-factly, as though it's nobody's business but her own. Again, the agency here is Ginny's; she has moved on yet again, not letting the breakup or Harry's lack of attention affect her. However, in the *HBP* film, Ginny is only mentioned to be dating Dean Thomas as a device to make Harry jealous. This is the first time, in the films, Ginny is reduced to being Harry's love interest.

Ginny's romantic life, in the novels, is very much a topic of conversation amongst her brothers. At the beginning of *HBP*, Fred and George take it in turns to question her about her boyfriends, because they have heard that "she's already got about five boys on the go," is currently dating Dean Thomas, recently broke up with Michael Corner, and is "moving through boyfriends a bit fast" (*HBP*, p. 121). Ginny's response to their paternalistic and patronizing inquisition—"It's none of your business. And I'll thank you ... not to tell tales about me" (*HBP*, p. 121)—again makes it clear that Ginny is in control of Ginny, independently of Harry Potter. It seems like a minor consideration to spend so much time explicating, but in reality, it is a vital point for readers of the books: Ginny is not a prop in Harry Potter's story; Ginny is the main character in her *own* story. While the films—particularly *HBP*—continually marginalize Ginny and reduce her to everything from MacGuffin to love interest, Ginny's actual character from the original text is a much more nuanced, multi-layered, dynamic and important figure.

Ginny is, in fact, so powerful that Horace Slughorn invites her to become a part of the "Slug Club," an elite group of students with the potential to become successful, all handpicked by Slughorn himself. She is invited to the group meeting aboard the Hogwarts Express because "He saw me hex Zacharias Smith ... when Slughorn came in I thought I was going to get detention, but he just thought it was a really good hex and invited me to lunch! Mad, eh?" (*HBP*, pp. 147–148). It is made clear that Ginny is the only person in the room invited by Slughorn not for who she is related to, but because of her individual merit. Even Harry Potter is there because of association, not because of achievement.

Ginny is moved from Quidditch seeker to chaser with Harry's rejoining of the team, and by all accounts, she is a pretty fantastic player. This is played for contrast with Ron, who struggles with confidence as the team's keeper, but it should be noted that Ginny is an outstanding player in her own right (in the match against Slytherin, Ginny racks up four out of Gryffindor's six goals). Eventually, Ginny will become Gryffindor's Quidditch captain in the absence of Harry Potter, and, according to the *Pottermore* extended canon, a professional Quidditch player and sports journalist for the *Daily Prophet*. This integral part of Ginny's character is significantly reduced in the films; although she does stand behind Harry and shouts, "Shut it!" at the Gryffindor Quidditch tryouts (00:45:06, Yates, 2009), and fires off goal shots at the Keepers, both of these actions are played in service to Harry's and Ron's stories respectively, not in service to her own. Ginny is quieting the players *for Quidditch captain Harry*; Ginny is shooting at the goal *for Ron's tryout*.

Ginny's main role in *HBP*, because of the construction of this particular story, is to make the transition back to being interested in Harry Potter. There is quite a bit of romantic undercurrent to the sixth book, with both Harry and Hermione realizing the Weasley with whom each is in love. For Harry's part, his focus on Ginny begins in Slughorn's potions class, when he smells a peculiar flowery scent in the Amortentia potion—a love potion that smells like whatever one finds attractive. Later, he encounters Ginny in the hallway and realizes that she smells identically. It is interesting that at the same time Harry begins to make the connection between the scents, Ginny is scolding him for "taking orders from something someone wrote in a book" (*HBP*, p. 102), a callback to her earlier possession by Riddle's diary. Harry's interest in Ginny is brought to the forefront when he and Ron stumble upon her and Dean Thomas in a darkened corridor, "who were locked in a close embrace and kissing fiercely as though glued together" (*HBP*, p. 286).

The ensuing scene is important because, again, it reinforces the idea of Ginny as agent, in charge of her own story, and because it is expressly missing from the film. Ron immediately confronts Ginny, who dismisses Dean so that she can focus on her brother. The tone of Ron's questioning is possessive and patriarchal—it is clear that he is worried about Ginny's behavior as a reflection of him, not in and of itself:

> "Right," said Ginny, tossing her long red hair out of her face and glaring at Ron, "let's get this straight once and for all. It is none of your business who I go out with or what I do with them, Ron—"
> "Yeah, it is!" said Ron, just as angrily. "D'you think I want people saying my sister's a—"
> "A what?" shouted Ginny, drawing her wand. "A *what*, exactly?" [*HBP*, p. 287].

Ginny counters Ron's judgmental slut-shaming with derision, claiming that Ron is the only person in their friendship group that has never kissed anyone, calling him out for mooning over his brother's fiancée, Fleur Delacouer, and reminding Ron of Hermione's tryst with Viktor Krum. Ginny makes it absolutely clear that she is not willing to let her brothers dictate what her romantic life looks like. Her proclamation that Ron has "got about as much experience as a twelve-year-old" (*HBP*, p. 288) is not only an in-character criticism of Ron's jealousy, but a meta-commentary by Rowling herself of the realities of being a contemporary teenager. This idea that, in a high school full of teenagers with hundreds of darkened corridors and corners and relatively little supervision, there would be no secondary sexual contact (at the *very* least) is patently ridiculous. At this point, Ginny Weasley is fifteen years old and has had several boyfriends—clearly, she has been kissing boys. Ron's insinuation that somehow that would make her a ("A what? A what exactly?" [*HBP*, p. 287]) is not only insulting, but catastrophically chauvinistic. Even more catastrophic for Ginny, as a character, is the fact that not just this scene, but this entire storyline and aspect of her character has been excised from the films. At 00:50:00, we see Dean Thomas sitting close to Ginny in the Three Broomsticks tavern, whispering in her ear, holding her hand, and eventually kissing her, but it is a relatively chaste portrayal of their relationship. Certainly, they are not locked in any sort of embrace as if glued together. At any rate, this particular scene is played out not for Ginny's benefit, but again, as character development for Ron (and Hermione). Ginny's kiss with Dean is there to provide an opportunity for Hermione to bring up kissing Ron, not as any sort of character movement for Ginny herself. It serves to awaken Harry's feelings for her. Later, lying in bed, Harry muses about Ginny when Ron asks what Dean sees in Ginny. Harry comments on Ginny's better qualities: "'She's smart, funny, attractive (…) she's got nice skin'" (00:59:30, Yates, 2009). Ginny has been, once again, reduced to the MacGuffin; she is a thing that Harry wants, and little more than that.

In the novel, Harry's use of the Felix Felicis potion inadvertently (and luckily) spurs Ginny to break up with Dean, leaving her free for Harry's affections. When Harry receives high school detention for committing attempted murder on Draco, using the *sectumsempra* spell, it is portrayed as the larger consequence is Harry being forced to sit out the finals of the Quidditch House Cup. Ginny is played as seeker in his stead (symbolically, against Harry's former love interest, Cho Chang), and she leads the team to a 450 to 140 victory over Ravenclaw. In the common room after, when Ginny finally does kiss Harry, she does it boldly, in front of everyone, with "a hard, blazing look in her face as she threw her arms around him ... without thinking, without planning it, without worrying about the fact that fifty people were watching" (*HBP*, p. 333). This is incredibly important for Ginny's development as a character; the girl who squeaked and hid at the first meeting of Rockstar Harry Potter is the one who instigates and effectuates their romantic sexual relationship. This relationship is Ginny's choice, not Harry's, and is done in the open and broadcast, effectively, to everyone they both know.

In contrast, in the film, her first kiss with Harry is in the Room of Requirement, in a scene that seems more like a dream sequence than actual plot. Ginny and Harry are alone, in the secret depository room, with no one around to witness the birth of their relationship. More significantly, Ginny kisses Harry not because of her euphoria over her own achievement, but because Harry needs a distraction while she hides the Half-Blood Prince's potion book from him. Once again, Ginny's agency is stripped in service to instrumentality for Harry. She doesn't kiss Harry because she decides to; she kisses Harry because it serves the needs of Harry's plot.

In both versions of the narrative, when Dumbledore is killed by Snape, it is Ginny who provides Harry comfort as he sobs atop Dumbledore's corpse. However, in the novel, this is following Ginny's Felix Felicis-powered wand duel with multiple adult Death Eaters. In the film, Voldemort's minions meet no resistance whatsoever. In the novel, Ginny has to physically pull Harry from Dumbledore's body; in the film, she merely holds him in her arms as he cries.

Following the death of Dumbledore, Harry makes the decision to leave Hogwarts to pursue Voldemort's horcruxes. For him, this means ending his relationship with Ginny, for her own protection. But Harry also knows that she will fight him on this, and that he owes her an explanation. She is not simply his girlfriend, but a fellow revolutionary soldier; she cannot accompany him on this fight, and they both know it. In fact, when Harry breaks things off with her, "she [does] not cry, she simply look[s] at him" (*HBP*, p. 646).[6] Ginny is strong enough in herself to know that she wants to be with Harry, but does need to be with Harry. She will be fine without him while he's off trying to save the world. In the film, there is no such conversation between Ginny and Harry. Harry informs Hermione and Ron that he is not returning to Hogwarts, but he never shares this information with Ginny. He basically chooses to abandon their relationship, and we as viewers are unconcerned about her feelings on the matter.

For most of *DH,* Ginny is necessarily absent from the narrative in both iterations. Harry spends much of the beginning of the book unsuccessfully attempting to avoid her, although they do end up kissing in the kitchen prior to Bill Weasley and Fleur Delacouer's wedding. Once the hunt for horcruxes begins in earnest, though, Ginny is out of the story. However, even in her absence, the presence of her agency can be felt. While hiding in the woods, Harry overhears a conversation between Ted Tonks and Dean Thomas about how Ginny attempted to steal the Sword of Gryffindor from the headmaster's office—a headmaster that is widely thought to be one of the most prominent Death Eaters in the world. Though she was caught, Harry also finds out that she, Neville and Luna have been heading up the rebellion within Hogwarts. Ginny is not simply sitting around waiting for Harry to return; she is taking active steps to oppose the occupation of Hogwarts on her own (though Neville later reveals Ginny stopped attending school around Easter time).

Ginny returns to Hogwarts with her twin brothers and Lee Jordan just prior to the Battle of Hogwarts. In one of the key events leading up to the fight, the entire Weasley family volunteers to enter the fray, but Ginny is expressly forbidden by her parents because she is underage. Ginny argues with her family about letting her stay and fight: "'I can't go home!' Ginny shouted, angry tears sparkling in her eyes. 'My whole family's here, I can't stand waiting there alone and not knowing and—'" (*DH,* p. 605). Arthur Weasley compromises with her and allows her to remain in the castle within the Room of Requirement, but every moment of Ginny's character up to this point tells the reader that there is no way she is going to stay put. Like most of Ginny's character, this scene is missing from the *DH2* film. We don't get to hear about her escapades at Hogwarts or how she's working to bring down the terrorist regime that's taken over her school. Instead, the film focuses on her reunion with Harry, in an "eyes-meet-across-the-room" moment. Sweet, but it gives nothing to Ginny's character. There is never a question that Ginny will fight, because all of the Hogwarts Gryffindors fight, underage or not. Ginny is robbed of the opportunity to display her own agency, deliberately making the adult decision to defy her parents and enter the fight after the Room of Requirement is destroyed.

In the novel, we see Ginny taking active part in the battle, firing jinxes out of the windows and comforting injured students. After Harry's death and resurrection, when the reader rejoins the battle in the Great Hall, Ginny (with Luna and Hermione) is dueling Bellatrix Lestrange, second in command to Voldemort and the last Death Eater standing. When Molly Weasley steps into the fray with her iconic, "NOT MY DAUGHTER, YOU BITCH," (*DH,* p. 736), it is because Ginny narrowly escapes an *Avada Kedavra* by an inch. Ginny has fought the best fight she can against the most powerful dark witch in the world and survived. When this moment arrives in the film, Ginny is flanked not by Hermione and Luna, but by George and Arthur Weasley. She deflects an unnamed curse before Molly steps in front of her. This final betrayal of Ginny's character cements her, not as a fully capable adult witch, equal in skill and power to those around her, but the last remaining child of the Weasleys, in need of assistance from her father and older brother and of protection from her mother. We don't see Ginny again until the "nineteen years later" coda, in awkward aging makeup, at the side of her husband and children. Her forceful admonition to her son, James, to "give it a rest!" (*DH,* p. 753), her playful poke at her older brother ("You interrupted them? … You are *so* like Ron" [*DH,* p. 756]), and her reassurance to Harry that their son Albus "[will] be all right" (*DH,* p. 759) are all gone. Even as an adult parent of two, in the film epilogue, she is stripped of all of the fire, competence, and strong will Rowling packs into her in seven short pages. She has no lines in this scene, and stands deferentially just behind Harry every time she is shown. She is the captured MacGuffin in full, serving her purpose as Potter's reward.

Ginny Interrupted

While *otaku* of *Harry Potter* have the full wealth of Ginny's story across seven novels to fall back upon, to fill the gaps in her character and storyline in the films, many, many *Potter* fans do not. For those fans who have the singular experience of the films as their only canon, they are fundamentally robbed of the essence of Ginny Weasley. The transmediated experience is imperative to a true understanding of the character. Bonnie Wright's Ginny Weasley of the films is a weak shell of the full character, bearing almost no resemblance to Rowling's original conception. For a franchise so committed to snowball transmediating the novels on screen in faith, both the casting of Wright and the continuing characterization of Ginny Weasley are curious, unfortunate choices. The Ginny Weasley of the books is strong, competent, and so much more than just "Harry Potter's girlfriend" or "Ron Weasley's sister." She is tough, talented, complex, and ferocious. She stands up for the small, grows in skill and agency through her own personal battles with Voldemort's horcrux and his minions, and will fight for her friends at the drop of the hat.

Rowling once said:

> [T]he plan was, which I really hope I fulfilled, is that the reader, like Harry, would gradually discover Ginny as pretty much the ideal girl for Harry. She's tough, not in an unpleasant way, but she's gutsy. He needs to be with someone who can stand the

demands of being with Harry Potter, because he's a scary boyfriend in a lot of ways. He's a marked man. I think she's funny, and I think that she's very warm and compassionate. These are all things that Harry requires in his ideal woman. But, I felt—and I'm talking years ago when all this was planned—initially, she's terrified by his image. I mean, he's a bit of a rock god to her when she sees him first, at 10 or 11, and he's this famous boy. So Ginny had to go through a journey as well.... And I feel that Ginny and Harry ... they are total equals. They are worthy of each other [Rowling, as quoted in Anelli & Spartz, 2005].

But movie Ginny is not tough, or gutsy, or on a journey, or, ultimately, worthy. By diminishing, or in many cases, outright removing Ginny's best qualities in the films for the sake of plot expediency, young girls without the novel canon learn to be nothing more than an accessory first and their own persons second. In a world where women earn seventy-nine cents to their male counterparts' dollar, and often have their value judged by men (with or without a right to do so), role models that teach girls to be strong and fierce on their own are very important. The films fall into the *Highlander* trap of "There Can Be Only One" (Mulcahy, 1986). Hermione is centralized and gets to have character development, growth, and both internal and external power. Therefore, by Hollywood rules, no other girl or woman her age is allowed to in the same text. This is a tragic consequence of having a male screenwriter and male directors for every single installment in the series. Ginny's character is seen as secondary and expendable, when in reality, she is just as important to the telling of the tale as anyone. There can be more than one important girl in the story. It *is* possible. In a cultural work as popular and important as *Harry Potter*, it is critical that young women get to see strong female characters they can strive to emulate, but perhaps equally as important, it is vital that young men get to see strong *female* characters they can *also* strive to emulate.

NOTES

1. One of the best parts of Harry Potter Studies as a scholarly discipline is our commitment to the creation, development, and mentoring of the next generation of Potter scholars, and our belief that the importance of what one has to say is not arbitrarily dictated by age, title, or rank. This essay is the result of our first ever high school *Potter* scholar search. Celina Smith presented the key concept of this paper at the Chestnut Hill Harry Potter Conference in October of 2017, and was selected by the leadership of Harry Potter Studies for this collaboration. We are proud to present this work to you, and encourage you to share it with other high school students who may be ready to take the next scholarly step into academia.

2. It should be noted here that adaptation, as a concept, has an incredibly wide body of literature detailing the subject. This body of literature is well outside the scope of this essay—for our purposes here, we are considering adaptation a transmediation process, one which necessarily fundamentally alters the original text, and dealing with it accordingly.

3. The use of the term "otaku" is a contested space, particularly when used in connection to Western media. For purposes of this essay, we use the term because Rose used the term in a more general sense. Wide use of this term is certainly an area for future further inquiry.

4. A "MacGuffin" is "an object, event, or person that the characters in a story value greatly—so much so that nearly the whole plot revolves around it, despite that the thing itself isn't actually terribly important to the actual unfolding story" (Blitz, 2017). The most classic example of a MacGuffin is the black statue in *The Maltese Falcon*, but everything from *The Avengers'* tesseract to the briefcase in *Pulp Fiction* to the Ark of the Covenant in *Raiders of the Lost Ark* has served in this capacity. The term "MacGuffin" is often credited to Alfred Hitchcock, although Hitchcock himself credited writer Angus MacPhail for coming up with the word.

5. Surely there must have been many, many important prophesies on those shelves about things other than Harry Potter. The filmic wizarding world will never know…

6. "She was not tearful; that was one of the many wonderful things about Ginny, she was rarely weepy … having six brothers must have toughened her up" (*DH*, p. 116). It is unfortunate that Rowling attributes this clearly innate characteristic of Ginny to her brothers' influence rather than to her own inner fortitude.

References

Anelli, M., & Spartz, E. (2005). The Leaky Cauldron and Mugglenet interview Joanne Kathleen Rowling: Part three. *The Leaky Cauldron.* http://www.accio-quote.org/articles/2005/0705-tlc_mugglenet-anelli-3.htm Accessed 13 December 2017.

Blitz, M. (2017). What's a MacGuffin in films and why is it called that? *Today I Found Out.* April 1, 2017. http://www.todayifoundout.com/index.php/2017/04/whats-a-macguffin/ Accessed 12 December 2017.

Jenkins, H. (2006). *Convergence culture: Where old and new media collide.* New York: New York University Press.

Mulcahy, R. (Director). (1986). *Highlander* [motion picture]. USA: 20th Century–Fox.

Rose, F. (2011). *The art of immersion: How the digital generation is remaking Hollywood, Madison Avenue, and the way we tell stories.* New York: W.W. Norton & Company.

Rowling, J.K. (1997). *Harry Potter and the sorcerer's stone.* New York: Scholastic.

Rowling, J.K. (1998). *Harry Potter and the chamber of secrets.* New York: Scholastic.

Rowling, J.K. (1999). *Harry Potter and the prisoner of Azkaban.* New York: Scholastic.

Rowling, J.K. (2000). *Harry Potter and the goblet of fire.* New York: Scholastic.

Rowling, J.K. (2003). *Harry Potter and the order of the phoenix.* New York: Scholastic.

Rowling, J.K. (2005). *Harry Potter and the half-blood prince.* New York: Scholastic.

Rowling, J.K. (2007). *Harry Potter and the deathly hallows.* New York: Scholastic.

Ryan, M.L. (2013). Transmedial storytelling and transfictionality. *Poetics Today, 34*(3), 361–388.

Siegel, M. (1995). More than words: The generative power of transmediation for learning. *Canadian Journal of Education, 20*(4), 455–475.

Yates, D. (2009). *Harry Potter and the Half-Blood Prince* [motion picture]. USA: Warner Bros. Pictures.

Performing Memories Through Fandom Talk
What a Focus Group Interview Reveals About Growing Up with Harry Potter

BRONWYN E. BEATTY

Once it was easy to define and identify a fan: a socially inept, emasculated male or hysterical female who is inappropriately obsessed with and emotionally attached to a popular culture media product, thereby calling into question his or her maturity, identity, and grip on reality. So described, the fan was, at best, belittled, with William Shatner's infamous 1986 exhortation to Trekkers to "get a life!" (Jenkins, 1992, p. 10) exemplifying the exasperation even the cultural industry often felt towards the more zealous members of its audience.

Current discussion around fandom, however, invokes a more varied and descriptive terminology, such as "mainstream fandom" (Jenkins, 2006), "casual fans" (Busse & Gray, 2011), "post-object fandom" (Williams, 2011), "aca-fans" (Jenkins, 2012), "fandom-is-a-way-of-life" (Busse, 2006), "media fans" (Booth & Kelly, 2013, p. 57), "anti-fans" (Pinkowitz, 2011), "online fandom" (Baym, 2000), and even "non-fans" (Gray, 2010). As the language implies, the epistemology of a fan has become more nuanced and normalized in the age of the internet and neo-liberal politics (Booth, 2015). Since recognizing the untapped commercial potential of fandom, the cultural industries have endeavored to foster and, importantly, manage "fannish behavior" (Stein, 2006) in order to deepen engagement and instill loyalty, and thereby improve their bottom line. So emerges "industry-sanctioned fans" (Busse & Gray, 2011, p. 439), being those who "play within the confines of the industry-set rules" (p. 438).

This mainstreaming of fandom contrasts with the early understanding of fandom as subcultural and marginalized. Yet the widespread uptake and expression of fannish practices creates a dilemma for fandom studies; as Busse (2006) asks, "How can we define fans without invoking a category so expansive that it includes all media audiences or one so narrow that it excludes large numbers of individualist fans?" This is a relevant question in the age of participatory culture when individuals increasingly regard themselves as fans and fannish practices are encouraged by the cultural industries.

This essay examines a focus group interview centered on the *Harry Potter* phenomenon. The participants self-identify as fans and members of the *Potter* generation, but given the problematizing of fandom noted above, what can we learn about their fandom through this research method? The first section clarifies the methodology, noting the focus group interview tends to collective agreement and as such it suggests, but does not mirror, everyday social exchanges which also look to bring about mutual understanding. The second section considers the fandom expressed in the group interview, concluding that they are predominantly mainstream fans. The third and fourth sections consider the memory work undertaken to achieve this collective understanding of their fandom during their "extended talk." Their memory work, including narrative, is discussed in the third section, and this story telling enables the participants to project an autobiography as a *Harry Potter* fan with recourse to a readily understood cultural imaginary. The fourth, and final, section reveals the group's efforts at consensus. There is much they collectively agree upon, but there is also censure; when one participant apparently oversteps the group's normalization of an industry-led fandom experience, her memories are rejected, thereby ensuring consensus is achieved. This essay therefore captures memories of mainstream *Harry Potter* fandom and considers how this common experience is normalized against a more fannish subject position.

Methodology

In November 2014, a group of students undertaking a broadcasting communication degree attended a discussion focused on the *Harry Potter* phenomenon. The group was self-selecting; having been advised that there would be a group discussion where they could share their experiences of growing up with the *Harry Potter* franchise during the lunch break, 25 of a possible 65 students opted to attend. Opportunely, there was a gender balance in the group with 13 females and 12 males attending, and they were aged between 18 and 23 years. As to be expected of a self-selecting group, those attending were fans of the series; no one who was either uninterested in or actively disliked the franchise (an anti-fan) chose to participate. It is important to emphasize the extent to which the participants knew each other, as this has implications for the "spirit of spontaneity and authenticity" (Schrøder et al., 2003, p. 148) of their responses, as will be evidenced below. Having been engaged on the same immersion mode tertiary-level course for the previous nine months, the students were comfortable and confident with each other, with the researcher and with the television studio environment in which the discussion took place. In addition to attending class together 9–5 daily, their study included group work, and in some instances they socialized and rented accommodation together. All of these factors contributed to their willingness to openly share memories of growing up with *Harry Potter*.

It is also worth recording the participants' homogeneity. While class is not typically invoked in New Zealand, these participants were predominantly middle class and educated (they were undertaking tertiary study). The majority were Pākehā (white European) and neither nationality nor ethnicity played a significant part in the discussion, despite there being Pasifika, Māori, English, and American individuals in the group.

To start the 60-minute semi-structured conversation, each individual responded in turn to the opening question I posed, "What first springs to mind when you hear the words 'Harry Potter'?" The group discussion was entirely discursive, with no physical or visual items to prompt or aid recollection. Once each person had had a chance to offer an initial memory of their engagement with Pottermania, the floor was open for general discussion. I endeavored to intervene as little as possible, moderating with questions or prompts only when necessary to maintain the flow of conversation, clarify a point, or to direct the discussion. As such, this "speech event" (Schrøder et al., 2003, p. 149) reflects Halkier's evaluation of group interviews as "accounts *in* action" (2002 cited in Schrøder et al., 2003, p. 151, italics in original). While the individual interview allows subjects to provide "accounts *about* action" (Halkier 2002 cited in Schrøder et al., 2003, p. 151, italics in original) focus groups enable group interactions to be observed, with the primary data analyzed being the "complex and varying processes through which group norms and meanings are shaped, elaborated and applied" (Bloor et al. 2001, p. 71 cited Schrøder et al., 2003, p. 152). Group discussions are marked by "consensus-forming negotiations" (Schrøder et al., 2003, p. 110) and the one examined in this study was no exception.

These participants were willing to impart their memories of growing up with *Harry Potter*; for them it enabled an occasion during which they could assert themselves as fans of *Harry Potter* as well as more broadly connect with their peers as part of the *Potter* Generation. Equally they could withhold details as they wished. Lance's[1] comment "I think we should tell [author]…"

before regaling an anecdote points to the fact that participants have a choice about what they reveal, and therefore are active or "agentic" in the discussion.

A key value of the focus group interview is that participants "collectively enact a negotiation of the meaning of a media product, and thus ... reflect, the way the social production of meaning normally takes place in interpersonal encounters, in more extended spans of time and contexts of space" (Schrøder et al. 2003, p. 152). Although not suggesting the focus group directly replicates real life situations in which identity and meaning are socially established, reception research agrees that the method goes some way towards this by exploring "media experiences through the medium of extended talk" (p. 147). This particular "extended talk" is now examined for what it can tell us about this group's experience of growing up as part of the *Potter* Generation.

Performing Fandom

That the *Harry Potter* franchise was—is—a "phenomenon" is indisputable; Jenkins (2007) even suggests that it is "subcultural" to not be a fan when he blogs that, "statistically speaking, the people who are not fans of *Harry Potter* are outside of the mainstream." True, too, is the fact that many young people who grew up with the book and then film series count themselves as part of a "*Potter* Generation," with their childhood, their very identity, marked by Rowling's bildungsroman which unfolded across seven books and eight films over the 14 years from 1997 to 2011 (Beatty, 2015; Gierzinsky & Eddy 2013; Siede, 2014). Millennials are therefore frequently recorded as proclaiming some variation of "I grew up with Harry Potter" (Lee, 2015, p. 71; Tapaleo, 2011; Owen, 2011) and this focus group study is no exception. Lizzie declared that the series "is a natural part of us!," indicating there is no separating the franchise from their life stories. They describe a lifelong immersion in the franchise, with some of the participants only born when the first book was published: first being read the early books, then reading and rereading all the books themselves; eagerly anticipating the books and film releases; playing *Harry Potter*-inspired games with friends; desiring and/or receiving *Harry Potter* gifts; valorizing particular merchandise and peripherals such as the official Lego and PlayStation games; engaging with online *Harry Potter* resources such as *Pottermore*; feeling special as members of the *Potter* Generation. That they are fans was therefore taken for granted by the participants in the talk; no explicit mention of fandom was forthcoming until specifically asked if they were fans, when they all returned an emphatic "yes!" in chorus.

Differing levels of fandom were indicated within the group. They ranged across having: only watched the films; read the books and watched the films but purposefully not engaged with the merchandise (Simon); read the books, watched the films, enjoyed the merchandising as a child and the official online resources as they matured (the majority—for example, Christine, Rhonda, Rosemary, Lance, Ben, Owen); read the books, watched the films and continue to purchase the merchandise as an adult (Vessie). Simon's preference to ignore the merchandising reflects comments made by some young fans at the height of Pottermania; in 2002, 13-year-old, John claimed, "If there is too much hype it destroys the whole thing. I think that is what has happened with Harry Potter" and 15-year-old Claire felt, "It's almost too commercial … [the merchandising] cheapens it for me" (cited in Beatty, 2006, p. 163). Vessie's attitude toward the merchandise is contrary to this position. She talks about her long-term love of the merchandise and purchasing new items at considerable expense into her adulthood. She finds the merchandise is every bit as important to the *Harry Potter* franchise as the books that underpin the transmedia product.

Vessie's relationship with the merchandise sets her fandom apart from that of the others in the group, more so than Simon's disavowal of *Harry Potter*-themed products. Her level of fandom perhaps goes some way towards the "superfans" named but not described by Lance ("there are fans and there are super fans") while the majority position themselves more modestly as mere "fans." For the latter, the merchandise is primarily aligned with a nostalgic recollection of their childhood media practices and with contemporary small gifts (a chocolate frog, a Polyjuice hipflask) that symbolize friendship and not with an ongoing desire to possess such items.

But even Vessie did not mention "superfan fandom" practices, such as attending conventions, writing fan fiction or blogs, communicating with other fans in online spaces, making *Harry Potter*-inspired media content. Nor did these particular members of the *Potter* Generation indicate any willingness or desire to engage directly with the wider fandom. Rachel notes there is pleasure in knowing that she is part of a global fandom and that she would be able to connect with strangers through a shared love of *Harry Potter* if she were travelling overseas, but it is of the type Benedict Anderson (1983) describes: an "imagined community" that does not necessarily require the member to know or engage with the others, it is enough to enjoy the feeling of communitas or "we-feeling" (Reulecke, 2008, p. 119). This diffidence toward the global fandom is unlike the online fans that Lee (2015) describes who post on the We Owe J.K. Rowling Our Childhood Facebook page or the politically-oriented fans who act through the Harry Potter Alliance (Jenkins, 2012).

The type of fandom described by the majority of the participants and summarized here seems to reflect the "mainstream fandom" that Busse (2006) refers to as "a commercially constructed position." That is, the individual's fannish behavior is exhibited primarily through official opportunities, rather than creating their own resources such as fan fiction. They are emotionally invested in *Harry Potter* and self-identify as fans on the basis of both this investment and their lifelong engagement with the various elements of the franchise. With the "fan" no longer a clear-cut identity (if indeed it ever was), it is constructive to consider how to map out the various ways of being a fan. While there are an increasing number of labels as identified at the beginning of the chapter, Busse suggests regarding the various possibilities of being a fan as part of a spectrum, with investment and involvement the means of tracing (and placing) a fan's practice. By this reasoning, Vessie's fannish engagement places her further along the spectrum towards "proper fans"[2] than her peers, given her strong focus on the merchandise in addition to the primary texts of books and films, and that she continues to purchase merchandise to the present day. Nevertheless, Busse and Gray sum up the dominant characteristics of this particular group when they write:

> an intense emotional investment in a text that is wholly singular may create a fan but it does not make the individual part of a larger fandom, where its members are characterized not only by their affect and engagement with the source text but also by their engagement with one another [p. 426].

"Community" becomes the defining element of a "superfan" (to use Lance's parlance) with their expectation and desire to seek out and engage with likeminded people. The fans engaged in fandoms describe resulting relationships in terms of instant friendship and family; an online fan explains, "Whenever I meet a new person and I come to know that he/she is a Potterhead, I don't ask more from them because this connection makes me feel that I'm with the right person" (cited in Lee, 2015, p. 67). This experience is applicable, of course, across fandoms. Meg, a "filker" (a fan who writes songs about fandom), refers to the common cultural knowledge shared by fans as "reinforcing the sense of belonging, of 'family'" (cited in Jenkins, 1992, p. 260) and Booth and Kelly record that *Dr Who* fans "share a familial sense of recognition" (2013, p. 68) when they meet up with likeminded people at a convention.

However, it should not be concluded that the mainstream fans represented here in the focus group do not seek shared opportunities when they arise. As the ensuing section demonstrates, more modest levels of community (family, peers, fellow students) than global online spaces and international fan conventions are adequate for their purposes. While this section has been about the dominance of mainstream fandom expressed in the focus group, the next reflects on specific nostalgic remembrances of growing up with *Harry*

Potter as well as the memory work undertaken to determine these as the cultural norm.

Memory Work

For Jan Assman, "Memory is the faculty that enables us to form an awareness of selfhood (identity), both on the personal and on the collective level" (2008, p. 109). Although common sense might suggest that memory is a private experience, an interiorized practice that marks out the individual as unique amongst the masses, the line between personal and social memory is blurred. Indeed, Halbwachs wrote in 1925 that it is impossible to conceive of a clear-cut distinction between the two forms of memory (cited in Kansteiner, 2002, p. 185). Therefore, "what we typically call 'memory' is ... the social-communicative act of remembering and forgetting with others in the course of some activity" (Brown & Reavey, 2013, p. 47).

There were many examples in the group discussion of the participants demonstrating Brown and Reavey's idea of remembering as a "social accomplishment performed as a joint activity with others" (2013, pp. 47–48). Co-construction, for example, involved the participants corroborating each other's memories. Rhonda asked, "Do you guys remember those Scholastic book club little magazines?" and only proceeded with her recollection about ordering a spellbook when her peers confirmed their awareness of the service. Similarly, Angela sought the group's confirmation of the character Hermione's messy hair when outlining how she would backbrush her own in order to emulate her heroine's standout physical feature, prefixing her story with, "You guys will probably remember..." The speaker's narrative only makes sense if they can assume a common cultural imaginary with their listener and a quick request for confirmation (verbal or physical, such as nods of the head) enables the story to proceed without further elaboration. "It is this shared cultural imaginary," Brown and Reavey claim, "which makes the participants 'at ease' in the habitable world produced in the recollection" (2013, p. 54). The listener automatically fills in the gaps of the narrative with their own memories which are much in accord with those of the speaker, leading to agreement.

Cross-cueing also reflects the collaborative effort of memory work, with one person's memory prompting or cross-cueing a new memory for another, which would otherwise not have been recalled (Hirst & Echterhoff, 2012, p. 59). The prompt was typically recognized by the speaker before recounting their revitalized memory, as indicated in this abridged part of the group discussion:

CHRISTINE: ...And along with Vessie and her limited edition things, one of my friends went to Australia for a holiday and she came back with ... this kind of Polly Pocket version of the Weasley's house ...
VESSIE: That reminds me of the Harry Potter Lego....
...
SIMON: Going on from what Rosemary has just said...

Each of the participants draws on memories previously expressed by their friends to recall their own, gradually building up a picture of both the individual and the collective "vision" of what growing up with *Harry Potter* was like, how the phenomenon inflects their ongoing sense of identity, and what it continues to mean to them in adulthood. Christine and Vessie prompt each other's distant memories, and Simon is reminded of a detail about food in the books by a prior point from Rosemary, demonstrating that conversational remembering aids personal recall. Summarizing Halbwachs, Olick writes that "The social frameworks in which we are called on to recall are inevitably tied up with what and how we recall. Groups provide us the stimulus or opportunity to recall, they shape the ways in which we do so, and often provide the materials" (2008, p. 155). Just as memory is aligned with the occasion in which it is actively constructed, so too is fandom. In this way fandom is performative, as "fandom is performed differently and can mean different things in different micro-contexts, in different moments of social interaction, and even on different platforms" (Hills, 2015, p. 149).

As part of the memory work undertaken, narrative was used to link past and present, with the fandom talk acting as a bridge between then and now for the participants. Telling stories was demonstrably a pleasurable performance of reaching back into their younger selves. Such "Autobiographical memory is the core of identity," Fivush advises, "To a large extent, we are the stories we tell about ourselves" (2013, p. 13). The group discussion included many autobiographical stories: pretending to be the erratic owl Pigwidgeon while playing with friends, attending the films with family, being disappointed with the gift of a *Harry Potter* doll until learning of the cultural cache attached to it, listening to the audiobooks while in the family car, and desperately wanting to play with a friend's *Harry Potter* toys. These personal narratives were conveyed with relish; the students enjoyed the opportunity to share their warm memories of growing up with *Harry Potter*. The memories recalled reflect a willingness to step outside normal roles and realities, with one story particularly striking in this regard: when specifically asked late in the discussion "What is a fan?," Ben responded, not with a definition, but with a personal story:

BEN: At high school, and this kind of feels like I'm in an AA meeting [general laughter] like I'm coming out about something, but none of my friends probably know but back in high school I was in the Harry Potter Secret Club ...

[laughter] I was one of the first XV, rugby macho boys, and I'm 6th and 7th form, but I also had this dirty little secret [big laugh from group]. So we would meet at lunchtime on Thursdays and discuss *Harry Potter*, like the book or that sort of thing [big laugh from group] and we would go on the internet and go on the likes of Wikipedia and go down like wormholes of *Harry Potter* ... [general laughter] and we had houses that we were sorted into.... Every second Thursday, none of the lads knew what I was up to but for two years I was attending this *Harry Potter* club ... it was awesome. Sometimes we would dress up and I think I was maybe one of two guys and the rest were like 20 girls [ohhh, ahhhh from others] It was just great fun! We would discuss all sorts of things and then from that I've moved into the internet side of things. I don't know if anyone here is a member of *Pottermore*? [chorus of "yes" from group] So *Pottermore*, for those of you who don't know, is a very social and interactive website where you can go to Ollivander's and get your wand and sorted into a house and my wand is elder with a unicorn hair core [general laughter at this knowledge] ... I don't know, I've had a lot of great experiences with *Harry Potter*, I get all the *Pottermore* updates every week and I don't go on there so much anymore, but it's a good thing to do when you've got some down time and I get immersed in the "interactiveness" of *Harry Potter*. [Ben is laughing at himself now, and others too.] Everyone knows!

This excerpt conveys the friendly and confessional tone of the conversation where the participants felt safe to offer up personal memories. But it also demonstrates how narrative was used to establish an identity as a fan of *Harry Potter*. Telling stories about ourselves helps to establish our identities (Fivush, 2013, p. 16; Fisher, 1985; Hood, 2012; Straub, 2008). Ben's recollections of intimate knowledge, long-term engagement, and social interaction serve to reveal himself and his peers as fans of *Harry Potter*, and that this generationally significant cultural phenomenon is vital to their identities.

A friend went on to corroborate Ben's fandom (and that of others in the group) with another story:

LANCE: ...two or three weeks ago, Ben was in the common room and I was there and there were a couple of other people and he got up ... a quiz site, and [addressing Ben] what was the quiz? Name 200...?
BEN: The top 200 names of characters...
LANCE: From *Harry Potter*. And how many do you think we got, 90 or something?
BEN: No we got more than that. We ended up being on 114.
LANCE: But how many people were in the common room? Like, people just kept coming in.
BEN: Five of us?
ROSEMARY: It started off with, like, five of us but ended up with 10 people in there...
BEN: Yeah, 10 or so...
LANCE: Just shouting out [character names], at school, at lunchtime. It took, like, 20 minutes of our lunchbreak.
BEN: Yeah, and some of these characters were only mentioned once or twice in the

books; they were very, very minor characters. It was something to do, another social thing to do!

Once more, Ben and his peers work together through co-constructing and storytelling to validate their claims in this group discussion to be *Harry Potter* fans. If recalling memories as stories creates identity, it is necessarily an interactive and ongoing process as new information is incorporated and old forgotten, and experiences re-versioned to account for a different social context in which it is told. Each telling is therefore "motivated and agentic" (Fivush, 2013, p. 14), as indicated here with the participants selecting what narrative elements to reveal. The participants' reassessment of the number of people involved in the quiz and the number of characters' names recalled accords with the view that:

> memory [is] not simply about an accurate record of the past; remembering [is] an "effort after meaning." Memory is about making sense of what has happened to us. This does not mean that accuracy does not matter, but rather changes the question to whose accuracy for what purpose? [Fivush, 2013, p. 26].

Given the focus of the group discussion being about the *Harry Potter* phenomenon, it is unsurprising that the numbers relating to the lunchtime quiz went up rather than down, thereby enhancing their claim to be knowledgeable fans of the franchise.

Cross-cueing, co-construction and story constitute the dominant memory work conducted by these individuals as they recalled their past and present experiences connected with Pottermania. Those participating in the group discussion were afforded the opportunity to augment their identity as *Harry Potter* fans. Within the conversation, the speaker is purposeful, and the listener "hear[s] and acknowledge[s]" (Fivush, 2013, p. 27) the recollection; together they confirm a memory and thereby affirm an identity. Within this context, the students narrated the continuity of their identity through these memories; they were fans as children, and remain so as young adults, as revealed by their ongoing engagement through movie marathons, accessing online sources such as *Pottermore* and utilizing spare time on campus with quizzes. The group interview provides a glimpse into the dynamic nature of memories of childhood media use, revealing how being a fan of *Harry Potter* elides into growing up for them. However, their memory work not only operates to link the individual's past and present through nostalgic narratives, it also connects those remembrances of individual experiences to a wider collective—the Potter Generation and *Harry Potter* fandom more generally. As Booth and Kelly write, "Fandom as an identity necessarily entails duality; one is oneself, but also one is part of a larger group" (2013, p. 69). The following section considers this element of group memory work, especially reflecting on how the participants strive for consensus.

Achieving Consensus

The group discussion here under close analysis can be considered a moment at which collective memory is achieved. "Thus," Fivush claims,

> from a socio-cultural theoretical perspective, autobiographical memory is socially constructed in everyday storytelling that is itself shaped by cultural narrative frames. Critically, these stories are constructed and reconstructed in social interaction in which listeners hear the stories, contribute to the stories, confirm, validate, negate and question, in situations where there may or may not be a shared social and cultural understanding of how to frame and evaluate specific kinds of experiences [2013, p. 17].

There is significant agreement in this group discussion about all things *Harry Potter* as members of the *Potter* Generation; as Beatrice observes, "Everyone knows what *wingardium leviosa* means!" Schrøder et al. note that as focus groups tend to consensus they enable "the researcher to directly observe the social production of meaning as participants negotiate their readings of media material in an environment with strong consensual constraints" (2003, p. 125). Two instances exemplify contrasting modes of establishing a consensus in this group context: mutual agreement and rejection of a counter view.

Mutual agreement was evident when the group jointly established certain narrative points and reflected on the merits and demerits of film adaptations:

> OWEN: I got really annoyed with, I think my memory is a bit off, but I think it's the fourth movie, where Dobby gives him the gillyweed, or whatever it is, to go in the water, and in the book it's someone different who gives it to him.
> [hubbub as the group discusses this point between individuals]
> KARL: Neville gives it to him.
> OWEN: Yeah, Neville gives it to him in the book and Dobby gives it to him in the film or something.
> ROSEMARY: Other way round.
> CHORUS: Other way round.
> OWEN: Okay, other way round. Sorry ... I just wanted [the film] to be exactly like the books...
> JASON: In saying that, it was probably one of the best book to movie translations I have ever seen.
> OWEN: Oh yeah.
> JASON: And I don't know how they do it. It might have been when I read the first one I was so young I wasn't really taking in as much information as I do now but for some reason even if there was the odd slip up it was still a near perfect translation.
> SAM: I don't know, not even slips ups. I'm kind of happy that they didn't put like Peeves in and stuff. It would have been so weird. For some scenes it was too difficult. You know, like the scene with all the ghosts in the dungeon in the book? ... I think they picked it really well.

ROSEMARY: Yeah, they chose what to put in and what to leave out really well. They didn't miss out any of the story which is what a lot of book to movie translations are doing these days, they're missing out important things from the books that would help, like, enhance the story. And with *Harry Potter* they lift out the perfect amount rather than putting in everything.

VESSIE: If you go back and read the books or whatever you get that added "extra" as well, like an Easter egg I guess at the end of a movie or something like that. It's kind of the same, if you read the books there are added bits that aren't in the movies.

This part of the group discussion demonstrates the participants collectively establishing the facts (exactly who gave Harry the gillyweed in the books and the films) and contesting the directors' filmic interpretations of Rowling's "urtext" (Jason's "slip up" is Sam's intentional and successful omission during adaptation). What began as a complaint (alterations to Rowling's story in the film adaptation) becomes a positive attribute, with Jason, Sam, and Rosemary indicating the adaptations respect the new medium, and Vessie suggesting that the deliberate and necessary elisions from the film give the reader greater value when they return to the books. Consensus is "actively accomplished" (Brown & Reavey, 2013, p. 49) in the course of the conversation, through what Henry Jenkins refers to as "collective intelligence"; "None of us can know everything; each of us knows something; and we can put the pieces together if we pool our resources and combine our skills" (2006, p. 4).

However, a second example shows consensus being achieved by marginalizing the memories of one of the group members. In discussing their personal memories of growing up with *Harry Potter*, these fans together express their own particular "collective memory." Olick records that collective memory "is a process not a thing" and "is something—or rather many things—we *do*, not something—or many things—we *have*" (Olick, 2008, p. 159, italics in original). Not only is collective memory an ongoing process, such memories are multiple, complex and "far from monolithic" (Olick, 2008, p. 159). As such, collective memories require continued iteration in which the details are debated and consensus sought. Contesting collective memories is important as they are "representations of the past in the minds of members of a community that contribute to the community's sense of identity" (Manier & Hirst, 2008, p. 253). This particular community (those participating in the focus group) had agreed to an ideal of mainstream fandom, yet there was one participant whose recollections sometimes challenged this tacit understanding.

Some of Vessie's personal narratives valorize the merchandise itself and its cost over the social possibilities these items can facilitate. She talks at length of the items she had as a younger fan (*Harry Potter* Lego, for example) as well as those items she has purchased more recently (the Wizarding set).

The monetary value of these items is important ($500 for the Wizarding set, the Lego set was "expensive") as is their "untouched" quality:

> VESSIE: After the last movie, I was waiting because I knew that they were going to release all the movies in some shape or form ... and then they announced they were going to do this Wizard Collection and I thought, "Sweet! I'll be in on that no matter what it costs and it might be 5 or 600 dollars." I got it from Mighty Ape, pre-ordered it, and it's just this huge box, and I got it and took it out and inside the box is another box and then there's all these secret places. So you open up one bit and there might be a couple of discs and then you open up another bit and there might be a locket and there's a map. But I haven't taken [the map] out of the plastic. It's still in there. There's just all this really cool stuff, and down the bottom there's this certificate of authenticity which has got a stamp on it and all the codes for the digital copies and I haven't used anything except the codes because you have to use the code before it expires. But everything else in the box, I've kept in the box and not really touched it because it's quite expensive.

This detailed description of the Wizard Collection purchased at significant expense as part of her current fan practices distinguishes Vessie's experience of *Harry Potter* fandom from that of the others in the group. Nevertheless, Vessie also greatly appreciated the social connections which arise from her fandom. She enjoys playing the PlayStation games with her boyfriend and "For the final movie, I dressed up. My nana made me a robe and I had a Slytherin badge on and she stuffed a hand puppet owl and put velcro on it so it would stay on my shoulder which was really cool. That was awesome."

Vessie's experience of Pottermania mixes the homemade with the mass produced, with each as "valuable" as the other, and fosters social connections, such as with her grandmother and boyfriend. However, other members of the group were offended by the importance she places on the cost of trademarked merchandise, that she covets the commodities in a way that goes beyond that of their own collective memories as *Harry Potter* fans. Despite their own experiences being littered with merchandise, an agreement emerged in the discussion that the purpose of the goods was oriented toward connecting with others, even if, as in Christine's experience, this was to increase her mana within her childhood playgroup by possessing toys (a *Harry Potter* doll) not then available in New Zealand.

Consequently, Vessie's memories are challenged by her peers:

> VESSIE: That reminds me of the *Harry Potter* Lego. [General murmuring by the group in recognition of the brand] It's just this amazing thing where you can just be in the castle or whatever. I got all the little sets because they were quite cheap, but for my birthday one year my parents bought me, it was the first one, the whole castle worth a couple of hundred [mumbling from group] because I really wanted it, but they didn't actually give it to me until after my party

because they didn't want any of my friends stealing anything or breaking anything.
OWEN: Who are your friends?! Jeez!
[Some awkward laughter from the group]
VESSIE: I'm also very particular with things. I won't let anyone touch my stuff. Yeah. That was so cool.
LANCE: Just thinking about merchandise and *Harry Potter* everyday life, something I forgot until now: for my 18th birthday, so only this year in February, my girlfriend got me a hipflask that said Polyjuice on the front of it. And, like, even this year I've been to a few parties and been sitting there and I've got some sort of concoction in there—"Have a hit of polyjuice! Go on, you know you want to!"
[General laughter]
LANCE: So that's how *Harry Potter* influences me!

As this passage indicates, there was a subtle rejection of Vessie's memories. No one says that the events portrayed in her narrative did not occur; rather, they refuse to legitimate the memories first by voicing offense at the implication that friends cannot be trusted with the merchandise, and then by immediately offering a counter-narrative, one in which the merchandise is recalled as a tool for socializing rather than as a rarefied object (despite its mass production) of particular monetary value. Vessie's fandom is perceived as analogous to the more industry-led fandom followed by the majority, and is therefore critiqued for going beyond the agreed collective experiences of sharing and developing social relations through merchandise, as demonstrated by Lance's narrative of the Polyjuice hipflask.

There were moments, then, when some participants undertook memory work that served to police the parameters of acceptable fandom, lending support to the observation by Gray, Sandvoss and Harrington that "fans are seen not as a counterforce to existing social hierarchies and structures but, in sharp contrast, as agents of maintaining social and cultural systems of classification and thus existing hierarchies" (2007, p. 6). In the process of performing memory work, this group establishes and clarifies normative boundaries to their particular collective memory of *Harry Potter* fandom, at times chastising Vessie for her alternative vision, which embraces material value in the merchandise. Manier and Hirst assert that "a collective memory is not simply a memory shared across a community. It must serve a function for the community" (2008, p. 253). In this instance, the agreed collective memory extols an intensely commercial global franchise as facilitating a sharing and social experience and rejects the perceived more "super-fannish" memories put forward by Vessie. That Vessie's attachment to the merchandise does not diminish her experiences of socializing through the franchise is lost in collective affront; when Vessie describes how "disgusting" polyjuice potion tastes, Beatrice interjects, "That was another $300!" Such "fan-tagonism"

(Johnson, 2007) is neither new nor exclusive to this specific group; but here, Vessie's fandom is called out in order to assert the mainstream vision of growing up with *Harry Potter* as normal.

Conclusion

Annette Kuhn observes that, "Memory work is a conscious and purposeful staging of memory" (Kuhn, 2010, p. 186). Her assertion is confirmed by this close analysis of a particular fan community's memory work conducted during a focus group interview in which they proclaim their eligibility to be called *Harry Potter* fans. But there is an edge to the collective spirit and warmth conveyed in the group discussion, with one participant modestly chided for her differing relationship with the merchandise; for Vessie, at times the social possibilities of the franchise were trumped by the monetary value of her collectibles during her memory work, and this did not sit well for all the participants in the conversation as they worked to establish a collective memory of a socially-oriented mainstream fan experience. If this group discussion was a moment of memory work in which the students recollected treasured memories of growing up with *Harry Potter* that were intrinsic to their ongoing identities as members of the *Potter* generation, the majority did not want them sullied by incongruent memories of the minority.

Yet, this was a performance of memories of fandom at a particular time, in a particular group, with a particular intention. Each of these elements influence the memories recalled and their articulation. Thus, it would be informative to re-interview these participants in the near future. How do their recollections compare with those expressed in this group discussion? Do their current stories of sociality remain? Do particular examples of childhood fandom persist? Do the participants continue to socialize through *Harry Potter* or have they outgrown the franchise? Fivush writes that "Some stories become canonical and quite stable, and may provide for a consistent and coherent sense of self over time (Conway et al. 2004), whereas other stories remain fluid, changing with each retelling" (2013, p. 16). Future research will engage with this claim.

Notes

1. All participants in the focus group interview have been given a pseudonym.
2. Busse (2006) uses this descriptor in quotation marks to demarcate those fans at one end of the spectrum who exhibit both strong involvement and investment, with involvement specifically including participation in the fandom community. That is, "*fans* as members of *fandom*" (Busse & Gray, 2011, p. 426, italics in original).

References

Anderson, B. (1983). *Imagined communities: Reflections on the origin and spread of nationalism*. London: Verso.
Assman, J. (2008). Communicative and cultural memory. In A. Erll & A. Nunning (Eds.), *Media and cultural memory* (pp. 109–118). Berlin: Walter de Gruyter.
Baym, N. (2000). *Tune in, log on: Soaps, fandom, and online community*. London: Sage.
Beatty, B. (2006). *The currency of heroic fantasy: The* Lord of the Rings *and* Harry Potter *from ideology to industry*. (Unpublished Doctoral thesis, Massey University, Auckland, New Zealand). Retrieved from https://mro.massey.ac.nz/bitstream/handle/10179/512/01front.pdf
Beatty, B. (2015). "It's a natural part of us!": The Potter generation reflect on their ongoing relationship with a cultural phenomenon. In C.E. Bell (Ed.), *From here to Hogwarts: Essays on Harry Potter fandom and fiction* (pp. 99–122). Jefferson, NC: McFarland.
Booth, P. (2015). *Playing fans: Negotiating fandom and media in the digital age*. Iowa City: University of Iowa Press.
Booth, P., & Kelly, P. (2013). The changing faces of *Doctor Who* fandom: New fans, new technologies, old practices? *Participations: Journal of Audience and Reception studies, 10*(1), 56–72.
Brown, S.D., & Reavey, P. (2013). Experience and memory. In E. Keightley & M. Pickering (Eds.), *Research Methods for Memory Studies* (pp. 45–59). Edinburgh: Edinburgh University Press.
Busse, K. (2006). Fandom-is-a-way-of-life versus Watercooler Discussion; or, The geek hierarchy as fannish identity politics. [Website]. Retrieved September 18, 2017, https://www.flowjournal.org/2006/11/taste-and-fandom/
Busse, K., & Gray, J. (2011). Fan cultures and fan communities. In V. Nightingale (Ed.), *The handbook of media audiences* (pp. 425–443). Hoboken, NJ: Wiley-Blackwell Publishing Ltd.
Fisher, W. (1985). The narrative paradigm: In the beginning. *Journal of Communication, 35*, 74–89.
Fivush, R. (2013). Autobiographical memory. In E. Keightley & M. Pickering (Eds.), *Research methods for memory studies* (pp. 13–28). Edinburgh: Edinburgh University Press.
Gierzynski, A., & Eddy, K. (2013). *Harry Potter and the Millennials: Research methods and the politics of the muggle generation*. Baltimore: Johns Hopkins University Press.
Gray, J. (2010). *Show sold separately: Promos, spoilers, and other media paratexts*. New York: New York University Press.
Gray, J., Sandvoss, C., & Harrington, C.L. (2007). Introduction: Why study fans? In J. Gray, C. Sandvoss & C.L. Harrington (Eds.), *Fandom: Identities and communities in a mediated world* (pp. 1–17). New York: New York University Press.
Hills, M. (2015). Fandom as an object and the objects of fandom: Interview with Matt Hills by Clarice Greco. *MATRIZes, 9*, 147–162. DOI:http://dx.doi.org/10.11606/issn.1982-8160.v9i1p147-163
Hirst, W., & Echterhoff, G. (2012). Remembering in conversations: The social sharing and reshaping of memories. *Annual Review of Psychology, 63*, 55–79.
Hood, B. (2012). *The self illusion: How the social brain creates identity*. Oxford: Oxford University Press.
Jenkins, H. (1992). *Textual Poachers: Television Fans and Participatory Culture*. London: Routledge.
Jenkins, H. (2006). *Convergence culture: Where old and new media collide*. New York: New York University Press.
Jenkins, H. (2012). "Cultural acupuncture": Fan activism and the Harry Potter Alliance. *Transformative Works and Cultures, 10*, http://dx.doi.org/10.3983/twc.2012.0305
Johnson, D. (2007). Fan-tagonism: Factions, institutions, and constitutive hegemonies of fandom. In J. Gray, C. Sandvoss & C.L. Harrington (Eds.), *Fandom: Identities and communities in a mediated world* (pp. 285–300). New York: New York University Press.

Kansteiner, W. (2002). Finding meaning in memory: A methodological critique of collective memory studies. *History and Theory*, *41*, 179–197.
Kuhn. A. (2010, August 2). Memory texts and memory work: Performances of memory in and with visual media. *Memory Studies*, 1–16. doi: 10.1177/1750698010370034. Retrieved from https://qmro.qmul.ac.uk/xmlui/bitstream/handle/123456789/4640/KUHNMemoryTexts2010POST.pdf?sequence=2
Lee, C-T. Keeping the magic alive: The fandom and "*Harry Potter* experience" after the franchise. In C.E. Bell (Ed.), *From here to Hogwarts: Essays on Harry Potter fandom and fiction* (pp. 54–77). Jefferson, NC: McFarland.
Manier, D., & Hirst, W. (2008). A cognitive taxonomy of collective memories. In A. Erll & A. Nunning (Eds.), *Media and cultural memory* (pp. 253–262). Berlin: Walter de Gruyter.
Olick, J. (2008). From collective memory to the sociology of mnemonic practices and products. In A. Erll & A. Nunning (Eds.), *Media and cultural memory* (pp. 151–161). Berlin: Walter de Gruyter.
Owen, J. (2011, July 10). For the Harry Potter generation, it all ends with tears and applause. *The Guardian*. Retrieved from https://www.theguardian.com/film/2011/jul/10/harry-potter-fans-last-film
Pinkowitz, J. (2011). "The rabid fans that take [Twilight] much too seriously": The construction and rejection of excess in Twilight antifandom. *Transformative Works and Cultures*, *7*, http://dx.doi.org/10.3983/twc.2011.0247
Reulecke, J. (2008). Generation/generationality, generativity, and memory. In A. Erll & A. Nunning (Eds.), *Media and cultural memory* (pp. 119–125). Berlin: Walter de Gruyter.
Ross, K., & Nightingale, V. (2008). *Media and audiences: New perspectives*. Maidenhead, Berkshire, UK: Open University Press.
Schrøder, K., Drotner, K., Kline, S., & Murray, C. (2003). *Researching audiences*. London: Arnold.
Siede, C. (2014). How *Harry Potter* shaped a generation. [website] Retrieved September 18, 2017, https://boingboing.net/2014/07/23/how-harry-potter-shaped-a-gene.html
Straub, J. (2008). Psychology, narrative, and cultural memory: Past and present. In A. Erll & A. Nunning (Eds.), *Media and cultural memory* (pp. 215–228). Berlin: Walter de Gruyter.
Tapaleao, V. (2011, July 14). Growing up with Harry. *NZHerald.co.nz* Retrieved from http://www.nzherald.co.nz/movies/news/article.cfm?c_id=200&objectid=10738277

Magical and Mundane Narrative Devices

Jørgen Riber Christensen
and Thessa Jensen

This essay addresses the narrative modes of the *Harry Potter* novels and films and concludes with a brief discussion of *Harry Potter* fan fiction. The combination of the magical and traditional—or mundane—narrative modes is considered with the inclusion of a comparative reading of the Dumbledore murder scene in *HBP*. The methodological framework is literary narratology and film narratology. This narratological approach is augmented by theories about fantasy, narcissism and fandom. The appeal of the advanced and complex narrative modes to readers and cinema audience can be found in the unity of themes and narration made possible by the genre of low fantasy. The themes of family and coming of age is tied to narrative devices that reflect the narcissist peer group positively. This unity is further augmented through fan fiction, where the readers identify strongly with the novels and become co-authors by continuing and transforming the Potter universe. In this essay, we define fan fiction as the transformation of an original text, using the original text's characters and focusing on the development of a relationship between the chosen characters. While fanfiction.net is the largest fan fiction site on the Internet, we use archiveofourown.org for collecting data, since this site provides easier access to statistical data and overviews.

Narcissism, Fan Fiction and Narrative

A theme running through the novels and the play *Harry Potter and the Cursed Child* is the quest for a father figure. Similarly, most families are problematic or disintegrated (Christensen, 2009). The sociologist Thomas Ziehe sees changes in the traditional nuclear family as the source of the rise of a new character formation; the narcissist (Ziehe, 1975, pp. 106–107). His conception of narcissism is less negative than is usually found. For instance, the narcissist's lack of a strong Freudian superego is compensated for by the inclusion of the narcissist in a peer group of friends (pp. 192–193). Ron, Harry, and Hermione form such a group, and together they are strong. This group serves three functions. It may reflect the readers' own uncertainties about family, it offers an alternative to a nuclear family, and it is the perfect vessel for expositional dialogue, which as we shall see below is a central narrative device in both novels and films. Another pertinent aspect of narcissism is the wish for the omnipotence of thought (pp. 108, 198). In the Harry Potter universe, this omnipotence has its expression in the supremacy of magic and magic as a theme is combined with a narrative function. Without these magical narrative devices, neither the plot nor the general narrative of the novels could proceed, as the following analysis will show. The narcissist peer group reaches beyond the original *Harry Potter* texts, and it is here that the fan fiction based on the *Harry Potter* universe comes into play. Ziehe connects the socialization type of narcissism and its concept of the peer group to subcultures and their aesthetic expressions, which help define identities and the presentation of the self. Within each singular subculture, Ziehe writes,

> these aesthetic expressions and narcissist reflections are highly standardized, and they include "emotionality, subjectivity and metacommunication," and this metacommunication allows intersubjective interpretations and critique within the peer-like subcultural group [pp. 192–193].

Fan fiction communities are such peer-like subcultural groups. Using the original texts and movies as their tent-pole (Davidson et al., 2010), *Harry Potter* fans are emotionally involved in understanding, analyzing, and transforming Rowling's story. While the books were written, the *Harry Potter* fandom tried to predict the storylines, development of characters, as well as the final outcome. Sandvoss (2005, p. 95) points to further implications of narcissism. Fandom becomes an extension of the self of the fan by using the object of fandom, be that a football team or Rowling's books, to form an inner dialogue with the material presented. To Sandvoss, narcissism is the lack of realizing that the object the fan falls in love with in fact is a mirror of the fan's self. The text itself gains its meaning through the fan's self-recognition in the text, rather than through a semiotic interpretation of the text itself (Sandvoss, 2005, p. 108). The process of transformation, as found in the writing of fan fiction, can be seen as an inner dialogue of the fan with the text; effectively turning the text into an extension of the fan's self. This process is by no means done uncritically or devoutly to the original text, as the following will demonstrate.

Thus, both the search for a father figure as well as the use of the peer group as compensation and narratological device are less obvious or totally absent in *Harry Potter* fan fiction. Instead, the main plot in fan fiction is the development of a relationship between two characters from the original texts. The character's inner dialogue seen from a third person perspective is the main fulcrum of any fan fiction. This mode of narration is also called selective omniscience and will be further elaborated on.

Relationships	Characters	Additional Tags
☐ Draco Malfoy/Harry Potter (29650)	☐ Harry Potter (75093)	☐ Romance (22143)
☐ Sirius Black/Remus Lupin (12880)	☐ Draco Malfoy (45451)	☐ Angst (17780)
☐ Harry Potter/Severus Snape (10728)	☐ Hermione Granger (43563)	☐ Fluff (15162)
☐ Hermione Granger/Ron Weasley (8308)	☐ Severus Snape (32806)	☐ Alternate Universe (12779)
☐ James Potter/Lilly Evans Potter (6595)	☐ Ron Weasley (31297)	☐ Humor (12022)
☐ Harry Potter/Ginny Weasley (6340)	☐ Remus Lupin (26290)	☐ Drama (9078)
☐ Hermione Granger/Draco Malfoy (6231)	☐ Sirius Black (26151)	☐ Drabble (7698)
☐ Hermione Granger/Severus Snape (3237)	☐ Ginny Weasley (17755)	☐ Slash (7349)
☐ Remus Lupin/Severus Snape (2602)	☐ James Potter (15384)	☐ Hurt/Comfort (6836)
☐ Harry Potter/Tom Riddle (2500)	☐ Albus Dumbledore (13876)	☐ Explicit Language (6305)

Figure 1. Fan fiction pairings and number of fics with certain characters. The third column shows additional tags. AO3, 30 August 2018.

Figure 1 shows the most written pairings (Draco Malfoy and Harry Potter leading with 29,650 fics) and most used characters on archiveofour own.org (AO3). The additional tags shown in Figure 1 give an indication of the favorite genres of Potter fics: romance, angst, and fluff. While "romance" explains itself, "angst" typically describes fics based on one or both characters in the chosen pairing being afraid of the other not loving him. "Fluff" can be seen as the opposite of angst, meaning the relationship between the characters is sweet and tender without any signs of angst or hurt.

The wealth of characters in the *Potter* universe can be seen as one contribution to its success especially in transformative fandom as found on fan fiction sites. Several of the characters have a perceived chemistry with each other, a few are directly shown as pairs. Fan fiction makes it possible to give a beloved character a different storyline, even resurrect them and let them have a happy ever after with their chosen lover. The readers of the original books can use this transformation to extend their own self, both by unconsciously mirroring the chosen character, and using the character's story as a way to self-reflect; or, in a more constructive and creative way, to transform the story by writing it anew and in this process not only self-reflect, but also expand the reader's own skillset. The passion for the story invites the reader to create a new story or develop the existing story.

Finally, fan fiction is a way of prolonging the pleasure of the original text (Barthes, 1975). By transforming certain main events of the original story, fic writers and readers are able to give new meaning to the same plot by changing perspectives, even rewrite and recreate the same trope over and over again (Coppa, 2017, p. 135).

A Hierarchy of Knowledge

The storyteller's undertaking in mainstream fiction is as much to withhold as to distribute information in a hierarchy of knowledge (Branigan, 1992/1998, pp. 72–76). Who is to know what and when are they to know it? The author as storyteller is at the top of this hierarchy. Some characters may be higher in the hierarchy of knowledge and they, on their part, may also choose not to tell other characters what they know. Especially in *OOTP,* Harry Potter has the feeling that Dumbledore has chosen secrecy rather than divulging to him that his master plot was to keep Voldemort out of Harry's mind, and with growing frustration Harry is kept in the dark. It is not until the penultimate chapter that Dumbledore comes clean.

The narrator has various narrative mechanisms at her disposal. Branigan mentions "speakers, presenters, listeners, and watchers who are in a (spatial and temporal) position to know" (p. 96). In the magical realm of narration, the question of giving information or holding it back is reflected in the contrast between legilimency (magically entering a person's mind) and occlumency (magically closing one's mind against legilimency). Harry's and Snape's duels to enter each other's minds or each shutting their own mind to the other illustrate how information is not only given, albeit involuntarily, to another character, but also gradually to the readers. The scenes in the books describing legilimency are akin to the literary technique, stream of consciousness, which has many forms, but in general is equivalent to an expression of a character's thoughts and feelings (Booth, 1961/1983, pp. 163–165). Booth identifies the narrative privilege of an omniscient knowledge based on "an inside view of another character" with "what could not be learned by strictly natural means or limited to realistic vision and interference" (p. 160). Rowling manages to harmonize this knowledge of what cannot "be learned by strictly natural means" with "realistic vision and interference." In a universe where magic exists, it is realistic that Snape and Harry, together with the readers, have the privilege of searching each other's minds for the characters' motivations, which shape the action. Even a deeper unconscious layer of Harry's mind is told to the readers through magical means. The Mirror of Erised reveals his innermost desire and longing for his parents. Dumbledore explains this to Harry, and the readers also gain this understanding of the mirror scene.

The Limited and the Omniscient Point of View

The principle of the hierarchy of knowledge is apparent in the first and the second chapter of *PS*. The mode of narration of the first chapter demonstrates how Mrs. and especially Mr. Dursley have access only to a certain amount of knowledge, and he is able to notice "something peculiar—a cat reading a map" (Rowling, 1997/2014, p. 2). Yet, it is also made perfectly clear that his place is low in the hierarchy of knowledge, and an intrusive omniscient narrator corrects Mr. Dursley: "How very wrong he was" (p. 8) in his understanding of what had happened during his day. His third person point of view is, as is the case with all Muggles, very limited. From chapter two and throughout the entire book series, the point of view almost exclusively becomes Harry's.

Wellek and Warren (1949/1970, pp. 222–223) describe the "omniscient narrator," who is the author's representative that "can tell a story without laying claim to having witnessed or participated in what he narrates." An alternative to this omniscient narrator is the first-person point of view, where the action is filtered through the consciousness of a character. Another alternative is the third person point of view, which is more direct as it does not have the self-conscious distance of a first-person narrator, but the readers are offered not only the action of a scene, but also the character as he is responding to it and reflecting directly upon it. This is how the readers of the Harry Potter novels are brought into direct contact with him and his world. This aspect of directness has bearing on the fantasy genre where the readers' involvement as a result of this narrative technique is one of the ways that the suspension of disbelief is facilitated.

With the limited third person point of view as the dominant one, it is typical of the Harry Potter novels that each chapter centers on one character. The Muggle Prime Minister is an example in *HBP*'s chapter called "The Other Minister." We are told that his pulse quickens and what his thoughts are. Almost the same narrative structure can be seen in the first chapter of *GOF*, where an omniscient narrator first relates local history, then the chapter moves to the present with the groundkeeper Frank Bryce as its subject, until he is murdered by Voldemort and Wormtail. The last line of the chapter, however, introduces Harry: "Two hundred miles away, the boy called Harry Potter awoke with a start" (Rowling, 2000/2014, p. 13), and the novel connects this scene of murder with its eponymous character. From now on it employs the limited third person point of view with Harry as its subject with what Wellek and Warren call "a controlled point of view with some characters' consciousness of what is going on (within and without) distinct from a 'scene'" with "the voluntary absence from the novel of the 'omniscient novelist'" (1949/1970, pp. 223–224). This "objective rendering of a specific subjectivity" constitutes the bulk of the series so that Harry Potter is the center of subjectivity.

By their very names, "omniscient" and "limited," these two points of view are subsumed under a hierarchy of knowledge. A single sentence will illustrate this: "Unfortunately, the teachers seemed to be thinking along the same lines as Hermione" (*PS*, Rowling, 1997/2014, p. 246). The context is that in dialogue Ron and Harry argue against Hermione's nagging about studying for the coming exams, and the teachers piling huge amounts of homework on the students. The omniscient narrator is guarded in her approach, and does not have the privileged access to the teachers' thoughts. The narrator can only use the word "seem" about the teachers. They only seem to share Hermione's point of view, which on the other hand is not qualified as it has been stated openly in dialogue in the presence of Harry's third person point of view. His point of view is also limited, as like the narrator, he can only know the status of affairs from the actions he witnesses, i.e., Hermione's opinions spoken to him and the increasing amount of homework.

For our purpose, Friedman's comprehensive typology of narrative modes (Friedman, 1955) may illustrate the many-faceted narration of the *Harry Potter* novels; but as we shall see this inclusive narratological model does not suffice for Rowling's method. Friedman has six versions of third person narration. The omniscient point of view has two forms. There is (1) *editorial omniscience* with an intrusive narrator, who offers "authorial intrusions and generalizations about life, manners and morals, which may or may not be explicitly related to the story at hand" (p. 1171), and there is (2) *neutral omniscience* but without "direct authorial intrusions" (p. 1172). These two kinds of the omniscient narrator with varying degrees of intrusion are present in the *Harry Potter* novels, yet we must go to paratexts; e.g., Rowling's Twitter account to read her "generalizations about life, manners and morals," and the authorial intrusion can for instance be seen in direct character descriptions, also external descriptions, as when Rowling writes, as she often does, "Snape/Malfoy sneered" instead of the neutral "said."

The narrator can relegate her function to one or more characters, so there can be (3) *multiple selective omniscience* from the point of view of different characters. "The appearance of the characters, what they do and say, the setting—all the story materials, therefore—can only be transmitted to the reader through the mind of someone present" (p. 1176), and to a single character with (4) *selective omniscience*. It is like the multiple selective omniscience, with the obvious difference that this character's mind is the focal point. The author may choose how deep into the consciousness of this character she goes (p. 1177), as when narration in (5) *the dramatic mode* is limited largely to what the characters do and say. Their appearance and the setting may be supplied by the author as in stage directions. However, there is never any direct indication of what they perceive" (p. 1178), or even more externally, there is (6) *the camera mode*, which is like the dramatic mode, but less selective in its presentation of the action, and Friedman compares it to "the final extinction of the author" (p. 1179).

It is only when we enlarge upon these six narrative modes by adding combinations of them that we can encompass the narration of the *Harry Potter* novels. The last four categories are relevant with different degrees of privilege to knowledge in the hierarchy. "'Multiple selective omniscience" from the point of view of several characters in succession can be found in a few instances, mainly in the first chapters of some of the novels, e.g., the Muggle Prime Minister in *HBP*. "'Selective omniscience" from the point of view of one single character is the dominant point of view, i.e., Harry's; but the last four points of view cannot be applied as they stand. It is only when "the dramatic mode" and "the camera" are applied to "multiple selective omniscience" and "selective omniscience," so that the privilege of omniscience is reduced, that Rowling's complex narrative modes appear. Harry's dominant limited point of view does contain inside views of his own mind, and sometimes also of others' minds, e.g., Snape's and Voldemort's. "The camera" mode is also present, when Harry can only observe, but not interfere with the action that he is witnessing, e.g., when he is wearing his invisibility cloak. As we shall see below in "Magical Narration," this complexity is dependent on the fantasy genre.

Expositional Dialogue

In the original texts, Harry Potter's subjectivity is treated realistically. In the universe of the book series this includes the use of magic to gain and communicate knowledge, but there are some simpler means. Access to Harry's mind and most of his feelings and access to the knowledge, which he has the privilege to obtain, are not provided by a narrator. The readers get this knowledge and these insights from listening to the almost uninterrupted conversations between Harry, Ron and Hermione. This kind of distribution of information is called expositional dialogue (Edgar-Hunt, Marland, Richards, 2009, p. 84). Expositional dialogue has the function of telling the readers what some of the characters already know, or as is often the case, what Harry and Ron have not yet grasped so that Hermione must explain matters to them.

The narrative use of expositional dialogue has two other functions that are not solely connected to the distribution of information, but are a combination of narrative and thematics. The narrative aspect is the character function of the nearest relation. This character has its origin in film dramaturgy. The nearest relation is the confidante of the main character, and her function is to listen to the main character, yet the actual function is distribution of the main character's thoughts and feelings to the audience (Olsson, 1982/1986, pp. 63–67). In literature, an intrusive omniscient narrator can impart this information directly to readers, but with the use of a limited third person point of view the nearest relation is the tool to convey inside information of the main character to the readers. The nearest relation is high in the hierarchy of knowledge; but only as high as the main character allows her to be. For instance, in *DH,* Harry acts without the knowledge of his nearest relations: "Ron and Hermione seemed a long way away.... There would be no goodbyes and no explanations, he was determined of that" (Rowling, 2007/2014, p. 566). Ron and Hermione do not only fulfill the relatively neutral dramaturgical function of being Harry's nearest relations. They are his nearest relations in a much more real sense, they are his friends, and as we have seen, they are his social peer group. This aspect of these three characters is perhaps the thematic strength of the novels, and regarded in this way, the theme of the peer group is integrated not only in the action and plot of the novels, but also in their narrative mode.

Setups and Payoffs

Like the mechanism of the nearest relation, the pair of setup and payoff combine a narrative function with a thematic function. This narrative function runs through the seven novels and their span of seven years, plus the nineteen years between the last two chapters of the whole series. The chronological progression of seven school years structures the 3,733 book pages with some clearly marked flashbacks. The development of the complicated action with its huge number of characters is tied together with strings of setups and payoffs. Larsen (2003, p. 141, our translation) defines the two: "Setup—payoff—chain of expression consisting of at least two small parts. The first (setup) camouflages information, and its deeper significance that is only revealed later through the second part (payoff)."

Rowling consistently works with a system of setups and payoffs, and there may well be quite a span of time between them, so that a setup established in one volume reappears as its payoff in a later volume. For instance, already in the second volume, *COS,* the Polyjuice Potion is used to trick Draco Malfoy. This situation turns out as comedy when Hermione by mistake is transformed into a cat. The comedy distracts the readers from the narrative function of this setup, so when the Polyjuice Potion is used cruelly against

Mad-Eye Moody, who is incarcerated in a trunk through most of the fourth volume, *GOF*, the much earlier introduction of the effect of the potion will verify and make probable this decisive plot element.

The developing mood of the series, which grows more and more somber and tragic, is also seen in setups and payoffs. Polyjuice must again be used in the last volume, *DH*. To try to avert the Death Eaters' attempt on Harry's life, Hermione, Ron, Fred and George Weasley, Mundungus and Fleur Delacour take Polyjuice Potion to transform into Harry Potter look-alikes for their escape from Privet Drive. By doing this they are all prepared to risk their own lives to save Harry. Behr describes this movement, where she writes that "clues and references planted by Rowling in earlier books are only appreciated by later events" (2005, pp. 113–114). This appreciation must include the readers' belief in the probability of the subsequent, often fantastic, payoffs. The thematic function of the darkening and often tragic payoffs reflects Harry's development from his infant innocence into a tragic and traumatized hero.

Paratextual Narration

When Genette quotes Philippe Lejeune about the "fringe of a printed text which in reality controls one's whole reading of the text" he refers to his own theoretical system of paratexts, and these paratexts are "the conveyer of a commentary that is authorial or more or less legitimized by the author" (1987/1997, p. 2). This paratextual system and Genette's terminology are condensed here. Paratexts are texts that are placed around the main text to add extra meaning to it. The main text is called the *hypotext*. Basically, but as we shall see, not totally, the hypotext is the seven Harry Potter novels written by the author J.K. Rowling. Paratexts with the example of a book's cover can be physically connected to the hypotext without being an integral part of it. These are called *peritexts*. When the paratext is physically removed from the hypotext as for instance a review of it, we are dealing with an *epitext*. There is also the distinction between *autographic* and *allographic* paratexts. The former is produced by the author of the hypotext, and the latter by someone else. The volume of these four types of paratexts connected to the seven *Harry Potter* novels is staggering. We now discuss some of the autographic paratexts, which Rowling employs as part of her narration and as an integral part of the thematics of the novels.

Information is not only provided to readers through Harry Potter's point of view and through conversations with the nearest relations. There is also textual information in different forms. These include letters by owl post, the tabloid *The Daily Prophet*, a section of the ancient book *The Tales of Beedle the Bard*, the Hogwarts library book *Quidditch Through the Ages*, the Hogwarts textbook *Fantastic Beasts and Where to Find Them*, the journalist Rita Skeeter's biography *The Life and Lies of Albus Dumbledore*, and there are broadcasts from the pirate radio station *Potterwatch*.

Some of these supplementary paratexts, which have different plot-bearing properties, have their own independent existence outside the novels, and they have the double existence of being both epitexts and peritexts. *The Tales of Beedle the Bard, Quidditch Through the Ages, Fantastic Beasts and Where to Find Them* have their own publication history. Hermione inherits *The Tales of Beedle the Bard* from Dumbledore. One of its stories, "The Tale of the Three Brothers," provides a clue for the genesis of the Deathly Hallows. *Quidditch Through the Ages* has a cursory appearance in *PS* when Snape confiscates it from Harry. *Fantastic Beasts and Where to Find Them* is a required textbook on Harry's supply list for his first year at Hogwarts. In 2016, this textbook has been expanded into an independent film series, which connects to the Harry Potter novels and films as a loosely tied prequel with Newt Scamander as the main character.

The sensationalist *The Life and Lies of Albus Dumbledore* and Dumbledore's obituary in *The Daily Prophet* contain clues to Harry's, Ron's and Hermione's understanding of Dumbledore and his motivation, and the biography helps them find one of the Hallows. This book with its partially unreliable narrator, Rita Skeeter, has a place in the hierarchy of knowledge. Though written by Rita Skeeter, it is an autographic paratext, and it offers a commentary to its hypotext and is part of it. *The Daily Prophet* itself has a double role. It provides information that is valuable and necessary for both characters and readers, but personalized by Rita Skeeter it gradually becomes an antagonist to Harry and his friends and tends to be a propaganda mouthpiece for The Ministry of Magic.

In *DH,* when Harry, Ron and Hermione are isolated in their tent, the third person limited point of view has the consequence that the progression of the plot outside the tent can only be told to the readers when the three fugitives listen to the radio station *Potterwatch*. It is run by the Order of the Phoenix, and its narrative function is combined with the theme of solidarity and friendship in the underground movement.

Magical Narration

With Harry Potter as the focus of the narration with only a few scenes in the novels outside his hearing and vision, the narrator is faced with the challenge that his point of view is limited, both in place and time. How can the narrator relate information found in other places and times to the readers and to him? The omniscient narrator has an expedition into the past with the local history of the village of Little Hangleton. Harry does not have to be present and have a direct sensory experience of what is going on or has been going on. Other characters can give him this information, though we have seen that often he is held in the dark, and not only by Dumbledore.

Harry, Ron, Hermione and the readers are helped higher in the hierarchy of knowledge by the genre. The fantasy format allows magic, and one important example is how Harry can listen to other characters' conversations undetected when he is wearing his invisibility cloak, and in the same way he can witness situations at places he should not be, as when Hagrid is arrested by the Ministry of Magic in COS, and Harry, Ron and Hermione are present under the cloak in Hagrid's cottage (Rowling, 1998/2014, pp. 273–279). The pattern of both a comic and a more serious use of setups and payoffs can be seen regarding the invisibility cloak. Harry, being invisible, can throw snowballs at Draco Malfoy; but the cloak is also one of the Deathly Hallows, and in HBP, Harry overhears Snape offer his help to Draco (Rowling, 2005/2014, p. 268). This comes after Harry in the cloak has been listening to Malfoy in the Hogwarts Express telling some other Slytherins that he may not return to the school next year. The invisibility cloak has its most crucial narrative function in Dumbledore's murder scene.

Fred and George Weasley's invention, extendable ears, serves the same narrative function as the invisibility cloak, i.e., they allow Harry, Ron and Hermione together with the readers to listen to conversations where they are not allowed to be. The ears are at the end of a long flesh-colored string, which is inserted into the listener's ear so that he can eavesdrop on conversations, and they can be shoved under a closed door. They are used when the Order of the Phoenix does not allow the children to be present at a meeting (Rowling, 2003/2014, p. 64), and again from the tent when Harry, Ron and Hermione are on the run and they listen to a group of Muggle fugitives in DH (Rowling, 2007/2014, pp. 239–244).

Harry—and the readers—obtain the privilege of not only looking into the past but also into other characters' memories when peering into Dumbledore's Pensieve. This is a major expansion of the limited point of view. The Pensieve is a shallow basin filled with a silvery liquid and memories that have been siphoned from a person can be poured into it and viewed. The viewer is pulled into the viewed scene but in a non-participatory way, which narratologically makes it correspond to Friedman's camera mode. The Pensieve allows numerous flashbacks, which are necessary to develop the plot and to educate Harry to take his part in it. There is the trial of Barty Crouch's son by the Wizengamot juror, Snape's painful memories of Lily Potter, Dumbledore's first visit with the young Tom Riddle at the orphanage, and there is the complex retrieval of Horace Slughorn's true memory.

The narrative function of the Pensieve with views into decisive moments of the past is supplemented with Harry's access to other characters' minds during his Legilimency lessons. Legilimency is an expansion of Harry's limited point of view, e.g., into Snape's tortured mind. The readers share Harry's involuntary excursions into Voldemort's mind, sometimes in the form of Harry's dreams.

All these magical narrative mechanisms contribute to an expansion of the limited point of view, so that omniscience is imported into the novels, but it is also often imported into Harry's mind, which makes him more efficient in the plot's conflict between himself and the forces of evil. Again, we have seen how the narrative modes and the thematics of the novels work together. The doubling of narrative modes, traditional and magical, limited and omniscient, must be seen in the context of the genre, low fantasy.

Low Fantasy

The relationship between the world of the reader and the fantasy world of fiction was expressed by J.R.R. Tolkien in "On Fairy-Stories." The fantasy writer is a sub-creator who creates a secondary, independent universe, which the reader can enter and leave her own primary world with its everyday life (Tolkien, 1964/1977, pp. 40–41). This double universe can be duplicated in the fantasy text itself. Boyer and Zahorski (1984, p. 5) establish two subgenres, high and low fantasy. High fantasy only contains the secondary fantasy world, and Tolkien's own writings exemplify this subgenre. Low fantasy is a conglomerate of the primary and secondary world. It contains a world like the reader's own world and a fantasy world, where the *Harry Potter* universe is a mixture of the magic world with brooms you can fly and spells that work, and then the Muggle world like Great Britain today with company cars and neat front gardens in Privet Drive. These two worlds coexist within the same universe.

This doubling of worlds, one magic and one real, corresponds to the doubling of narrative modes. Harry's limited third person point of view is anchored within the real world, and the aspects of an omniscient narration added to his limited point of view through magical means, belong in the secondary fantasy world. Both modes coexist, as the two worlds coexist in the subgenre of low fantasy.

Film Narration

Already during the prelude to the first adaptation, *PS*, the double world of low fantasy is established by cinematographic means. The film begins with the street sign "Privet Drive," and the camera pans to Dumbledore, dressed in wizard garb. The camera now trails the walking Dumbledore until it reaches a sitting cat in a close-up image. Dumbledore now extinguishes the street lamps in front of the houses in Privet Drive with a Deluminator. The atmosphere-filled underscoring music is interrupted by the cat meowing, and there is a reaction shot of Dumbledore looking down at it, and he says to the cat: "I should have known that you would be here, Professor McGonagall." The cat's shadow on a wall grows into McGonagall's shadow, and she walks into shot. In conversation, they walk along the front gardens and the parked cars followed by a camera tracking. In less than two minutes the stereotypical suburb in the primary world has been tied to the magical secondary world.

As Harry is the focus of the narration, there is a bond between him and the audience's reception of the fantasy films. Initially, Harry and the readers share their position in the primary world, and they must learn to accept the existence of the secondary fantasy world. A cinematographic technique is employed to convey to the audience the validity of this fantasy world and thus suspend disbelief. This general technique uses point of view shots and reaction shots. First there is a close-up of Harry looking at something, often with an expression of surprise and disbelief. This is followed by a point of view shot of what he is looking at, often something magical from the secondary world, and finally the third element is a reaction shot of Harry's face, which now has an expression of joyful acceptance, and the audience can share Harry's acceptance of the world of magic. This technique particularly features in the first films.

Magic is involved when the traditional technique of flashbacks is employed, but in a manner that is an expansion of this technique. When in *POA* Hermione uses the Time-Turner, the audience is brought back in time while she and Harry are embedded in the time shift so that this flashback facilitates interaction between the characters and the past, and they must take care not to be seen in the past. This magic use of time is connected to the Pensieve with the difference of its inability to change the past.

Setups and payoffs take on cinematographic forms. In *GOF*, there is the tragic setup of Cedric's fate. The scene in which he adds his name to the tournament goblet has been toned in cold blue with color grading as a premonition of his death; but in the same film there is a romantic use of a setup. Editing between close-ups of Hermione's and Victor Krum's faces paves the way for their dating later in the film.

The third person point of view of the novels is reflected in the adaptations. Though Harry is not always in shot, he is present in most scenes of the films. His point of view is reflected in a pattern of his point of view shots followed by his reaction shots, and in the magical sequences in which Harry enters Voldemort's mind in his dreams, the same narrative cinematographic pattern appears in a similar way with first a dream montage of Voldemort's actions, corresponding to the point of view shots, and the reaction shots are then close-up shots of Harry's agonized face as he wakes up. Harry as the main character and the focal narrative point can for instance be seen when Harry is knocked unconscious during the Death Eaters riots at the Quidditch world cup in *GOF*. There is a cut-away from violence, and it is caused solely by Harry's (un)consciousness.

Dumbledore's Murder Scene

The murder of Dumbledore is described in the chapter "The Lightning-Struck Tower" in *HBP* (Rowling, 2005/2014, pp. 486–496), and the point of view is Harry's. It is significant that this is all that Harry is allowed; i.e., to witness the murder and not being able to interfere. He can only watch and listen. At first to the expositional dialogue between Dumbledore and Draco Malfoy, which explains the mysterious assassination attempts earlier in the novel. Then to Snape's *Avada Kedavra!*. Harry has already put his invisibility cloak on, and it is not until the next chapter after Dumbledore's death that he pulls it off. He could not do it sooner because Dumbledore had immobilized him with the *Petrificus Totalus* charm, nor can he yet seek to defend Dumbledore. He might just as well not have been present, apart from the fact that because of the third person point of view, he must be there for narrative purposes. The combination of the invisibility cloak and *Petrificus Totalus* has reduced Harry to a narrative tool, he has become Friedman's camera mode. At the same time, the omnipotence of magic has been tragically demonstrated.

In the film adaptation of the scene, Harry does not wear the invisibility cloak and he is not petrified, but sent below in the astronomy tower by Dumbledore: "Hide yourself below, Harry. Don't speak or be seen by anybody without my permission. Whatever happens, it is imperative that you stay below." The scene is now edited between three camera positions. They are close-up shots of Draco and Dumbledore in conversation, and Harry's reactions are shown in close ups with slow camera movements, and these have the semblance of point of view shots. The scene is underscored by low and suspenseful music. When the Death Eaters arrive the camera necessarily moves back so this group comes into shot, and this also means that Draco's tortured face is no longer in an emotional close-up image. Snape arrives below at Harry's level, points his wand at him and gestures Harry to keep silent. This is different from the novel where Harry is invisible and unable to move. Here it is only his promise to Dumbledore and not magic that prevents Harry from taking part in the action. When Snape's *Avada Kedavra* is uttered Harry's horrified reaction is shown in two shots, the final one in ultra-close-up, and Dumbledore falls from the tower in slow motion with the music rising. Harry as Friedman's camera in the novel has been supplanted by a real camera, and the magic of Harry's passivity has been replaced by his obedience to the headmaster.

Fan Fiction

The sheer amount of *Harry Potter* fan fiction, 184,860 fics on AO3 and 794,000 on FFnet with new fics uploaded on a daily basis, makes it impossible to give a fully comprehensive representation of the wealth of narrative devices used to tell these stories. Instead, we will attempt to show the clear differences between fan fiction and the original tent-pole, i.e., Rowling's novels and their movie adaptations.

> **Freeform:** Manipulative Dumbledore Evil Dumbledore Weasley Bashing Dark Harry Good Death Eaters Good Voldemort Time Travel Master of Death Harry Potter Ravenclaw Ravenclaw Harry Do-Over Pre-Slash Independent Harry Smart Harry Master of Death Soul Bond apparently the dark side does indeed have cookies Hermione Granger Bashing OOC characters OOC Harry BAMF!Harry Time Travel Fix-It Dumbledore Bashing Slow Build Prisoner of Azkaban AU Alternate Universe - Canon Divergence

Figure 2: Freeform tagging on AO3. The author chooses the tags and can create new tags if necessary.

Many of the literary narrative devices described in this essay also hold true for fan fiction, as any fan fiction story would include warnings and tags for the reader. While the author is still at the top of the knowledge hierarchy, the reader is given an advantage over the narrator and characters; e.g., knowing if a given character dies or is abused. Figure 2 shows an example of freeform tagging on AO3. The first tags reveal how Dumbledore is portrayed in this story, i.e., manipulative and evil. Likewise, Harry Potter is portrayed as "dark." Among other interesting tags is the "OOC" tag, which indicates "out of character" both for Harry Potter and "other original characters," implying that the author has invented new characters. Tagging in this form is necessary for fan fiction readers. Readers want to avoid potential triggers, which are plot twists or depictions of violence or abuse that could be unpleasant for the reader, e.g., triggering unwanted memories. At the same time, tagging allows readers to find certain fan fictions or fics to read for pleasure. In this, the mirror and extension of the self can be found. The text should deliver a recognizable universe and also mirror the mood of the reader.

Basic tagging can be found on most fan fiction sites. AO3 allows writers extensive use of tagging, to the extent of giving away major plot points and other potentially triggering content. Fanfiction.net offers fewer possibilities for tagging. Basically, it only provides rating for the sexual content ("mature" being a tag denoting the most sexual descriptions allowed, as explicit content might be censored), language of the story and a very basic description of the genre. The author must choose from a given list and can only give extra tags or warnings in the very short summary. Tagging must be regarded as part of the narrative, like the title or name of the author. The list of tags for a given fic is presented at the top of every chapter, giving the reader the possibility to choose or dismiss reading a fic.

To further facilitate identification with the characters in the story, the point-of-view (POV) of a fic is important. This to such an extent that tags can include from which POV a given fic is written.

An example will illustrate some of the narrative principles of fan fiction. In the German fan fiction *Wahrheit und Wagnis*, part 4, Lorelei Lee (2006) writes the story from the point of view of Remus, who finds Severus Snape in his flat waiting for him. Lee uses the third person selective omniscience, which makes it possible for the reader to follow Remus' line of thinking but keeps Snape's motivation and behavior a mystery. The story unfolds in the aftermath of Dumbledore's murder by Snape while Remus, who is in love with Snape, is both terrified by and attracted to Snape. During the four chapters of the story we see the increasing tension between the two characters, resulting in Snape attacking Remus, apparently by taking away his memories of their time together. Remus puts up a fight but is overpowered by Snape. The point of view changes after the attack, which leaves Remus unconscious. Now, the reader is treated to an insight into Snape's motivation for the attack; i.e., wanting to keep Remus safe. This change in POV gives the author the possibility to make use of hidden knowledge and continue to surprise her readers.

The number of fan fiction tropes is as diverse as the fics themselves. From different kinds of character transformations, which would include werewolves or zombies, over domesticity, arranged marriage, or being trapped on a desert island. Using the trope as a setting enables both writers and readers to adjust their expectations to the text itself.

The typical nature of fan fiction is that of a work in progress (Busse & Hellekson, 2001). The setup and payoff in fan fiction have to be within the same chapter. Chapters are being posted one at a time, and a new story is sometimes uploaded even before the author has completed the whole story. So-called cliffhangers are useful to keep up suspense, though they are dreaded by the readers because of the unfinished nature of the story. Reading a work in progress has the risk of never reaching the payoff; the resolved happy-ending.

Reading and writing fan fiction presupposes a profound knowledge of the original text, which is used even if the narrative itself is heavily transformed. Using Genette's classification, fan fiction can be labeled allographic paratexts.

Paratextual narration, like magical narration and magic as such, is used to further the relationship between the chosen characters in a given fic. In Lee's fan fiction, Snape uses a spell, he has developed himself, to push the memories of Remus away from conscious thought; not erasing them, but keeping them hidden for Remus' safety. There is no need to explain its use, since the readers will know how spells work from their prior knowledge of the *Potter* universe.

Dumbledore's murder in the original texts is used as a plot device, pushing Harry Potter forward along the storyline and into adulthood. In fan fiction, the murder of Dumbledore is either absent or used as a background story, especially when the pairing includes Severus Snape. Dumbledore himself was adopted by the LGBTQ+ fandom community even before Rowling explicitly mentioned his sexuality (Cuntz-Leng, 2015). Again, this points to the narcissistic use of the object of fandom as a mirror and extension of the fan's own ego.

While Dumbledore's murder is referenced in fan fictions, not all fan fictions are compliant with the original text. The genre "AU" means alternative universe, which can include anything from a setting in a coffee shop in which Harry Potter is a barista or Dumbledore not being murdered. Of the 184,860 fan fiction works on Harry Potter, only 787 have the pairing Dumbledore/Grindelwald and a further 53 the pairing of Dumbledore & Grindelwald on AO3, 30 August 2018. The "/" normally indicates a romantic relationship between the two characters, while the "&" denotes friendship.

All of this indicates that fan fiction should be recognized as a form of archontic literature. Archontic in the sense of an ever expanding and never completely closed body of text (Derecho, 2006, p. 64). Fan fiction communities write and develop fanart to increase content. Readers seek fics, which nourish their current mood; the pleasure of the text being at the forefront of their reading. Fan fiction's focus on bodies and the relationship between the protagonists might explain why an analysis of the used narrative devices only captures part of a fics essence. Instead, Coppa (2006) proposes using theatrical performance theory to understand fan fiction. Coppa further develops the notion of the unfinished text by showing how the original books and subsequent films by themselves were open-ended for a long time. This led fans to develop their own endings, discussions on plot points and possible pairings (Coppa, 2006, p. 241). Thus, the whole universe of *Harry Potter* should be recognized as a creative universe with strong reader involvement, which continues to expand—now even including new works by Rowling herself.

Conclusion: The Unity of Narration and Thematics

The hierarchy of knowledge has been central in the chapter reaching from ignorant Muggles to readers, who have been raised to omniscient fan fiction authors. Harry Potter himself, has different positions in this hierarchy during his development. The hierarchy of knowledge is not limited to a narrative mechanism. It is also part and parcel of the themes of the *Harry Potter* novels and films. The same goes for the theme of the peer group. With its expositional dialogue the peer group is integrated not only in the action and plots, but also in their narrative mode, and reflections of the social function of narcissist peer groups can be seen in the aesthetics and communicative modes of fandom. Similarly, setups and payoff are narrative devices that tie the thousands of pages together, and thematically, they trace the increasing somber moods of the development of Harry himself. The large amount of autographic paratexts supports the genre of low fantasy, and it is with this genre in mind that it has become clear how the narrative modes and the themes of the novels work keenly together. The doubling of narrative modes, traditional and magical, limited and omniscient, has been seen in the context of this genre during the chapter. The innovative combination of magical and mundane narrative devices and themes in the novels, films and the affordance these offer to fan fiction has been seen in the chapter as a defining trait of Rowling's *Harry Potter* universe.

The significance of the complex narrative devices of the *Harry Potter* universe is that this advanced, yet coherent, mode of narration helps the readers accept magic as a way of coming to terms with their lives in their own secondary world. Through reading *Harry Potter*, the primary magical world becomes an acceptable and useful way of seeking to understand family life and the challenges of childhood and coming of age.

REFERENCES

Barthes, R. (1975). *The pleasure of the text*. New York: Hill and Wang.
Behr, K. (2005). Same-as-difference: Narrative transformations and intersecting cultures in Harry Potter. *Journal of Narrative Theory*, 35(1), 112–132.
Booth, W.C. (1961/1983). *The rhetoric of fiction*. Chicago: The University of Chicago Press.
Boyer, R.H., & Zahorski, K. (Eds.) (1984). *Fantasists on fantasy*. New York: Avon Books.
Branigan, E. (1992/1998). *Narrative comprehension and film*. London: Routledge.
Busse, K., & Hellekson, K. (2001). Introduction: Work in progress. In K. Hellekson & K. Busse (Eds.), *Fan fiction and fan communities in the age of the internet*. Jefferson, NC: McFarland.
Christensen, J.R. (2009). Certain regressive tendencies in Rowling and Tolkien. In J.R. Christensen (Ed.), *Marvellous fantasy*. Aalborg: Aalborg University Press, 2009 (pp. 45–57).
Coppa, F. (2006). Writing bodies in space: Media fan fiction as theatrical performance. In: K. Hellekson & K. Busse (Eds.), *Fan fiction and fan communities in the age of the internet*. Jefferson, NC: McFarland.

Coppa, F. (2017). *The fanfiction reader: Folk tales for the digital age.* Ann Arbor: University of Michigan Press.
Cuntz-Leng, V. (2015). *Harry Potter que(e)r: Eine filmsaga im spannungsfeld von queer reading, slash-fandom und fantasy film genre.* Bielefeld: [transcript].
Davidson, D., et al. (2010). *Crossmedia communications: An introduction to the art of creating integrated media experiences.* Pittsburgh: ETC Press.
Derecho, A. (2006). Archontic literature: A definition, a history, and several theories of fan fiction. In: K. Hellekson & K. Busse (Eds.), *Fan fiction and fan communities in the age of the internet.* Jefferson, NC: McFarland.
Edgar-Hunt, R., Marland, J., & Richards, J. (2009). *Screenwriting.* Lausanne: AVA Academia.
Friedman, N. (1955). Point of view in fiction: The development of a critical concept. In: *PMLA*, 70(5) (December 1955): 1160–1184.
Genette, G. (1987/1997). *Paratexts. Thresholds of interpretation.* Cambridge: Cambridge University Press.
Larsen, P.H. (2003). *De levende billeders dramaturgi I.* København: Dr Multimedie.
Lee, L. (2006). *Wahrheit und Wagnis, Teil 4.* on https://www.fanfiction.net/s/2731872/1/Wahrheit-oder-Wagnis-Teil-4
Olsson, O. (1982/1986). *Några Anteckningar om dramaturgi. Rapport från seminaret "Dramatikern i dialog med sin samtid."* Oslo: Nordiska Teaterkommitten.
Rowling, J.K. (1997/2014). *Harry Potter and the philosopher's stone.* London: Bloomsbury.
Rowling, J.K. (1998/2014). *Harry Potter and the chamber of secrets.* London: Bloomsbury.
Rowling, J.K. (2000/2014). *Harry Potter and the goblet of fire.* London: Bloomsbury.
Rowling, J.K. (2001/2017). *Fantastic beasts and where to find them.* London: Bloomsbury.
Rowling, J.K. (2001/2017). *Quidditch through the ages.* London: Bloomsbury.
Rowling, J.K. (2003/2014). *Harry Potter and the order of the phoenix.* London: Bloomsbury.
Rowling, J.K. (2005/2014). *Harry Potter and the half blood prince.* London: Bloomsbury.
Rowling, J.K. (2007/2014). *Harry Potter and the deathly hallows.* London: Bloomsbury.
Rowling, J.K. (2008). *The tales of Beedle the Bard.* London: Bloomsbury.
Sandvoss, C. (2005). *Fans: The mirror of consumption.* Cambridge: Polity Press.
Tolkien, J.R.R. (1964/1977). *Tree and leaf Smith of Wooton major: The homecoming of Beorhtnoth Beorhthelm's son.* London: Allan and Unwin.
Wellek, R., & Warren, A. (1949/1970). *Theory of literature.* Harmondsworth: Penguin.
Ziehe, T. (1975). *Pubertät und narzissmus.* Frankfurt am Main: Europäische Verlagsanstalt.

The Magic of Harry Potter for Children in Care

SARAH JAYNE MOKRZYCKI

I was introduced to the *Harry Potter* series quite by chance when my mother came home with a hardcover copy of *OotP*, having bought it on a whim after seeing it on display at a department store. I hadn't even heard of *Harry Potter*, nor did I realize at first that *OotP* (Rowling, 2003) was part of a series. After devouring the story, I was gifted second-hand paperback copies of the first four books. The sixth book, *HBP* (Rowling, 2005), came out while I was in America, working at a summer camp in Pennsylvania. The only means of transport out of the camp for international staff was a once-a-week bus on Sundays; fortunately, an American camp counselor took pity on me and brought me a copy. *HBP* is my only American copy of the entire series (the rest being Australian), and I still get a kick out of all the little differences between publications.

Harry Potter has been a treasured part of my life for over a decade. My books are now a bit worse for wear (particularly *HBP*, having traveled across the world with me) but they remain a timeless and much-loved addition to my bookcase. Several years ago, when I became a foster carer, my new role presented an entirely new way of experiencing my well-loved collection.

As a foster carer, I have witnessed first-hand the therapeutic benefits of *Harry Potter* for children in out-of-home care. My husband and I read the series to our eight-year-old foster child, who reveled in the vitality and vividness of J.K. Rowling's wizarding world: the sights and sounds of Diagon Alley, the excitement of a quidditch match, and the awe-inspiring grandeur of Hogwarts castle. But for him, and the hundreds of thousands of children like him living in care around the world, *Harry Potter* is more than just an engaging literary experience; it is salvation.

Children in care personally identify with the character of Harry Potter in a way that the average reader cannot: they identify not only with his more broadly understandable challenges like fitting in at school and forming new relationships, but with his abuse and subsequent early childhood trauma during his life with the Dursleys. The *Harry Potter* series helps to show children that they are not alone in their circumstances, and provides a valuable means for them to deal with their trauma. In this way, it is a valuable bibliotherapuetic resource (literature that promotes emotional and mental wellbeing).

This essay uses an autoethnographic approach to examine the series' use in bibliotherapy, as well as its use as a therapeutic tool in role play and discussion. It firstly investigates the effects of early childhood trauma and the neurological damage and lasting impacts it has on the developing brain. It then looks at the therapeutic uses of the *Harry Potter* series, and finally delves deeper into Harry's abuse and its lasting impact as evidenced in *HBP*.

There have been many academic studies on the benefits and importance of J.K. Rowling's iconic wizarding world—from the series' scientifically proven ability to reduce prejudice (Vezzali et al., 2015) to its clinical assistance in helping patients in therapy cope with loss and grief (McNulty, 2008). In this essay, I examine *Harry Potter* through a fostering lens; exploring the series' specific therapeutic benefits for children in care.

The Effects of Early Childhood Trauma

To say that Harry experiences extraordinary hardship during his years at Hogwarts is an understatement. The series explores some of the darkest depravities of human (or wizarding) kind, and every year Harry faces life threatening battles against dark forces; the danger in each new story eclipsing the last. Upon my first reading of the series as a young adult, it was these later experiences in Harry's life that carried the most impact. However, after becoming a foster carer, it became clear that it is not Harry's perilous experiences as an older child that truly delve the depths of trauma, but his early childhood at Privet Drive with the Dursleys. Put simply, even the Battle of Hogwarts does not compare to being locked in a cupboard.

Studies show that early childhood trauma impacts healthy brain development and has lifelong effects, increasing the risk of "emotional, behavioral, academic, social and physical problems throughout life" (Perry, n.d.). An increase in research on trauma and its effects on neurobiology show that trauma has an undeniable impact on children's development, (Archer, 2003, p. 78) resulting in "distorted neural pathways" (Archer, 2003, p. 85). The brain goes through critical periods of development and these are altered by abuse. The undeveloped infant brain develops and matures during childhood in a sequential fashion: the more basic or automatic functions developing first (like respiration), followed by the more complex functions (like regulating emotions).

This early brain development is impacted by experiences. If the experiences are healthy then the brain is healthy; however, if the sequential development of the brain is disrupted by abuse the impact on neurodevelopment can be devastating (Perry, n.d.). The developing brain becomes hyperalert for danger and the distorted neuro pathways strengthen in the abusive environment as a means of survival (Children's Bureau, 2015, p. 5). Trauma quite literally changes the shape and growth of the brain, which in turn affects a person's capabilities as an adult. Issues like excessive anger, chronic illness, incarceration and substance abuse later in life are regularly linked to early childhood experiences (Sound Medicine, 2015).

Harry's start to life is fraught with trauma. Even if he had not been placed in the care of his abusive aunt and uncle, Petunia and Vernon, Harry had already survived an attempt on his life and witnessed his parents murdered in front of him (although infants lack the cognitive ability to comprehend or process stress, research indicates that they are hypervigilant and vulnerable to stimuli [Archer, 2003, p. 79]). Under the care of his aunt and uncle, Harry endures ongoing emotional, psychological and, at times, physical abuse. He is severely neglected and, most distressingly, denied love and affection from his family. Arguably, the most famous of the Dursleys' abuse is their forcing Harry to sleep in the cupboard under the stairs—indeed, the "cupboard under the stairs" is synonymous with the character of Harry Potter.

Troubling as it is to accept, such child abuse is not limited to the safe confines of storybooks but exists unflinchingly in reality for hundreds of thousands of children the world over—there are approximately 415,000 children living in care in the United States alone (Children's Bureau, 2017). In Harry, children in care have a hero with whom they relate to on a level that others cannot. It is this identification with Harry that opens up doors for emotional healing, as foster carers Margie and Darren Fink have observed. The Finks, foster and adoptive parents from Tennessee, created a non-profit program called Transfiguring Adoption that provides media resources to assist foster and adoptive families. The program originated from a family reading of *SS* where they discovered that the foster care-related topics explored in the book provided a safe way for their children to discuss their experiences. In an email interview with Transfiguring Adoption co-founder, Darren Fink, he explained the noted benefits of the series for children in care:

> We have read the *Harry Potter* series to foster children, and noted that they seem to identify with Harry as being a child separated from his parents. Although none of the children we have read the stories to have lost their parents through death, the children still seem to resonate with the loss and grief that Harry feels. Children are allowed to indirectly speak about their fears, their dreams, and their pasts through

Harry or other characters in the books. They allow for an indirect way for children to talk about issues they need to work through [D. Fink, personal communication, September 2017].

Fink went on to describe a particular experience in which one of his adopted sons was personally impacted by Harry's story, finding that he was able to relate it to his own history with trauma:

> The most memorable reaction we have encountered with children in our home was the reaction of our middle-adopted son. Upon reading the first couple of chapters of *SS*, the then twelve-year-old boy teared up and proceeded to talk to us, the caregivers, about various trauma that he had suffered in his birth home from years past. Upon discovery, the conveyed traumas were feelings and events that had never before been shared by this child [D. Fink, personal communication, September 2017].

SS enabled this child to unlock and explore previously guarded memories and gave him a voice to share his feelings in a way he had never been able to before (D. Fink, personal communication, September 2017). Fink also explained what he felt was one of the most powerful aspects of *Harry Potter*: its ability to normalize the separation of a child from his or her birth parents; an experience that is often viewed as an "abnormal situation" (D. Fink, personal communication, September 2017) by society:

> Children in care are able to read and explore a world of magic through the eyes of an orphan—or someone who is also separated from his birth parents. For foster children, who often feel they are in the minority or unusual for being in the situation they find themselves in, Harry Potter offers them a literary friend who looks a bit more like their life. The stories allow children to look at themselves and realise that there really are other children going through similar situations as themselves [D. Fink, personal communication, September 2017].

Early childhood trauma has lasting effects, but the knowledge that they are not alone in their circumstances is a powerful healing tool for children in care. Through this, children who have experienced early childhood trauma can better communicate their experiences; and in doing so, better learn to overcome them.

Harry Potter *as Bibliotherapy*

There have been many studies and, consequently, many developments in our understanding and use of bibliotherapy over the past several decades (Jalongo, 1983). The practice of bibliotherapy has long been used to assist children with trauma through difficult or confusing life situations. Bibliotherapy serves to provide insight, reflection and support, and provides a means in which those dealing with problems can find guidance through literature. The benefits of bibliotherapy for children in care have been studied predominantly by Jean and John Pardeck (1987, 1994), whose research highlights the importance of believable characters in stories, and bibliotherapy's ability to support the "unique needs and problems" of children in care (Pardeck & Pardeck, 1987, p. 269).

Interviews I conducted with child welfare stakeholders in 2015 highlighted the important role bibliotherapy plays in the wellbeing of children in care. Doctor Daniel Hughes, clinical psychologist and leading expert in childhood trauma, noted that "it helps children to know that other children have had similar stories" and that bibliotherapy helps children in care "make sense of their trauma" (D. Hughes, personal communication, August 2015). Similarly, Doctor Susan Straus, clinical child psychologist and author of *Healing Days*, said:

> It helps for a child to identify with the characters [of a story] so that they don't feel alone. So many of the children that have experienced trauma and are in the foster care system feel as if they're the only ones.... They feel alone and isolated, but knowing that other children have had the same experience and have come out okay in the end is reassuring to them [S. Straus, personal communication, August 2015].

These thoughts were echoed by Coram BAAF (British Association for Adoption and Fostering) publisher Shaila Shah, who stressed that "children need to see themselves at the heart of their stories … showing the child that they are at the centre of their story can give them the confidence that they have value" (S. Shah, personal communication, August 2015).

Bibliotherapy allows children to investigate feelings in a safe and comforting space (Rizza, 1997). There is a fundamental maxim that reverberates throughout bibliotherapy: You are not alone. This is perhaps the most vital component of the process and is bound to the idea of "relatability." This is the key to bibliotherapy and serves to help unlock a child's trauma and open up healthy dialogues (Shechtman, 2009). Academic journals such as *Reading Horizons* (Perez, 1984) and *Young Children* (S. Mankiw & J. Strasser, 2013) have published studies on the importance of children identifying with characters in stories. Relating to characters is what engages early readers and helps foster a lifelong love of reading. It connects children to the world around them and, vitally, it validates their own reality.

In my studies of bibliotherapy and children's literature, I have found that relatability in literature tends to fall under three of the five W's: Who, What and Where. "Who" refers to a relatable character, someone the reader personally identifies with, and is arguably the most effective form of relatability. "What" refers to a relatable situation, such as being bullied or feeling stressed. "Where" refers to a relatable setting, such as a classroom or family home. These three forms may act as bibliotherapeutic tools together or individually.

There is an underlying relatability to the *Harry Potter* series, particularly for children in care. We have the hero, Harry Potter ("Who"), and his struggles with early childhood trauma and issues like confidence, self-worth, and identity ("What") in a primarily school-based setting ("Where"). The fact that Harry is a wizard, his school is a castle, and the majority of the series takes place in a magical world does not detract from the relatability of the series. In fact, this has no adverse impact at all. The crux of relatability does not lie in realism, but in the authenticity of the "Who," "What" and/or "Where" it presents. The *Harry Potter* series may be about a boy who is discovering magic and overcoming fantastical foes; however, even more so, it is about a boy who is discovering who he is and overcoming trauma.

This is why the *Harry Potter* series is not just popular amongst children in care, but a valuable bibliotherapuetic resource that assists their healing. Children in care identify with Harry Potter, and through his experiences, they are better able to talk about and overcome their own. The experiences of children in care are often overlooked or not properly explored; not just in literature but in life. Thus, the ability to relate to Harry Potter—not just a main character but the hero of the story—is a truly empowering gift for children so often forgotten by society.

Harry Potter *as a Therapeutic Vehicle*

The use of *Harry Potter* in therapy can take many forms. As well as bibliotherapy, the *Harry Potter* series is used by clinicians as a topic for therapeutic role play (McNulty, 2008) and group therapy discussions (Noctor, 2006) with children who have experienced trauma. The positive impact of the *Harry Potter* series, as studied by clinicians like McNulty (2008) and Noctor (2006), lies in the ability to relate Rowling's fantastical creations to real world problems and solutions. While the studies by McNulty and Noctor are not specific to children in care, the issues they cover (such as the loss of a parent and self-harming) overlap with issues and the subsequent associated behaviors commonly faced by children in care.

McNulty describes the *Harry Potter* series is an effective "therapeutic vehicle" (2008, p. 25) for helping children cope with traumatic loss. In two case studies in which children have lost a biological parent (or biological family member in the role of a parent), he utilizes *Harry Potter* as a tool for therapeutic role play to address the trauma and any behavioral issues that presented themselves. Children in care go through a very similar sense of grief as those that have lost parents—in some cases their biological parent or parents may not be deceased, but they are likewise absent from their lives. Thus, the same types of behavioral issues like those presented in McNulty's case studies—emotional outbursts, stress and anxiety, regressive behavior and more (McNulty, 2008)—also present in children in care.

The *Harry Potter* series is also an effective means of facilitating discussion, as seen in studies by Noctor (2006), who has made breakthroughs using the series in group therapy sessions with adolescents:

> This very animated, or at other times very silent group, soon began to discuss their own difficulties and emotional problems out loud through the guise of the *Harry Potter* themes. This form of directed group storytelling allowed the young people to do something that previously they had found impossible to do: Speak [Noctor, 2006, p. 585].

The ability to speak about trauma is the only way children and adolescents can heal, and the use of the *Harry Potter* series as a discussion topic or "ice breaker" provides a safe framework for emotional exploration. Discussing the series opens up avenues for children and adolescents to examine their personal connection to the characters and their experiences, especially when fantastical elements of the stories are used to assist real-life examples and comparisons.

Using Rowling's creations to help children better understand and overcome their own trauma is a large component of *Harry Potter* as therapy. For example, McNulty has used the "metaphoric symbolism" of Harry's physical scar to help children in therapy discuss their emotional ones (McNulty, 2008, p. 32). He also found that children used magic (cast imaginary spells) as a means to combat trauma (McNulty, 2008, p. 34). Similarly, Noctor discussed what form a boggart would take for different members in a group therapy session. This was done in order to provide children with a safe environment to talk about their fears. He discovered that it encouraged supportive creative thinking, as children suggested different ways of helping others defeat their personal boggarts (Noctor, 2006, p. 585). These methods provide different ways to approach Harry's world beyond reading the text, creating a successful therapeutic framework for healing.

The Impact of Harry's Abuse

Rereading the *Harry Potter* series as a foster carer, the absence of any mandatory reporting of Harry's abuse to child protection services is something I am unable to fully comprehend. Granted, the reader learns through the introduction of family members like Aunt Marge, Vernon's sister, that the couple's extended family view Harry with the same contempt Vernon and Petunia do. Likewise, Marge views Vernon and Petunia's treatment of Harry as charitable rather than abusive. Vernon and Petunia share this viewpoint themselves—or at the very least, protest they do; but one does wonder if they doth protest too much.

Surely, however, there must have been some community member—a teacher, doctor or neighbor in Harry's life—that noticed the telltale signs of abuse? Of course, like many childhood heroes Harry's journey is tightly connected to—and begins with—his tragic backstory, and what would Harry Potter be without the imagery of the young boy living in the cupboard under the stairs? It is this image that the reader carries with them throughout their experience of the series, the cupboard having cemented itself in the psyche of the reader thanks to the bombardment of owl-delivered letters in the first book addressed to:

Mr H. Potter
The Cupboard under the Stairs
4 Privet Drive
Little Whinging
Surrey [Rowling, 2001, p. 30].

While the cupboard is a symbol of Harry's maltreatment, it accounts for a fraction of the abuse Harry suffered at the hands of his aunt and uncle, who employed a continual pattern of neglect and emotional and physical abuse throughout Harry's childhood.

Harry's early childhood trauma (and the continued abuse in his family home) directly affect Harry throughout his time at Hogwarts—although just how much he is impacted is a point of conjecture. Provenzano and Heyman (2006) argue that "the miracle of Harry is not the *Avada Kedavra*–defying Boy who Lived, but the maltreatment-resilient Boy Who Lives" (Provenzano & Heyman, 2006, p. 105). They further posit that Harry emerged from his abuse at the Dursleys' "relatively unscathed" (Provenzano & Heyman, 2006, p. 109) and accredit Harry's stability to his resilience.

However, as resilient and "well-adjusted" (Provenzano & Heyman, 2006, p. 105) as Harry may be, I argue that it is impossible for a child to live through the trauma Harry experienced and not be highly—and continually—impacted by it. Harry may not exhibit some of the more challenging behaviors of a child who has experienced abuse, such as compulsive stealing and physical aggression (Family Care for Children & Youth, 2016), but he showcases the common emotional struggles of blocked trust, low self-esteem, and fear of abandonment.

Evidence of the Impact of Trauma in The Half-Blood Prince

This impact of Harry's abuse is prevalent throughout the series, most notably in the form of blocked trust, a term first introduced by Hughes and Baylin:

> Blocked trust refers to the impact of abuse and neglect upon young children's ability to trust that they can rely on their caregivers to meet their basic psychological and physical needs ... having no confidence that adults will naturally want to do what is best for them [Hughes, 2017, p. 5].

Harry shows all the classic symptoms of a child from a care background struggling with blocked trust. While evidence of this can be found throughout the series, it is perhaps most noticeable in *HBP* (Rowling, 2005).

In *HBP*, Harry receives a letter from Dumbledore stating that he will pick Harry up from Privet Drive and escort him to the Weasleys,' where Harry will spend the rest of the school holidays. Harry's reaction to this is typical of the mistrust and fear often exhibited by children in care. In the interim between the arrival of the letter and Dumbledore's promised arrival, Harry reads the letter obsessively until he learns it by heart—though even then he is unable to stop reading it. On the night Dumbledore is to arrive, Harry sits himself by his window so he can monitor both ends of the street at once. This doesn't denote excitement so much as fear that Dumbledore may never arrive, which, indeed, is what Harry fears most.

Harry shows an incapability to be emotionally vulnerable and a clear fear of abandonment (no doubt cemented by the untimely death of his parents), issues both widespread amongst children with Harry's early childhood experiences. Harry is unable to entertain the thought that Dumbledore will come for him, so much so that he even refrains from packing: "It just seemed too good to be true that he was going to be rescued from the Dursleys" (Rowling, 2005, p. 44). Harry's fear is rooted fundamentally in a combination of his blocked trust and low self-esteem: although Harry does not appear to struggle with self-loathing, as many children in care do, he does struggle severely with the idea that others (notably adult caregiver figures) genuinely care for him, and questions it when they do.

As such, rather than packing, Harry instead lists all the worries he has as to why Dumbledore will not come for him—including that the letter he received may have been a forgery as a form of "trick" or "joke" (Rowling, 2005, p. 44). The heartbreaking implication here is that Harry is incapable of believing he is worthy of kindness. It makes more sense to him that someone would dangle the possibility of rescue in front of him as a mean joke than it does that Dumbledore will come as promised. Ultimately, it is Harry's unshakeable fear of being "let down" (Rowling, 2005, p. 44) that renders him incapable of any real trust.

The fear of being let down is one of the most pervasive issues faced by children in care. When children are neglected or abused, they learn they cannot trust adults to meet their needs, do what is right, or—like in Harry's case—keep their promises. Every child I have ever cared for has lived with a constant, if not overwhelming, belief that the adults in their lives will let them down. This belief is the essence of blocked trust. The child believes that any positive experiences or acts of kindness must surely be temporary: eventually the adult, no matter how much they say they love them or how much they care for them, will ultimately let them down.

I recently had a conversation with my five-year-old son in which his blocked trust, built up from years in the foster system, couldn't allow him to believe that I would stop him from being "taken away." Every response I gave to address his fear was met with a rebuttal: "But what if they search every house until they find yours?" "What if they smash all the windows and break down the doors?" "What if they hurt you?" Underlining every new question he fired at me was his unwavering belief that I couldn't—or perhaps wouldn't— keep him safe. Just as my son couldn't trust that he wouldn't be taken away, Harry couldn't trust that Dumbledore would come for him.

Of course, Dumbledore comes for Harry as he said he would. When he does, he says something to the Dursleys that has left a lasting imprint on many readers: that although Harry has "known nothing but neglect and often cruelty" (Rowling, 2005, p. 55) from the Dursleys, their treatment of Dudley is far worse. I can appreciate the message that raising a child the way Dudley was (who was spoiled and given no boundaries) is in itself a form of abuse. However, considering the neurological damage and lifelong effects of early childhood trauma, I must respectfully disagree with Dumbledore's assessment. I would argue, however, that the true abuse of Dudley was in exposing him to Harry's abuse—neglect and physical and emotional abuse of others was normalized throughout his childhood, and taught him that this behavior was justifiable.

Reflection

The trauma explored in the *Harry Potter* series could be viewed as indicative of the time in which it was written. Modern children's literature, particularly young adult novels, have a penchant for death-focused storylines (Cain, 2014). That being said, the use of trauma in children's storytelling is by no means limited to the modern age. The 19th and early 20th centuries were awash with literary orphans. Oliver Twist, David Copperfield, Mowgli from *The Jungle Book,* Anne from *Anne of Green Gables*—these characters were staples of children's literature and "paved the way for modern children's book heroines and heroes" (Mokrzycki, 2015); most notably Harry Potter.

Harry Potter is arguably the most famous literary orphan of the modern age. Like those that came before him, his story is rooted in trauma and adversity, and it is this that speaks to children in care across the globe. A hero born of early childhood trauma is a literary savior to children who believed they were walking the path of trauma alone.

The *Harry Potter* series has proven time and again to better the lives of those reading it. It is a valuable tool for healing, especially for children in care, but this quality is not limited to children who have experienced trauma—there is "therapeutic value for everyone in these books" (Noctor, 2006, p. 588). *Harry Potter* is, quite simply, irresistible. Its fan base spans the world. The books have been translated into over seventy languages and adapted into blockbuster films.

Harry clearly holds a very dear place in all of our hearts, but it is arguably what he means to children in care that is his greatest achievement. When Rowling created Harry, she created something very special: a child—a hero—that represented the children most often overlooked in the world. She created a mirror in which children in care could see themselves. As the World of Difference Institute (as cited in Mankiw & Strasser, 2013) explained: "When [children] are represented in the literature we read, they can see themselves as valuable and worthy of notice." This seemingly simple gift—the gift of representation—has the ability to change the lives of children in care, giving them all a little piece of the magic of Hogwarts in their daily lives.

REFERENCES

Archer, C. (2003). Developmental impact of trauma and implications for healing. In C. Archer & A. Burnell (Ed.), *Trauma, attachment and family permanence: Fear can stop you loving* (pp. 78–96). London: Jessica Kingsley.

Arehart-Treichel, J. (2002). Analyst discovers lessons in Harry Potter's ordeal. Retrieved from www.psychnews.psychiatryonline.org/doi/full/10.1176/pn.37.5.0033

Cain, S. (2014, May 11). YA books on death: Is young adult fiction becoming too dark? *The Guardian*. Retrieved from www.theguardian.com

Children's Bureau (2015). Understanding the effects of maltreatment on brain development. Retrieved from www.childwelfare.gov/pubPDFs/brain_development.pdf

Children's Bureau (2017). Child welfare outcomes 2010–2014: Report to Congress. Retrieved from www.acf.hhs.gov/cb/resource/cwo-10-14

Family Care for Children & Youth. (2016). *Problem behaviors in foster children following placement*. Retrieved from http://www.fccy.org/blog/foster-care-pa/problem-behaviors-in-foster-children-following-placement/

Hughes, D. (2017). *Building the bonds of attachment: Awakening love in deeply traumatized children* (3rd ed.). London: Rowman & Littlefield.

Jalongo, M.R. (1983). Bibliotherapy: Literature to promote socioemotional growth. *The Reading Teacher, 36*(8), 796–803. Retrieved from www.jstor.org/journal/readingteacher

Mankiw, S., & Strasser, J. (2013). Tender topics: Exploring sensitive issues with pre-k through first grade children through read-alouds. *Young Children, 68*(1), 84–89. Retrieved from www.naeyc.org/yc/

McNulty, W. (2008). Harry Potter and the prisoner within: Helping children with traumatic loss. In L.C. Rubin (Ed.), *Popular culture in counseling, psychotherapy, and play-based interventions* (pp. 25–42). New York: Springer.

Mokrzycki, S. (2015). *Fostering in fiction: The representation of foster care in children's publishing* (Unpublished master's dissertation). Monash University, Melbourne, Australia.

Noctor, C. (2006). Putting Harry Potter on the couch. *Clinical Child Psychology and Psychiatry, 11*(4), 579–589. doi: 10.1177/1359104506067879

Pardeck, J.T. (1994). Using literature to help adolescents cope with problems. *Adolescence, 29*(114), 421–427. Retrieved from www.ncbi.nlm.nih.gov/labs/journals/adolescence/

Pardeck, J.T., & Pardeck, J.A. (1987). Bibliotherapy for children in foster care and adoption. *Child Welfare, 66*(3), 269–278. Retrieved from www.cwla.org/child-welfare-journal/
Perez, S.A. (1984). Promote identifying with characters for motivation in reading stories. *Reading Horizons, 24*(2), 141–144. Retrieved from www.scholarworks.wmich.edu/reading_horizons/
Perry, B., & Marcellus, J. (n.d.). The impact of abuse and neglect on the developing brain. Retrieved from www.teacher.scholastic.com/professional/bruceperry/abuse_neglect.htm
Provenzano, D., & Heyman, E. (2006). Harry Potter and the resilience to adversity. In N. Mulholland (Ed.), *The psychology of Harry Potter: An unauthorized examination of the boy who lived* (pp. 105–120) Dallas: Benbella Books.
Rizza, M. (1997). A parent's guide to helping children: Using bibliotherapy at home. Retrieved from www.nrcgt.uconn.edu/newsletters/winter972/
Rowling, J.K. (2003). *Harry Potter and the order of the phoenix.* London: Bloomsbury.
Rowling, J.K. (2005). *Harry Potter and the half-blood prince.* New York: Scholastic.
Shechtman, Z. (2009). *Treating child and adolescent aggression through bibliotherapy.* New York: Springer Science+Business Media.
Sound Medicine (2015). *Childhood trauma leads to brains wired for fear* [Audio podcast]. Indiana University School of Medicine. Retrieved from www.tfttraumarelief.com/2015/05/04/effects-of-trauma-on-childrens-brains/
Vezzali, L., Stathi, S., Giovannini, D., Capozza, D., & Trifiletti, E. (2015). The greatest magic of Harry Potter: Reducing prejudice. *Journal of Applied Social Psychology, 45*(2), 105–121. doi: 10.1111/jasp.12279

House-Elves in Harlem

Stereotyping the Other in Fantastic Beasts and Where to Find Them

KRIS SWANK

At first glance, the American wizarding community of 1926 depicted in the film *Fantastic Beasts and Where to Find Them* (2016) appears to be an ethnically diverse and racially-integrated society. It is presided over by the Magical Congress of the United States of America (MACUSA), whose diverse employees work together without regard to race or ethnicity, while in the non-magical world (No-Maj), Jim Crow laws in the American South legalized segregation of the races. MACUSA's president in 1926 is Seraphina Picquery (Carmen Ejogo), an African American witch from Savannah, Georgia. According to *Pottermore*, women have been MACUSA presidents since the eighteenth century. By contrast, the first woman elected to the U.S. Congress was Jeannette Pickering Rankin (1880–1973) of Montana, who first served from 1917–1919, before No-Maj American women were even granted the right to vote by the 19th Amendment to the U.S. Constitution (1920).[1] A woman has yet to serve as the American No-Maj President, while the first African American No-Maj President was Barack Obama, whose 2008 election came more than eighty years after Madam Picquery's.

However, despite a surface appearance of racial toleration, the American wizarding community depicted in *Fantastic Beasts* is, at heart, a divided culture both in its relations with non-magical humans, and with other sentient magical beings, such as house-elves and goblins. In the film, British wizard Newt Scamander (Eddie Redmayne) travels to New York City in 1926 with a case full of magical creatures who escape into the city. The creatures risk exposing magic to No-Maj Americans, a fate the American wizarding community has been striving to avoid since the Salem Witch Trials (1692–1693).

With the help of American witches Tina and Queenie Goldstein (Katherine Waterston and Alison Sudol) and No-Maj Jacob Kowalski (Dan Fogler), Newt chases his escaped creatures across the city. To prevent exposure, and war with the No-Maj community, Rappaport's Law of 1790 enforces total segregation between American wizards and No-Majs. There is even a government sub-division dedicated to the enforcement of this segregation, an office with no counterpart in the British Ministry of Magic. As a British wizard, Newt is critical of the law, telling Tina, "I know you [Americans] have rather backwards laws about relations with non-magic people. That you're not meant to befriend them, that you can't marry them, which seems mildly absurd to me" (Rowling, 2016, pp. 64–65). A key tension of the film is the budding romance between the witch Queenie and the No-Maj Jacob. Their situation is reminiscent of the U.S. Supreme Court case, Loving vs. Virginia (1967), where Mildred Jeter, a black woman, and her white husband, Richard Loving, successfully challenged the State of Virginia's anti-miscegenation laws which carried a twenty-five-year jail sentence for interracial marriage (Loving v. Virginia, n.d.). New York, though, was one of a handful of states which had never enacted anti-miscegenation laws, which makes the New York–based MACUSA's anti-miscegenation law ironic, at best. Nevertheless, it is unlikely that mixed couples like Queenie and Jacob will find much sympathy in the intolerant America of the 1920s depicted in this film.

Another layer of inherent bias in the American wizarding community is its treatment of non-human magical species, such as house-elves and goblins. While there are no equivalent restrictions on contact with magical non-humans, and different species of magical creatures live side-by-side with witches and wizards in America, as they do in Britain, the non-humans occupy different and unequal spheres. Additionally, Rowling portrays the non-human magical species in *Fantastic Beasts* in characteristically stereotypical terms which have also been used to portray various human groups, such as African Americans, European Americans, and Asian Americans. Instead of portraying a racially-integrated America, the film reinforces the past inconsistent treatment of stigmatized groups in Rowling's writings.

House-Elves and Slavery

Pottermore defines house-elves as "Loyal magical creatures bound to their owners as servants for life." In the *Harry Potter* books, Muggle-born Hermione Granger sees the house-elves as slaves and advocates for their liberation, despite resistance from her friends who were raised within the wizard community. Ron Weasley, for instance, tells Hermione that house-elves "*like* being enslaved" (Rowling, 2000, p. 224). Hagrid argues, "It's in their nature ter look after humans, that's what they like, see?" (Rowling, 2000, 265). Most of the house-elves themselves do not appear to desire freedom. When Hermione hides hats around the Gryffindor common room for the Hogwarts' house-elves to find (the gift of clothing automatically setting house-elves free), Dobby tells Harry the other house-elves find her efforts insulting (Rowling, 2003, p. 385).

The oppression of British house-elves has been the subject of significant critical debate, with various commentators viewing house-elves in terms of race, gender, and class. Farah Mendlesohn and Bryccan Carey compare the British house-elves to African American slaves. Mendlesohn likens Dobby to the stereotypical "happy darky," laughing and causing mayhem, while Winky resembles the Negro "mammy" in films like *Gone with the Wind* (1939) (Mendlesohn, 2002, p. 179). Although Dobby relishes freedom, Winky is distraught by it and turns to abusing butterbeer. Mendlesohn writes, "The images of Dobby and Winky neatly confirm Stanley Elkins's long-discredited argument for Sambo complex, in which oppression creates a range of childlike behaviors and remakes freedom into a punishment for the institutionalized" (Mendlesohn, 2002, p. 179). Carey equates Dobby with Harriet Beecher Stowe's title character from *Uncle Tom's Cabin* (1852) "in the modern, American, pejorative sense" as an emancipated slave whose loyalties continue to lie with the oppressors rather than his fellow oppressed (Carey, 2009, p. 167).[2] Kathryn N. McDaniel offers an alternate comparison, "If we think of the house-elves not as African-American slaves, but as 'unliberated' women, shackled by the chains of tradition to a circumscribed role in the domestic sphere, we can perhaps understand the source of their ambivalence" (McDaniel, 2015, p. 65). She notes that freedom for house-wives in the twentieth century usually came as the result of divorce, a shameful situation for many which led to their loss of home, income, and purpose. "The key similarity between house-elves and twentieth-century women," McDaniel argues, "rests in this problem of liberation: that it is not unequivocally desired, that it can be devastating, that it does not always seem to be a 'true' liberation at all, and that many in fact derive satisfaction from their status as 'helpmeet,' subordinate though it may be" (McDaniel, 2015, p. 67). Elizabeth E. Heilman and Anne E. Gregory view house-elves in terms of immigrants and the working class. They write that house-elves who consider freedom a disgrace and a threat to their way of life send a "deeply disturbing" message that "oppressed people can and should be satisfied with their lot" (244–245). Winky speaks for this view when she tells Harry that Dobby is getting "Ideas above his station, sir" (Rowling, 2000, p. 98). Heilman and Gregory note, "Like other marginalized peoples in England and the United States, the house elves do not speak standard English" and they argue Rowling "reinscribes and normalizes the marginalized status of the immigrant or dialectic speaker" (244–245).

Fantastic Beasts adds to this ongoing conversation by presenting house-elves outside of the domestic realm and in a 1920s American context. House-elves are briefly seen in the film serving both humans and goblins. In the MACUSA lobby, several wizards wait to have their wands shined by a rag-clad house-elf (Rowling, 2016, p. 39). Later, inside a goblin-owned speakeasy, The Blind Pig, several more house-elves work in low-skill service roles as bartender, waiter, and clerk (Rowling, 2016, pp. 191, 192, 194, and 195). Outside the home, working within a large government bureaucracy and an illicit saloon, it is hard to view the *Fantastic Beasts* house-elves as unliberated house-wives, but the analogy of the working-class immigrant resonates, especially in the 1920s context.

A post–Civil War economic boom and the shift to large-scale manufacturing created an enormous demand for labor in the United States, particularly in the industrial North. Between 1910 and 1914, over 4.5 million European immigrants came to work in American factories, mills, and shipyards (Zieger & Gall, 2002, p. 34). This abundance of cheap labor, combined with weak union leadership and a lack of government protections, led to low pay, long working hours, and deplorable conditions for the working-poor immigrant. A worker who agitated for better conditions could simply be replaced by another who was more compliant. It is not hard to extrapolate from these real-life working conditions for immigrants at the turn of the century to the rag-clad house-elves in MACUSA and the Blind Pig.

Mendlesohn's and Carey's comparisons of house-elves to African American slaves are particularly jarring in the context of *Fantastic Beasts*. New York was the locus of the 1920s New Negro Movement, also called the Harlem Renaissance, a time of unprecedented African American prosperity, social amelioration, and free expression. Harlem, a large neighborhood in northern Manhattan, had been by turns Dutch, Irish, and Jewish, until around 1900, when middle-class African Americans began moving into the area and making it their own. The onset of World War I (1914–1918) precipitated a reverse flow of European immigrants from the United States back "home" to fight in the war. Between 1915 and 1919, fewer than half a million European immigrants entered the United States (Zieger & Gall, 2002, p. 34). Next, the Immigration Act of 1924, also known as the Johnson–Reed Act, severely limited the number of immigrants who could be admitted annually to the United States. The resulting labor shortage sent employers looking south. From the Civil War until 1910, only 67,000 African Americans *per decade* moved to the industrial north, but during the 1910s—the first years of what became known as "The Great Migration" from rural south to industrial north—half a million African Americans came north *per year*. "Black men increasingly took their place in the foundries, steel mills, munitions works, and meatpacking plants as wartime conditions brought to northern cities some of the most economically ambitious, culturally dynamic, and politically conscious members of the South's agrarian proletariat" (Zieger & Gall, 2002, p. 35). Black colleges and universities, most established after the Civil War, were also graduating middle-class doctors, nurses, lawyers, bankers, entrepreneurs, college professors, and school teachers. Once established in Harlem, they all wanted to buy houses and live the American Dream. According to James Weldon Johnson (1871–1938), "Buying property became a fever. At the height of this activity, that is, 1920–21, it was not an uncommon thing for a colored washerwoman or cook to go into a real estate office and lay down from one thousand to five thousand dollars on a house" (28). Harlem blossomed in the 1920s as an African American utopia. Johnson wrote in 1925:

> Harlem is not merely a Negro colony or community, it is a city within a city, the greatest Negro city in the world. It is not a slum or a fringe, it is located in the heart of Manhattan and occupies one of the most beautiful and healthful sections of the city. It is not a "quarter" of dilapidated tenements, but is made up of new-law apartments and handsome dwellings, with well-paved and well-lighted streets. It has its own churches, social and civic centers, shops, theaters, and other places of amusement. And it contains more Negroes to the square mile than any other spot on earth [24].

Black intellectuals and artists also flocked to Harlem, leading to a flowering of African American poetry, prose, plays, essays, art, dance, and music. Prominent authors of the Harlem Renaissance included Langston Hughes, Zora Neale Hurston, Johnson, Alain Locke, Claude McKay, and Jean Toomer.

Conversely, African Americans were the first to lose their jobs to white soldiers returning home from World War I, and "the government stopped its tentative efforts to reach out to blacks" (Zieger & Gall, 2002, p. 35). During the 1920s, many black women turned to domestic work, while black men struggled to find employment as porters and elevator operators (King, 2017, p. 63). Educated blacks had trouble finding work in New York in their fields of expertise. Dr. Herman Warner noted, "you could go into an apartment house, and the elevator man would have a doctorate" (quoted in King, 2015, p. 61). The Harlem Renaissance eventually faded away in the 1930s, a victim of the Great Depression, as several of the era's most important intellectuals and artists emigrated to Europe. Harlem neighborhoods transformed into the impoverished ghettos now associated with that name. If the *Fantastic Beasts* house-elves are viewed as African Americans, they can only reflect a time before the Emancipation Proclamation (1863). Completely absent from the film is any depiction of house-elves enjoying the same type of social and cultural expression as the Harlem Renaissance. A single house-elf journalist or entrepreneur could have captured the true spirit of the age. Instead, there is only the wand-shiner, bartender, waiter, and clerk—although these are analogous to real jobs held by many blacks in 1920s New York, they represent only half the story.

Rather, the house-elves of New York closely echo the fictional portrayals of African Americans in films of the early twentieth-century. Despite such luminaries as Oscar Micheaux (1884–1951), the first major African American filmmaker, and Paul Robeson (1898–1976), the international super-star singer and actor, the Hollywood studio system mostly limited black actors to roles as butlers, plantation laborers, mammies, maids, criminals, and comic relief. Actors such as Bill "Bojangles" Robinson (1878–1949) and Lincoln "Stepin Fetchit" Perry (1902–1985) portrayed a string of dancing and comic slaves and servants. Hattie McDaniel's (1895–1952) role as Mammy in *Gone with Wind* became the iconic portrayal of the black female slave devoted to the caretaking of her white charges. Kimberly Fain writes,

> There were those films who portrayed servants and sidekicks with malicious racism. Yet most films treated racial diversity with condescension and indifference. According to the black press and the civil rights community, black characters playing in *Gone with the Wind* represented the most abhorrent characterization of African Americans' position in Hollywood…. Then and now, many audiences are still uncomfortable with the one-dimensional depiction of African Americans in *Gone with the Wind* [Fain, 2015, pp. 43–44].

Yet, this is exactly the characterization of house-elves in *Fantastic Beasts*, what little there is of it. The only house-elf with a notable character is the surly bartender who grumbles at Jacob's nervous, "I love house-elves…. My uncle's a house-elf" (Rowling, 2016, p. 191). Otherwise, the house-elves of the film appear only in the background, mostly unnoticed and invisible, treated with the same condescension and indifference as blacks in early Hollywood. For the house-elves of 1920s Harlem, there is no renaissance.

Working-Class Goblins

But if *Fantastic Beasts* fails to shed much light on house-elves in America, it is revolutionary in its depiction of goblins, which are shown here to be more diverse and individualistic than the goblins of the *Harry Potter* franchise. In *Harry Potter and the Sorcerer's Stone*, the first goblin Harry ever encounters, at the doors of Gringotts Bank, is described as short, swarthy, and clever, wearing a pointed beard (Rowling, 1997, p. 72). Once inside, Harry sees a hundred more goblins "scribbling in large ledgers, weighing coins in brass scales, examining precious stones through eyeglasses" (Rowling, 1997, p. 73). In his blog post "Harry Potter and the Jewish Goblins," Matthew Zeitlin argues the *Harry Potter* goblins exhibit a number of anti–Semitic stereotypes: "miserly, stingy, greedy and two-faced" (Zeitlin, 2007). The films also depict goblins as "universally hooked nosed, short, unattractive and green" (Zeitlin, 2007). A commenter on Zeitlin's blog lists additional Jewish stereotypes applicable to the Gringotts' goblins: "good with money, jewelers, persecuted historically, refuse to eat the same food as non-goblins ... different set of customary laws regarding e.g., property rights..." (James, 2009). Alternately, Giselle Liza Anatol links the Gringotts goblins to Oriental stereotypes (Anatol, 2009, p. 120). The goblins have "dark, slanting eyes" (Rowling, 2000, p. 446) and "swarthy" or "sallow skin" (Rowling, 2007, pp. 466 and 485). Edward Saïd's landmark study, *Orientalism* (1978), describes an "imaginary Orient" (i.e., the Middle East and Asia) historically and imaginatively fashioned by Europeans as a place which is "passive, seminal, feminine, even silent and supine," as well as "secret" (Saïd, 1978, p. 139). Anatol identifies Griphook as the quintessential Orientalized goblin (Anatol, 2009, p. 120). In *Harry Potter and the Deathly Hallows*, Griphook is injured and has to be carried to a bed in Shell Cottage where he lies supine and has his shoes removed for him (Rowling, 2007, p. 485). He sidles and slinks about the cottage, and slips silently beneath a table when fearful (Rowling, 2007, pp. 512, 513, and 515). Griphook also demonstrates a stereotypical Oriental duplicity, as Saïd calls it, the "incorrigibility of Orientals and therefore proves that they are not to be trusted" (Saïd, 1978, p. 322). Inside the Gringotts' vaults, Griphook betrays Harry, Ron, and Hermione, and then he vanishes (Rowling, 2007, p. 541).

But the *Fantastic Beasts* goblins are not the Semitic bankers of Gringotts, nor the Orientalized Griphook. At MACUSA, Tina speaks to Red, a goblin elevator operator. Viewers could be forgiven for thinking Red is a house-elf. Newt and Tina have just passed the wand-shine elf, and there is not much visual difference between the two except that Red wears clothes. Also, viewers have never before seen a goblin in a working-class job subservient to humans. But the *Original Screenplay* identifies Red as a goblin (Rowling, 2016, p. 39). Diverging from the more refined diction of the Gringott's goblins, Red speaks with an East Coast working-class accent, illustrating Heilman's and Gregory's view that Rowling marginalizes immigrants and dialect speakers. But Red also resonates with African American men of the era. By 1930, the two largest categories of employment for African American men in New York were as porters and elevator operators (King, 2017, p. 62). *Fantastic Beasts* also depicts the first female goblin in the Wizarding World, and she, too, resonates with African Americans of the time.

The Eighteenth Amendment to the U.S. Constitution (1919) and the Volstead Act (1920) prohibited alcohol sales in the United States until they were repealed in 1933. As a result, the 1920s saw hundreds of illegal nightclubs, or "speakeasies," open in New York City, many of them in Harlem. These offered illegal booze, drugs, prostitution, gambling, and jazz. Jazz was a uniquely African American musical form incubated in New Orleans prior to World War I and brought north during the Great Migration. The speakeasies run by Jewish or Italian gangsters frequently hired African American performers, and paid them better wages than black-owned establishments were able to afford (King, 2017, p. 131). Black jazz musicians also made their mark on early twentieth-century Hollywood. *Paradise in Harlem* (1939) and *Cabin in the Sky* (1943) both starred all-black casts. *Stormy Weather* (1943) featured notable performances by Lena Horne, Bojangles Williamson, Cab Calloway, and Fats Waller. *New Orleans* (1947) included music by Louis Armstrong, Billie Holliday, and others.

In the Wizarding World, the jazz musicians are goblins. Inside the Blind Pig, a speakeasy for wizards, "a glamorous goblin jazz singer croons on a stage full of goblin musicians, smoky images wafting from her wand to illustrate her lyrics" (Rowling, 2016, p. 190). While in the *Harry Potter* films, the goblins' appearances were achieved by live actors wearing prosthetics, in *Fantastic Beasts*, the goblins are fully-digital characters based on motion-capture performances (Yates and Rowling, "The Blind Pig," 2016). The goblin jazz singer is based on the performance of black British actress Aretha Ayeh, and the resulting digital character preserves much of Ayeh's own physical appearance (Yates and Rowling, "The Blind Pig," 2016).[3] Thus, like Red the goblin elevator operator, the jazz singer may also be considered analogous to African Americans of the time. She and the other jazz musicians further illustrate that goblin culture includes the creative arts. She also uses a wand, a subversive act performed in the subversive climate of the Blind Pig, for wands are forbidden to all non-humans by clause three of the Code of Wand Use (Rowling, 2000, p. 132). Thus, there appears to be an artistic and subversive subculture within goblin-kind which is significantly different from the "Semitic" goblins of Gringotts Bank. Goblins also have a criminal underworld.

If Red and the jazz singer can be viewed in terms of African Americans, Gnarlak, the proprietor of the Blind Pig, is entirely different. Larger and more intimidating than other goblins, Gnarlak is a stereotypical mob boss straight out of history and Hollywood. The New York underworld in the 1920s was dominated by ethnic groups which had emerged from the impoverished immigrant neighborhoods of the nineteenth century. Gnarlak may have been inspired by the Prohibition-era Jewish mob kingpin, Arnold Rothstein (1882–1928), the real-life inspiration for both Meyer Wolfsheim in F. Scott Fitzgerald's *The Great Gatsby* (1925) and Nathan Detroit in the musical *Guys and Dolls* (1950) (Abadinsky, 1981, 5). But more likely, Gnarlak is modeled upon the Italian mob boss archetype established by Al Capone (1899–1947) and actor Edward G. Robinson in the film *Little Caesar* (1930), whose character was based upon Capone (Phillips, 2014, p. 7). Like Robinson's cigar-smoking, dapper "Rico" Bandello, Gnarlak is "[s]moking a cigar and smartly dressed for a goblin, he has a sly, smooth demeanor like a Mafia boss" (Rowling, 2016, p. 194). Like Griphook—and "Rico"—Gnarlak is also duplicitous. He deals for information with Newt Scamander while simultaneously tipping off

MACUSA to the presence of the fugitive Newt and Tina (Rowling, 2016, p. 199).

In the *Harry Potter* series, the goblin bankers are arguably derived from a variety of Semitic and/or Asian stereotypes. In *Fantastic Beasts*, they are decidedly more working class and exhibit, rather, stereotypes based on European immigrants and African Americans. Gnarlak in particular is modeled upon Jewish-American or Italian-American mobsters. Yet, like the house-elves, the goblins are derived as much from pop culture stereotypes of the early twentieth century as from history. They are not the only ones derived from such stereotypes.

A Demiguise in Chinatown

The *Fantastic Beasts* film also features Dougal the Demiguise. That he is Asian is certain. Rowling, in the persona of Newt Scamander, writes in the feigned Hogwarts textbook, also called *Fantastic Beasts & Where to Find Them*, that the Demiguise lives in the Far East (Scamander & Rowling, 2001, p. 17). The Demiguise is described there "like a graceful ape in appearance, with large, black, doleful eyes.... The whole body is covered with long, fine, silky, silvery hair" (Scamander & Rowling, 2001, p. 17). This highly feminine description is reinforced by the purse Dougal carries in the film through Macy's department store. He is also enigmatic and silent, can perceive the future, and turns invisible when endangered. Dougal thus closely resembles the Oriental stereotypes articulated by Saïd, that is, feminine, silent, passive, and secret, as well as "mysterious" and "inscrutable" (Saïd, 1978, pp. 138 and 53). Dougal also resonates with Asian stereotypes from early twentieth century pop culture and film.

Kam Louie writes, "For most of the twentieth century, Chinese men inhabited a negative persona in the West.... Where the Chinese were once considered cultured and refined, this perception gave way to murky images of depravity, drugs and pagan barbarianism" (Louie, 2014, p. 57). Dr. Fu Manchu is a fictional criminal mastermind created by British novelist Sax Rohmer in *The Mystery of Dr. Fu-Manchu* (1913; U.S. title: *The Insidious Dr. Fu-Manchu*). The character was featured in numerous books, films, radio, and television programs in the twentieth century where he became the epitome of the sinister, inscrutable Asian, the "Yellow Peril" which sought to invade and dominate the "civilized" West. The character's distinctive facial hair—excessively-elongated mustaches—became known as "Fu Manchus." Contrasted against this negative stereotype was a more positive stereotype of the honorable Chinese man, exemplified by Honolulu detective, Charlie Chan. Created by American novelist Earl Derr Biggers in the novel *The House*

Without a Key (1925), Chan was also featured in numerous books, films, radio and television adaptations in the twentieth century. Louie writes, "Rather than being a devious mastermind, Chan was meant to be amusing and likeable" (Louie, 2014, p. 57). Chan was decidedly unthreatening, serene in the face of danger, wise and soft-spoken, though known to utter ancient Chinese wisdom in pidgin–English. In his most popular film appearances, he was played by a series of white actors in "yellow face."[4] Gloria Chun argues that Charlie Chan on film was "devoid of any assertiveness and sexuality ... [and was] self-effacing to a fault" (Chun, 2000, p. 19). Henry Yu writes of other stereotypical Asian film roles which were equally passive and gendered, "the Chinese laundryman and domestic workers or Japanese flower gardener, willing to do 'women's work' that no self-respecting white man would perform, served to feminize the portrayal of Oriental men" (Yu, 2002, p. 131). According to Louie, the "stereotypes of Chinese men as foul fiends or entertaining clowns were so powerful that for decades they were widely mimicked if not accepted as true reflections of the state of Chinese manhood in the West" (Louie, 2014, p. 57). Sometimes, the characteristics of Fu Manchu and Charlie Chan were combined into a single character who was both dangerous and beneficent, mysterious, wise, silent, passive, potentially-sinister, and inscrutable, such as Caine of the television series *Kung Fu* (1972–1975) and Mr. Miyagi in the movie, *The Karate Kid* (1984).

Both Fu Manchu and Charlie Chan stereotypes can be found in Rowling's Demiguise. The *Original Screenplay* describes Dougal as "a silvery-haired orangutan-like creature, with a curious, wizened face" (Rowling, 2016, p. 207). Both Minalima's sketch in the *Original Screenplay* and Dougal in the *Fantastic Beasts* film wear the prominent "Fu Manchu" mustaches (Rowling, 2016, p. 188; and Yates and Rowling, *Fantastic Beasts*, 2016). The Ministry of Magic classifies the Demiguise as "Dangerous" (Scamander & Rowling, 2001, p. 17). As an escaped and illegal creature, Dougal is considered dangerous by MACUSA President Picquery, who orders that he be secured. On the other hand, Newt claims the Demiguise are "fundamentally peaceful, but they can give a nasty nip if provoked" (Rowling, 2016, p. 207). Despite having a male name, Dougal is depicted with long lustrous hair and sad, feminine eyes. The film's heroes discover Dougal did not escape on his own behalf, but in order to "babysit" a nervous baby Occamy, which he placates with candy from his fashionable purse. Yet once the humans arrive on the scene, Dougal becomes infantilized, riding Jacob's shoulders like a small child, disappearing when frightened, and quiescently allowing Jacob to lead him by the hand back to Newt's case.

The Demiguise's status as an undesirable alien is another factor it has in common with early twentieth-century Chinese. Like all magical creatures, the Demiguise would have been barred from legally entering the United States during Newt's 1926 visit to New York. As *The New York Ghost* newspaper headline declares, the "Beast Ownership-Ban" makes the possession of magical creatures illegal in America (Yates and Rowling, *Fantastic beasts*, 2016). Tina informs Newt of another law prohibiting the breeding of magical creatures in New York (Rowling, 2016, 38). Likewise, the Angell Treaty of 1880 and the Chinese Exclusion Act of 1882 prohibited Chinese immigration to the United States (until the Magnuson Act of 1943). The Chinese Exclusion Act was the first law preventing a specific ethnic group from immigrating to the United States, and Charlie Chan, a citizen of Honolulu, Hawaii, had to routinely prove his citizenship to the mainland American whites he encountered (Chan). Yu writes,

> From the time Chinese arrived in the mid-nineteenth century, migrants from Asia were considered a threat to white labor and American society. Categorized as Orientals, these immigrants were demonized as exotic and non–American. From violent lynchings through the internment of Japanese Americans during World War II, Asian Americans were treated as a problem [Yu, 2002, p. 7].

The Demiguise, then, displays a full range of stereotypes associated with Asians in early-twentieth-century America, including their stock characterizations on television and film. They are considered a dangerous threat, yet they appear to be serene, wise, nurturing, and mostly docile, in other words, the embodiment of both Fu Manchu and Charlie Chan.

Othered Others

In the 2007 documentary, *J.K. Rowling: A Year in the Life*, Rowling stated the vice she most despised was "bigotry." More recently, in a YouTube featurette, Rowling said, "My heroes are always people who feel themselves to be set apart, stigmatized, or othered. That's at the heart of most of what I write, and it's certainly at the heart of this movie" (*Fantastic beasts and where to find them: A new hero*, 2016). The film *is* highly sensitive to the "Otheredness" of its human hero, Newt Scamander. It also portrays a multi-ethnic MACUSA headed by an African American woman. Yet, the film is less sensitive in its representation of "Other" non-human sentient species (the houseelf, goblin, and Demiguise), tending to portray them as pastiches of stock Hollywood stereotypes (the black servant, jazz musician, Italian mobster, and inscrutable Chinese). Just what is Rowling doing?

One possible answer is that Rowling is unaware she is perpetuating racial stereotypes. She has been the subject of this very critique before. In the run-up to the release of the *Fantastic Beasts* film, Rowling posted on *Pottermore* the essays "History of Magic in North America" and "Ilvermorny School of Witchcraft and Wizardry." Presumably, these essays were intended to both raise excitement for the new film and elucidate elements of the American wizarding community. However, the essays were widely panned for what readers believed to be inappropriate cultural appropriation of Native American history and beliefs, and the perpetuation of stereotypes.[5] Amy H. Sturgis observes that the essays were "plagued by what seem to be unexamined colonialist and nationalist assumptions" (Sturgis, 2016). She further writes, "Rowling simply doesn't appreciate how much she doesn't know about North America" (Sturgis, 2016).

The original *Harry Potter* novels received similar criticisms. McDaniel writes, "Two strong critiques of Rowling's fantasy world focus on her depictions of female characters and the house-elves; in both instances, readers have argued that she spoils the integrity of her fantasy world by injecting real-world prejudices that undermine her central message" (McDaniel, 2015, p. 64). Anatol concurs that Rowling's "inconsistent rendering of what it means to be an Other to society's hegemonic forces weakens the explicit antiracism theme of the books" (Anatol, 2009, p. 109). Many fans of the original series have expressed difficulty accepting the way some of its essentially good characters (Ron, Hagrid, and others) could accept or even condone house-elf slavery. The *Fantastic Beasts* film does nothing to alleviate such concerns as it perpetuates the oppression of house-elves and the equation of goblins with greed and duplicity. Ironically, Newt Scamander repeatedly risks his life to save the magical creatures in his case, yet he fails to comment upon the enslaved house-elves at MACUSA or the Blind Pig.

Compared to seven novels and eight movies for the *Harry Potter* franchise, a single "American" movie may not offer enough evidence with which to generalize about the beliefs and practices of the American wizarding world. Rowling may have wanted to do more with the non-human races in the film, but was constrained by the medium. While the *Harry Potter* novels are her singular vision, films represent the collaborative vision of hundreds of creative minds both in front of and behind the camera. A film can also be limited by available technology, budgets, and time. Hollywood blockbusters are also not often known for their nuanced scripts and characterizations. Furthermore, some powerful ideas on the page may simply not make it to the screen. For example, Hermione's elf-liberation organization from the books, S.P.E.W., was not included in the films. Yet, Rowling is this film's creator and screenwriter; a good portion of the responsibility for its portrayal of different races and species certainly falls to her. As in her essays on Native Americans, Rowling simply may not realize how much she doesn't know about North American race relations. Ultimately, as Carey argues, "It is impossible, of course, to fully understand an author's intentions with her work. Indeed, a writer's full and complex set of intentions may not even be clear to herself" (Carey, 2009, p. 163).

Another possibility, however, is that Rowling knows exactly what she is doing. McDaniel argues that readers of fantasy fiction often expect imaginary worlds to be ideal, but that "Importantly, for the fantasy writer the readers' ability to see the flaws in the fantasy world (as they perhaps cannot in their own) may serve to highlight those aspects of the 'real world' that need to be attended to and changed" (McDaniel, 2015, p. 64). When Hermione accuses Ron of propping up the unjust house-elf system just because he's lazy, Carey argues that Rowling is highlighting "the sort of causal misunderstanding of complex moral problems that allows ordinary and otherwise decent people to overlook great evils" (Rowling, 2000, p. 125; Carey, 2009, p. 166). Rowling could be doing something similar here. Newt Scamander is this film's "Hermione," the outsider who perceives institutionalized racism which is invisible to native-born citizens. When Newt criticizes the American prohibition against marrying No-Majs, Tina grimaces at Jacob, "Who's going to marry him?" (Rowling, 2016, 64–65). In that moment, Tina cannot conceive that her own sister will fall in love with such a seemingly oafish No-Maj. It is only through familiarity that Tina's sympathies toward Jacob soften. When Newt tells Tina he is writing a book on magical creatures, she replies, "Like— an extermination guide?" (Rowling, 2016, 45). From her perspective at the start of the film, the only good magical creature is a dead one. But the audience's sympathies lie with Newt. And even Tina comes to appreciate Jacob and the fantastic beasts, in time. Rowling might be encouraging her audience, like Tina, to look beyond the surface of stigmatized groups. In a twenty-first century America still actively engaged with complex issues of race and justice, the film might encourage viewers to search for "invisible Others" in their own societies, even amid some advances in ethnic and gender equality. In *Fantastic Beasts and Where to Find Them*, Rowling has opened the suitcase, but it is up to audiences to decide how they will treat the fantastic beings who emerge.[6]

NOTES

1. MACUSA President Seraphina *Picquery* likely owes her name to Representative Jeannette *Pickering* Rankin, and her birthplace in Georgia to Rebecca Latimer Felton (1835–1930) of Decatur, Georgia, the first woman in the U.S. Senate. Felton was appointed in 1922 by Georgia's governor to fill a short-term vacancy. She served for one day.
2. Carey continues, "But at the same time we should remember that is it far from clear whether Stowe's character—who dies as a martyr, defending other slaves, not Whites—can himself be described in these pejorative terms" (Carey, 2009, p. 167).
3. While Aretha Ayeh provided the physical performance, the goblin jazz singer's voice was provided by white British-Australian singer Emmi.
4. Charlie Chan was played early on by Asian actors—George Kuwa (1926), Kamiyama Sojin (1927), and E.L. Park (1929)—but the character finally gained widespread popularity as played by three Caucasian actors: Warner Oland (1931–1938), Sidney Toler (1938–1946), and Roland Winters (1947–1948).
5. Sturgis points specifically to the following articles: What J.K. Rowling's new story can teach us about cultural appropriation: Rowling messed up big time (*The Huffington Post*),

J.K. Rowling is getting major backlash for her depiction of Native Americans (*BuzzFeed*), and Four missed opportunities and problems with Pottermore's Ilvermorny (*Entertainment Monthly*) (Sturgis, 2016).

6. I am grateful for the comments and suggestions on this paper by Lélie Brémont, Katy McDaniel, and Travis Prinzi.

REFERENCES

Abadinsky, H. (1981). *The mafia in America: An oral history.* New York: Praeger.
Anatol, G.L. (2009). The replication of Victorian racial ideology in Harry Potter. In G.L. Anatol (Ed.), *Reading Harry Potter again: New critical essays* (pp. 109–126). Santa Barbara, CA: Praeger.
Carey, B. (2009). Hermione and the house-elves revisited: J.K. Rowling, antislavery campaigning, and the politics of Potter. In G.L. Anatol (Ed.), *Reading Harry Potter again: New critical essays* (pp. 159–173). Santa Barbara, CA: Praeger.
Chan, F. (2007, March 26). Charlie Chan: A hero of sorts. *California Literary Review, 39*. Retrieved September 3, 2017, from http://calitreview.com/39/charlie-chan-a-hero-of-sorts/
Chun, G.H. (2000). *Of orphans and warriors: Inventing Chinese American culture and identity.* New Brunswick, NJ: Rutgers University Press.
Fain, K. (2015). *Black Hollywood: From butlers to superheroes, the changing role of African American men in the movies.* Santa Barbara, CA: Praeger.
Fantastic Beasts and where to find them—A new hero [Video file]. (2016, June 23). United States: Warner Bros. Pictures. Retrieved September 3, 2017, from https://youtu.be/V8aYCm6WBHI
James. (2009, July 7). Re: Harry Potter and the Jewish goblins [Web log comment]. Retrieved September 3, 2017, from http://web.archive.org/web/20111124195205/http://whippersnapper.wordpress.com/2007/07/24/harry-potter-and-the-jewish-goblins/
Johnson, J.W. (1925). Harlem: The culture capital. In A. Locke (Ed.), *The new negro: An interpretation.* New York: Albert and Charles Boni. Reprinted as *The capital of Negro culture* (2003). In W.S. McConnell (Ed.), *Harlem Renaissance* (23–31). San Diego, CA: Greenhaven.
King, S. (2017). *Whose Harlem is this, anyway?: Community politics and grassroots activism during the New Negro era.* New York: New York University Press.
Louie, K. (2014). *Chinese masculinities in a globalizing world.* New Brunswick, NJ: Rutgers University Press.
Loving v. Virginia. (n.d.). Retrieved September 4, 2017, from https://www.law.cornell.edu/supremecourt/text/388/1
McDaniel, K.N. (2015). The "real house-elves" of J.K. Rowling: The elfin mystique revisited. In K. McDaniel & T. Prinzi (Eds.), *Harry Potter for nerds II* (pp. 63–92). Oklahoma City: Unlocking Press.
Mendlesohn, F. (2002). Crowning the king: Harry Potter and the construction of authority. In L.A. Whited (Ed.), *The ivory tower and Harry Potter: Perspectives on a literary phenomenon* (pp. 159–181). Columbia: University of Missouri Press.
Phillips, G.D. (2014). *Gangsters and g-men on screen: Crime cinema then and now.* Lanham, MD: Rowman & Littlefield.
Rowling, J.K. (n.d.) House-elves. Retrieved August 20, 2017, from https://www.pottermore.com/explore-the-story/house-elves
Rowling. J.K. (1997). *Harry Potter and the sorcerer's stone.* New York: Arthur A. Levine/Scholastic.
Rowling. J.K. (2000). *Harry Potter and the goblet of fire.* New York: Arthur A. Levine/Scholastic.
Rowling. J.K. (2003). *Harry Potter and the order of the phoenix.* New York: Arthur A. Levine/Scholastic.
Rowling, J.K. (2007). *Harry Potter and the deathly hallows.* New York: Arthur A. Levine/Scholastic.

Rowling, J.K. (2016). *Fantastic beasts and where to find them: The original screenplay.* New York: Arthur A. Levine, Scholastic.
Rowling, J.K. (2016, March 7). History of magic in North America. Retrieved September 1, 2017, from https://www.pottermore.com/collection-episodic/history-of-magic-in-north-america-en
Rowling, J.K. (2016, June 28) Ilvermorny school of witchcraft and wizardry. Retrieved September 1, 2017, from https://www.pottermore.com/writing-by-jk-rowling/ilvermorny
Rowling, J.K. (2016, ca. October 6). The magical congress of the United States of America (MACUSA). Pottermore. Accessed August 19, 2017. https://www.pottermore.com/writing-by-jk-rowling/macusa.
Runcie, J. (Director). (2007, December 30). J.K. Rowling: A year in the life [Television broadcast]. London, United Kingdom: ITV. On *Harry Potter and the Half-Blood Prince* [Motion picture on DVD]. (2009). United States: Warner Bros. Pictures. Disc 2: Special Features.
Saïd, Edward W. (1978). *Orientalism.* New York: Pantheon.
Scamander, N., & Rowling, J.K. (2001). *Fantastic beasts & where to find them* (2013 ed.). New York: Arthur A. Levine/Scholastic.
Sturgis, A.H. (2016, December). Hogwarts in America: In Fantastic beasts and where to find them, J.K. Rowling crosses the Atlantic and makes a hash of North American history and culture. *Reason.* Retrieved September 3, 2017, from http://reason.com/archives/2016/11/18/hogwarts-in-america
Yates, D. (Director), & Rowling, J.K. (Screenwriter). (2016). The blind pig. On *Fantastic Beasts and Where to Find Them* [Motion picture on DVD]. Warner Brothers. Disc 2: Special Features.
Yates, D. (Director), & Rowling, J.K. (Screenwriter). (2016). *Fantastic Beasts and Where to Find Them* [Motion picture on DVD]. Warner Brothers.
Yu, Henry. (2002). *Thinking orientals: Migration, contact and exoticism in Modern America.* New York: Oxford University Press.
Zeitlin, M. (2007, July 24). Harry Potter and the Jewish goblins [Web log post]. Retrieved September 3, 2017, from http://web.archive.org/web/20111124195205/http://whippersnapper.wordpress.com/2007/07/24/harry-potter-and-the-jewish-goblins/
Zieger, R.H., & Gall, G.J. (2002). *American workers, American unions: The twentieth century* (3rd ed.). Baltimore: Johns Hopkins University Press.

Harry Potter, the Boy with Many Faces
The Illustrated Harry Potter *Books in Transmedia Motion*

Sarah Mygind

The upsurge of digital media, the constant development of new technologies and the convergence of contemporary media industries have in recent years caused an intensification of cross- and transmedia practices. These include an increased emphasis in various fields of production on building strategies for delivering and marketing stories and entertainment experiences in and across several media at the same time. Children and young people compose a large market segment for these transmedia strategies, which in turn affects children's literature. In this situation, the role of the book as the designated carrier of literature is challenged as the literary mode of expression per se. Additionally, the concept of reading as the way to engage with literature enter into new complex interplays with other media, expression, and engagement forms. Children's literature is no longer only *adapted* from book to film and affiliated merchandise or *retold* in new book editions. The fictional universes first published in and thus originating in books are to a great extent also *adapted*, *expanded* and *elaborated on* in new ways in digital media, just like new fictional universes are now from the beginning created to be unfolded in and across several media at the same time.

The American media scholar Henry Jenkins has famously named this process "transmedia storytelling"; a notion that describes a new cultural, artistic as well as economic logic distinctive from, however not in direct opposition to the logic of franchising. Franchising refers in itself to a corporate system for the marketing of goods, services, and/or technology in which a brand, concept, or icon is moved across outlets such as media channels or countries.[1] Historically, franchises are based on reproduction and redundancy, and the concept of adaptation has to some degree been ascribed to this logic, as is evident in Steve Peters' of No Mimes Media and 4th Wall Entertainments distinction between "'franchising, stunt marketing, brand building or adaptations' in contrast to transmedia as 'the *new* types of *real* storytelling that we're seeing now'" (Hutcheon, 2013, p. 194). Unlike franchises, transmedia storytelling strategies are concerned with further developing and expanding the fictional universe through several media, striving after audience loyalty by means of consistency, not redundancy. However, changes in the media landscape, practices, and culture, including the rise of transmedia storytelling, have also had an impact on adaptive practices which challenge the idea of adaptations as mere reproductions and secondary productions in a media hierarchy; "as a lesser, more simplistic mode of reworking content" (Hutcheon, 2013, p. 196). The newly illustrated *SS* (2015) and its relation to the recent changes in the *Harry Potter* franchise will provide a case in point.

Ever since the first *Harry Potter* novel was published in 1997, Rowling's wizarding world and its characters have been extensively communicated and especially visualized in various media through both official, canonized works, products, and platforms, as well as fan produced texts and artifacts. In the light of the existing textual, visual, and animated level of detail which is already representative of this fictional universe, it was all the more remarkable when Rowling and her publishers, Bloomsbury and Scholastic, announced that the book series starting in 2015 would be published in new hardback editions fully illustrated by the artist Jim Kay. The illustrated *Harry Potter and the Sorcerer's Stone*—hereafter referred to as *SS*—was published in October 2015, *CoS* in October 2016, and *PoA* in October 2017. The publishers plan to release a new illustrated novel once a year, ending in 2021 (Paolone, 2015).[2]

Even though adaptation studies are increasingly moving beyond the discussion of adaptations' fidelity towards originating texts and the insulated study of novel-to-film adaptations to encompass negotiations between a wide range of media, images in illustrated novels are rarely discussed or even mentioned as adaptations in their own right (Newell, 2017). This is, however, precisely what this essay aims to do. The illustrated *SS* can be read and studied as an entity in itself, yet, it is principally impossible to regard it as an isolated work since it is both part of a book series and a larger network of media representations that, unlike when the text was first published in 1997, constitute the *Harry Potter* world and franchise today. Given this contemporary context of the publication, it seems justified to question whether this illustrated book even *can* contribute anything to the fictional universe other than the obvious: as a new opportunity for reaping financial profit off the popularity of the *Harry Potter* phenomenon.

This essay seeks to clarify the illustrated novel's way of being and explore its relation to the transmedia network that composes the *Harry Potter* world today. The analytical approach to the illustrated novel, inspired by N. Katherine Hayles' notion of media-specific analysis (2002), emphasizes the importance of the text's new materiality as creating and potentially altering meaning, while also recognizing that the publication of the illustrated book series is taking place in an entirely different context than the original publication of the book series (1997–2007) in which many associated media representations may infiltrate the reader's perception of the work. After a short outline of the current state of affairs in the *Harry Potter* franchise, which provides the necessary background for the analysis of the illustrated novel, I point to the means through which the illustrated book positions the illustrator, Jim Kay, as co-author and how this corresponds with a shift towards a more collaborative approach to the development—or revival—of the *Harry Potter* world. The greater part of the essay explores Kay's illustration approach, focusing on three significant aspects: the interplay that emerges between text and image, the incorporation of visual metafictional and intertextual elements, and the symbolism and role of the character portraits. The essay argues that this illustrated novel, this adaptation, engages in and is part of a transmedia storytelling strategy and reflects how adaptive practices today cannot be disregarded when discussing and theorizing contemporary transmedia practice.

Building J.K. Rowling's Wizarding World

The publication of the illustrated *Harry Potter* books comes at a time when the *Harry Potter* world and franchise is undergoing radical transformations. The storyworld has expanded forward and backward in time, but also in topography, most notably through the movie *Fantastic Beasts and Where to Find Them* (2016) (the first in a series of five movies) that takes place in New York 70 years before Harry Potter's story, the stage play *Harry Potter and the Cursed Child I–II* (2016) that continues Harry's own story by taking off from the epilogue "Nineteen Years Later" in *DH* (2007) telling the story of Harry as a father, husband and employee at the Ministry of Magic, and through the reconfiguration of the *Pottermore* website (2015). What makes the *Harry Potter* franchise unique in the entertainment industry and in contemporary culture is Rowling's own enduring influence on and control over the development of the fictional universe across media and especially the distinctive status of the digital platform *Pottermore*: "a unique digital franchise text that can be updated and rearranged according to shifting brand strategies" (Brummitt, 2016, p. 112).

It would, however, be inaccurate to claim that it is only in recent years that the *Harry Potter* world has undergone transmedia developments. The first Warner Bros. movie adaptation premiered as early as 2001, the same year that Rowling initiated her first world-building extension by publishing the book *Fantastic Beasts and Where to Find Them by Newt Scamander* and *Quidditch Through the Ages by Kennilworthy Whisp*. Both books are textbooks that appear or are mentioned in the *Harry Potter* series, but are, obviously, fictional books written by Rowling herself. The textbook form and content of these books, along with the later published collection of wizarding children's fairy tales *The Tales of Beedle the Bard* (2008), constitute an early turn from the unfolding of the plot in the book series toward an interest in the mapping or building of the storyworld—in these specific works focusing especially on the *mythos* or backstory of the fictional world (Klastrup & Tosca, 2004). In his historicizing of transmedia storytelling, Matthew Freeman (2017) reasons that transmedia storytelling "is not so much about multiple pre-existing textual forms 'converging' as it is about multiple textual forms being *built* in the first place—one component being added to another and another" (p. 22). Thus, transmedia storytelling is a process of building not only characters but storyworlds that can accommodate different plots as well as many different characters. Jenkins (2009) argues that among other traits the building of storyworlds across media is characterized by the way a storyworld lets the audience *immerse* themselves in it and at the same time gives them the opportunity to *extract* pieces of that world to take with them and use in their everyday life. The three books from within the *Harry Potter* storyworld create a gratifying tension between immersion and extractability, since they offer the reader a possibility of gaining more specialized knowledge about the storyworld, while also composing objects known from the storyworld that the reader can buy, read and use for fan related activities—such as cosplay.

The digital platform *Pottermore* has, since the relaunch in September 2015,[3] aspired to position itself centrally within the *Harry Potter* franchise and now works as a central "hub of information" (Jones, 2015, n.pag.) for all authorized *Potter* related activities, or as it is described on the website: "the digital heart of J.K. Rowling's Wizarding World" (Pottermore Limited, 2017a)—a trademark of J.K. Rowling and Warner Bros. Entertainment Inc. As Brummitt (2016) argues, the name of the trademark shows how the franchise is now focusing on "a more amorphous, easily expanded 'Wizarding World'" (p. 130) and thereby seeking to put *"Harry Potter"* to rest.[4] *Pottermore* can now be described as a curated online encyclopedia. The website weaves together texts of fiction and journalistic texts in a daily flow of information by publishing, e.g., both new narrative texts by Rowling and behind-the-scenes articles about the newest movie expansion *Fantastic Beasts*; interviews with the actors as well as background stories about the fictional Potter family:

"Get the latest Wizarding World news here. Faster than an owl and more accurate than the *Daily Prophet*" (Pottermore Limited, 2017c). The user navigates through curated "collections" of magical objects, characters, and locations. Michael Bhaskar (2016) defines curation as follows: "using acts of selection and arrangement (but also refining, reducing, displaying, simplifying, presenting, and explaining) to add value" (n. pag.) and argues that curation is a crucial business strategy for our age of information overload. Official curation seems to be the new strategy of the *Pottermore* platform as it claims to have the authentic, reliable information in an online world where information and not least speculation related to the *Harry Potter* world run amok and the right information becomes valuable. The Global Digital Director of *Pottermore*, Henriette Stuart-Reckling, states that through the newly announced official Wizarding World Book Club, which was kicked off in June 2017, "Members will be able to enjoy the shared experience of reading the books together, and then joining the discussions we're facilitating on our social channels, *all curated by Pottermore, the authentic and authoritative digital heart of the wizarding world*" (my emphasis, Sims, 2017, n. pag.).

In the light of the latest developments and changes in adaptation studies and in the *Harry Potter* world, where the story of the book series as well as the storyworld itself has been expanded, with Rowling as the driving force through a growing transmedia storytelling approach, it is all the more relevant to explore the adaptive practice employed in the new illustrated *Harry Potter* editions. In the following analysis, I will focus mainly on the illustrated *SS* (2015) in order to pay adequate attention to the strategies of the illustrated adaptation.

Establishing Co-Authorship and Canonicity

What motivates even discussing these illustrated books as part of the *Harry Potter* world and franchise is partly that the books are marketed and sold by the publishers of the original book series (Bloomsbury, UK and Scholastic, USA), and partly that J.K. Rowling has explicitly approved and backed the adaptation via several media channels. Along with feature articles about the illustrated edition and interviews with Jim Kay on *Pottermore*, Rowling announced the release of the first illustrated book on her personal Twitter profile (see Fig. 1). The tweet has a dual function, as it on one hand pays explicit tribute to Kay's "eyes," hereby authorizing his visual interpretation of Rowling's own written text, while Rowling on the other hand is distancing herself from the work by laying all attention on Kay, calling him "a genius." This validation is not only taking place outside the text and the printed volume—in what Gérard Genette (1997) has termed the *epitext*—but also as part of the text and the physical book (in the *peritext*).

Fig. 1. J.K. Rowling's tweet on October 6, 2015, about the illustrated *Sorcerer's Stone*.

When comparing various editions of *SS*, there is no question that the illustrated edition (2015) constitutes a new embodiment of the literary text, since the book format is remarkably larger than earlier editions, measuring 9.1 × 1.1 × 10.5 inches—an uncommon novel format.[5] Also, the book design draws on classic conventions, using a red hardback cover with no decorations other than the title, the publisher's logo, author, and illustrator name embossed on the back with metallic lettering, a red bookmark ribbon and a fully illustrated dustjacket. The illustration on the dustjacket extends from front to back and features an illustration of the Hogwarts Express in a scene shown from a bird's eye view in which Harry Potter is standing next to the train with his trolley looking up at the owls flying around the platform.[6] The peritext of the dustjacket also emphasizes the changed conditions surrounding this edition as a description of Jim Kay's work and achievements is now featured underneath the author description of J.K. Rowling on the back flap. Unlike the description of Rowling which highlights her status as public figure and bestselling author, more personal information is given about Kay, forming a more intimate, even whimsical image: "He now lives and works in Northamptonshire with his partner and a rescued greyhound." The intimate portrait of Kay as an artist is further elaborated on in the epitext through a promotional video published on the YouTube channel "Warner Bros. Pottermore Promotional Clips" on October 5, 2015, and distributed by both Bloomsbury and *Pottermore*. The video shows Kay in his studio, showing concept drawings for the books and working on a color illustration for *CoS*. The artist tells about his studio and how he uses his garden, wild life, and plants as inspiration for colors, shapes, and compositions. The video mixes documentary elements with "magical" elements, showing Kay painting next to a clay model of the house elf Dobby that suddenly starts to move. The rescued greyhound is also in the video following him in and out of the studio. The intimate portrait of Kay that is painted through interviews, this video, and in the peritext of the book establishes Kay as a creator and a person that has an influence on the *Harry Potter* world.

Lastly, the back cover of the dustjacket for the illustrated book features a quotation from Rowling: "Seeing Jim Kay's illustrations moved me profoundly. I love his interpretation of Harry Potter's world, and I feel honored and grateful that he has lent his talent to it." Genette (1997) defines the paratext as "a zone not only of transition but also of *transaction*" (p. 2). As part of this transactional paratextual zone that surrounds the text, Rowling's quote works as an explicit recognition—as a stamp of approval—of Kay as interpreter and, by extension, as co-author or co-creator of this new text, which she is hereby passing on to the buyer/reader. This idea of Kay as co-authoring the new *Harry Potter* books taps into Bryant's (2013) notion of the *fluid text*: "any work that exists in multiple versions in which the primary cause of those versions is some form of revision. Revisions may be performed by originating writers, by their editors and publishers, or by readers and audiences, who reshape the originating work to reflect their own desires for the text, themselves, their culture" (p. 48). Bryant has gone from theorizing mainly "the literary work" as a fluid text (2002) to more broadly "the work" (2013) as a fluid text. He is thereby extending beyond written text and books to include all genres and media in an attempt, as he argues, to breach the prevalent wall between "originating work and its adaptations when it comes to defining textually the *work*" (Bryant, 2013, p. 49). In the case of the illustrated *SS*, however, this conceptual wall is breached by the peritext and the originating author herself. The co-authoring illustrator is also highly present in the book: "Illustrated by JIM KAY" is written with only slightly smaller letters than "J.K. ROWLING" on the second title page and the next spread holds J.K. Rowling's original dedication, but is now also accompanied by Jim Kay's dedication: "for Louise/I went in search of strawberries,/and found unfathomable love" and an illustration of a black dog with one brown and one blue eye holding a pink toy rabbit.[7]

The presence of the illustrator is furthermore expressed throughout the book as part of the text's distinct materiality. All pages are painted with faint watercolors and visible color splashes appear throughout the book leaving no page unmarked by and so the text not ever entirely independent of the illustrator. Color splashes are usually a glitch or an accident that occurs in the painting process, which an artist might choose to remove or hide and which is hardly ever part of most illustrated books. Here, the "blunders" are integral to the work pointing both toward the illustrator's presence and the illustrator as fallible in his work, thus communicating a humble attitude toward the job of visually interpreting the text.[8]

Rowling's honored position as originating author is still dominant, but the presence of Kay both in the paratext and in the material expression of the book is so pronounced that the author's traditional sacrosanctity and sovereignty is destabilized and expanded to include the illustrator as co-author. As Freeman (2017) argues, the author has the power "to hold a fictional storyworld together [across media] (or even break it apart)" (p. 34). This has especially been the case with the *Harry Potter* franchise, as Rowling has made deliberate choices in denouncing certain adaptations and actively backing others, thereby dictating what is canonical. Freeman uses Jenkins' definition of "canon" to describe how the power of the author occurs in the link between the author and the perceived "canonicity" of given texts. According to Jenkins (2006), "canon" can be used to describe texts that are accepted by certain audiences as legitimate parts of a storyworld. Accordingly, "an author can always dictate what is canonical and thus holds the power to determine what does or does not constitute a part of a given storyworld" (Freeman, 2017, p. 34). These active strategies to incorporate Kay as co-author are precisely necessary in the current publishing context as the *Harry Potter* world is composed of many media representations all expanding the original *Harry Potter* book series and authorized by Rowling either through the presence of her name or through her public endorsement.[9] Corresponding to the new approach of *Pottermore*, I would argue that Rowling is engaging in a strategy of curating the adaptations of her own work, which is both commercially valuable but also valuable for the consistency of the wizarding world. In continuation of this, Brummitt (2016) points out that *Pottermore*'s transition to the open-commerce model that enables retailers to sell books, away from its original strategy of exclusivity regarding the sale of *Harry Potter* e- and audiobooks, shows a shift towards "a more collaborative authorial stance" (p. 118). Hence, as the illustrated edition shows, this new authorial stance seems also to be willing to incorporate other creative voices and expressions that accompany but are not above Rowling's own.

The Devil Is in the Details: Jim Kay's Illustrations

With the significant exception of picturebook studies, conventionally, illustrations in books are considered part of the paratext, that is elements that accompany the text and help present it to a reader. Genette categorizes illustrations as iconic paratexts (different from material and textual paratexts), but he also recognizes illustration as a practice that demands specific attention as it holds a vast paratextual capacity, especially when the author has provided the illustrations herself, and it requires "technical and iconological skill" to fully account for it. He concludes: "Clearly, [the study of illustration] exceeds the means of a plain "literary person" (Genette, 1997, p. 406). As I will argue in the following, this idea is challenged by Kay's approach in *SS* that comprises a distinct *iconotext*, meaning that to the reader, "the text" is a distinct interplay between text and image (Hallberg 1982).

As an uncommon feature for most novels, both endpapers of the book are illustrated. The front endpaper shows a close-up drawing of part of a large, elaborately ornamented building. The building is dramatically situated on a rock foundation with plants growing up around it, and as a curious detail the end walls of the building are decorated with the front and hind quarters of a wild boar. On the back endpaper, we see the building in its totality from a distance where its grotesque, fantastic architecture and position in the landscape become visible. These endpaper illustrations are kept in grey tones unlike the majority of illustrations that are in color. In most books, endpapers would not catch a reader attention. However, the utilization of endpapers is common in picturebooks where the paratextual zone of the endpapers is included to contribute to the story by establishing a scene—like a visual pro- and epilogue—or establish the storyworld (Nikolajeva & Scott, 2001, p. 247). In this way, the front endpaper introduces the uninitiated reader to a world that at first glance seems similar to the reader's own world but with humorous quirks and traces of the fantastic, while the initiated reader is introduced to a visual space that establishes that she—just like Harry—is on her way to Hogwarts School of Witchcraft and Wizardry, which is highlighted by the placement of the building in the right corner of the page, urging the reader to turn the page. The back endpaper complements the front by moving the viewer away from the building, away from Hogwarts, just like Harry who, at the end of the book, is on his way back to the Dursley family after the end of the school year. The drawings depict details of Hogwarts that no other medium has represented in this way. Not even the *Harry Potter* movies have managed to focus on these exterior details of Hogwarts, as the movies are fast paced and action driven when compared to the act of scanning these drawings. Thus, the fantastic elements of the illustrated Hogwarts seem to underline several textual descriptions from the books that imply that anything is possible at Hogwarts. Professor Dumbledore states in *HBP*: "the castle is a stronghold of ancient magic" (Rowling, 2005, p. 404).

Just like every page is marked with watercolor, so are the illustrations frequently invading or merging with the space of the text. All chapter titles are consequently integrated in the illustrations, and in both *SS* and *CoS*, double-spreads with a dark background are used for night scenes portraying the luminous ghosts of Hogwarts and verbal text with white letters. In their book *How Picturebooks Work* (2001), Nikolajeva and Scott argues for a wide-ranging spectrum for the diverse interrelationship between word and picture situating wordless picturebooks and texts without pictures as two extremes. The spectrum is furthermore divided into narrative and nonnarrative categories. According to Nikolajeva and Scott's categories, *SS* would be categorized as an *illustrated story*: "A verbal narrative [...] illustrated by one or several pictures" (p. 8) as the book does not contain at least one picture one each spread, which defines a picturebook (cf. Hallberg). However, as I have already hinted at above, the book mixes picturebook conventions with more traditional illustration tactics thereby creating an expressive interplay between text and image. This interplay emerges sporadically and inconsistently throughout the book—not counting the constant presence of the watercolor splashes. For example, on page 24–5, the verbal text is situated according to the shape of the illustration of a large snake that stretches across the spread. This arrangement creates a commotion in the flow of the text and a sense of movement to the image. The snake is the boa constrictor that is freed from its cage because of Harry's—at this point unknown—magical skills. Yet, the surrounding verbal text concerns Harry's thoughts right after the incident that the illustration portrays. Harry's thoughts circle around all the strange episodes he has experienced during his upbringing with the Dursleys—incidents that could indicate that there is something he does not know about himself. The magic scene with disappearing cage glass and the equally dreamlike friendly connection between Harry and the snake is extended through the illustration, where we see the snake from a bird's eye view and so from a distance. Consequently, this scene becomes an underlying theme for the end of the chapter. So, even though text and image work separately—as Nikolajeva and Scott elaborates: "the text is not dependent on illustrations to convey its essential message" (p. 8)—in the reading situation, however, a specific iconotext emerges as a consequence of the interplay between text and image.

Another aspect of the illustrated *SS*, which, I would argue, is significant due to its specific publishing context as part of a transmedia network and franchise and which complicates simply categorizing the book as an illustrated story, is its visual metafictional and intertextual elements. Specifically, the representation of pages from fictional books is a recurring feature in the book. In *SS*, a double-spread (p. 146–7) is devoted to an illustration entitled "Newt Scamander's Guide to Trolls." This guide is not mentioned anywhere in the verbal text and is therefore unique to the illustrated edition. Newt Scamander is the author of the textbook about magical creatures *Fantastic Beasts and Where to Find Them*, which is listed as one of the required books for first-year students at Hogwarts in Harry's acceptance letter (p. 57). But *Fantastic Beasts* is, as mentioned earlier, also a book in our world that Rowling wrote and published in 2001 under the pen name Newt Scamander. The real-world book pretends to be Harry Potter's copy of the textbook, including "handwritten" marginal notes.

The illustrated double-spread displays the three kinds of trolls that exist according to the "Troll" entry in *Fantastic Beasts* (2001), but the spread also adds information that is not mentioned anywhere else. For example, in the bottom right corner, we find two insects depicted, a so-called *troll cleg* and a *troll wig*, and the handwritten accompanying text indicates that these are the troll's parasites.[10] When comparing the handwritten text of the illustrated spread with text from both *SS* and *Fantastic Beasts*, it is clear that the spread is paraphrasing and adapting information from these texts to create a kind of meta-iconotext. The double-spread serves a layered agenda: It refers to Newt Scamander and, by extension, to the book *Fantastic Beasts*, which exists as a book in the fictional world but also as a book (and, as of 2016, also as a movie) in the reader's world. In this way, the reader is offered new information, new details about the fictional world as well as being led in the direction of other media works and new commercial products. But the double-spread also works as a metafictional entity in itself, as it imitates the design and format of a scientific fact book, or even an old anatomy chart with its own aesthetic expression. Consequently, the spread provides the reader with new information and details that potentially become the foundation for the reader's own imaginary connections across the different media representations and establish Kay as co-author in this distinctive contribution to the fictional world.[11]

A final aspect I would like to pay attention to, which is important in relation to the illustrated book's position in the transmedia network of the *Harry Potter* world, is the full-page individual portraits of the series' central characters that are scattered throughout the book and continued in *CoS*. The portraits are different in style and vary from simple bust portraits to half-length portraits in elaborate environments. The simplest ones include full face bust portraits of Ronald Weasley (p. 160) and Harry Potter (p. 238). Notably, the up-close portrait of Harry is featured at the end of the book and the drawing style is sketchy. What stands out in the portrait, however, apart from his round taped-together glasses, is his green eyes—a physical feature about Harry that is a recurring topic of conversation in the books and movies. In the verbal text on the opposite page, Harry is having a conversation with Dumbledore after the dramatic encounter with Professor Quirrell and Lord Voldemort. He is asking questions about his own background and Dumbledore replies: "You will know, one day … put it from your mind for now, Harry […] when you are ready, you will know" (p. 239). The interplay between the sketchy portrait and the verbal text hints at things to come; a development and maturity that lies ahead and is yet to be determined.

Other portraits, such as those of Draco Malfoy (p. 67), Severus Snape (p. 110), and Hermione Granger (p. 150), situate the portrayed characters in environments that hold a myriad of references. A third type of portraits are the ones that pretend to be actual portraits (similar to the representation of pages from fictional books) by stating the portrayed person's name in the illustration. In *SS,* these include a portrait of Albus Dumbledore (p. 84) and Minerva McGonagall (p. 200). The portrait of Dumbledore is, naturally, an interpretation of Dumbledore as a character or figure, his body and face—a visual adaptation or expansion of the Dumbledore that the text describes:

> He was tall, thin and very old, judging by the silver of his hair and beard, which were both long enough to tuck into his belt. He was wearing long robes, a purple cloak which swept the ground and high-heeled, bucked boots. His blue eyes were light, bright and sparkling behind half-mooned spectacles and his nose was very long and crooked, as though it had been broken at least twice [p. 7].

In this third category of portraits, Kay draws on a portrait painting tradition that incorporates objects into the painting which reflect the person's moral or religious character, such as Jan van Eyck's "The Arnolfini Portrait" (1434), Hans Holbein the Younger's "Portrait of the Merchant Georg Giese" (1532) or Niels Strøbek's "Queen Margrethe" (1977). This portrait of Dumbledore shows how Kay's illustrations are not only a visual *representation* of a single text but a visual *adaptation* and *interpretation* of Dumbledore as a character that is constructed and developed over a series of books and other media representations. In Kay's portrait of Dumbledore, he is holding a bag of yellow candy. In the first pages of *SS* (p. 8), Dumbledore stated that sherbet lemon is a muggle sweet he is fond of, and later on in the series, "sherbet lemon" is revealed to be one of the passwords to his office. At his side lies a knitting project in progress, but it is not until the sixth book, *HBP* (2005), that Dumbledore expresses his love for knitting patterns: "'I was merely reading the muggle magazines,' said Dumbledore. 'I do love knitting patterns'" (Rowling, 2005, p. 73). In the vase by his side is a branch from the plant in Latin known as *Lunaria Annua*, or *honesty* or *annual honesty* in English. The branch is carrying the characteristic seedpods of the plant, whose appearance is the source of the plant's name. *Lunaria* means "moon-shaped" in Latin and refers to the shape and semi-transparent appearance of the seedpods. The common name *honesty* may be connected to this translucent appearance. The plant also has many regional names, most of them referring to "coins" or "money" and thus associated with the round shape of the seedpod, but in the Scandinavian and the Dutch-speaking countries, the plant is known as "coins of Judas" ("Judaspenge" or "judaspenning"). This name alludes to the biblical story of Judas Iscariot and the thirty silver coins he was given for betraying Jesus Christ, and the name of Judas is thus often associated with betrayal and treason. Sitting on one of the branches in the portrait is an insect, namely a mantis. Originating from Greek, the word "mantis" means "soothsayer" (oracle or prophet), and in ancient civilizations they were considered to have magical powers, like the ability to show lost travelers the way home. Female mantises are, however, also known for practicing sexual cannibalism, meaning that they eat their mates after copulation. Consequently, the symbolism of the portrait is ambivalent; it apparently alludes to Dumbledore's honesty, wisdom and supernatural insight, but the elements in the portraits are not unambiguous and they raise doubts about Dumbledore's trustworthiness and curiosity about his character; a theme that is recurrent throughout the series, especially present with and vocalized by Harry in the last books. As I will return to in the next section, lately, special attention has likewise been given to Dumbledore's character on *Pottermore*.

This ambiguous and "thick" symbolism is repeated in many of Kay's portraits of the series' characters and has spiked detective-like activity in the *Harry Potter* fan community.[12] On his website, Kay comments while linking to a specific post on the fan website Mugglenet.com:

> you can't slip anything past Harry Potter fans. It [the post on Mugglenet.com] lists the "Easter Eggs" in the *Philosopher's Stone*. Now, there aren't any hidden things in the *Chamber of Secrets*, sorry about that, but I will make it my mission to work something into [*Prisoner of Azkaban*]! The portraits should lend themselves to that. I've been doing a lot of research into the imagery & symbolism of portraits [Kay, 2017b, n.pag.].

Kay is pointing towards two significant aspects of the context in which these new illustrated books are published. Firstly, the books are published in a time where *Harry Potter* fan communities are a transnational phenomenon where the meaning of names in different languages, such as Lunaria Annua, becomes part of transnational discussion and not just a specific national translation or reading. Secondly, Kay is describing these symbolic elements and hidden things as "Easter Eggs," a concept that, by evoking the idea of the traditional Easter egg hunt, originates from video game culture, referring to inside jokes, hidden messages, or features deliberately incorporated into a game by the developers for players to find. Kay therefore seems to be conscious of the nature of the fan communities and culture in which these new books now take part, a culture where "consumers become hunters and gatherers" (Jenkins, 2007, n.pag.), as Jenkins characterizes consumers in relation to transmedia storytelling. Hence, when regarded as part of a transmedia storytelling strategy, the illustrated *SS* can, as other transmedia narratives, work as a "textual activator": "setting into motion the production, assessment, and archiving [of] information" (*ibid.*), as the post on Mugglenet.com (Jennette 2016) demonstrates.¹³

Based on this analysis, I would argue that the illustrated book addresses a dual audience: On the one hand, the relatively large amount of illustrations makes the book more accessible for reading aloud for younger children than the original that were specifically targeted at a teenage audience. This means that the book targets a new generation of readers who will grow up as the illustrated books are published year by year, thus potentially, recreating the hype around the release of the original series. On the other hand, the illustrated book with its "Easter Eggs" and metafictional elements is also addressing an older readership who will already be familiar with the *Harry Potter* world and who will enjoy picking up on the different intertextual references and discovering the hidden messages. But what does it entail that Harry Potter is given yet another face? As Kay indicates in the quotation above, the portraits will be a recurrent element in the coming illustrated editions. One might ask what purpose these detailed and lifelike portraits serve when actor Daniel Radcliffe's face already serves as the face of Harry Potter? The distinctive new depictions of the characters tap into the previously discussed more collaborative attitude exemplified by recent developments in the *Harry Potter* franchise. Through paratextual strategies, Rowling is sanctioning Kay to interpret the novel, entrusting her work to his eyes. This includes his envisioning of, among other things, the characters. Rowling's approval works as a way of foregrounding the illustrated novel as an adaptation and not as either a replacement or a supplement to the originating text. As Linda Hutcheon (2013) explains: "adaptation is an act of appropriating or salvaging, and this is always a double process of interpreting and then creating something new" (p. 20). In this way, Kay's adaptation as a new artistic creation and envisioning becomes part of an extensive reconfiguring of and attempt to "prolong engagement with the transmedial wizarding world" (Brummitt, 2016, p. 112).

Conclusion: Adaptation with Transmedia Attitude

Children's classics have long been adapted to match changing tastes, new commercial potentials offered by new media and changes in the conceptualization childhood. Following recent shifts in adaptation studies, spearheaded by among others Linda Hutcheon's *A Theory of Adaption* (2013), this essay has specifically not focused on Jim Kay's illustration's loyalty toward J.K. Rowling's verbal text in the illustrated *SS*. Rather, the premise has been that the adaptation is "always already in conversation with the adapted text"

(Lefebvre 2013, p. 2), and in continuation hereof, as Kate Newell argues, to regard an illustrated novel as an adaptation and an artistic creation in its own right allows us, among other things, to see "how that work has been shaped by its connections and collisions with different media" (Newell, 2017, p. 490). What is significant about the illustrated *SS* is the context of the transmedia franchise and transmedia storytelling strategy in which it is published and the way this external condition influences the adaptation and the adaptive practice. Consequently, the aim of this essay has been to study the illustrated *SS* as an adaptation and its interplay with the overall *Harry Potter* franchise.

An eloquent, summarizing example of this interplay between the illustrated *SS* and the surrounding franchise is Kay's portrait of Albus Dumbledore. Like many of Kay's illustrations, the portrait is reproduced on *Pottermore* and its social media (e.g., Facebook, Twitter and Instagram) where it accompanies various entries. Recently, the portrait was used to complement the promotion of the *Pottermore* entry "What we learned about Professor Dumbledore from the Mirror of Erised." In an essayistic style, the text focuses specifically on the impossibility of not including all the information we learn about Dumbledore later on in the book series when reading *SS* and on the ambiguity of his character; all of this condensed in Kay's accompanying portrait as clarified above. The text's point of departure is to ponder the reasons for Dumbledore's words to Harry in front of the Mirror of Erised (cf. Rowling, 2015, p. 174): "Dumbledore's words to Harry about the Mirror are not to dwell on dreams and forget to live. Again he could be speaking of his own history—his obsession with the Deathly Hallows, perhaps, and his neglect of his family" (Pottermore Limited, 2017d, n. pag.). Conveniently, these speculations about Dumbledore's character and his motives play into the anticipation of the coming movies in the announced Fantastic Beasts series, which will unfold the story of Dumbledore's relation to and history with Newt Scamander and Gellert Grindelwald and thus most likely shed author-produced light on these speculations.[14]

In this way, the illustrated edition contributes to the transmedia world that is J.K. Rowling's "wizarding world" today by visualizing and adding never-before-seen material to this world, but also weaving the different media works closer together by adding new visual, intertextual references to later works and to the original text. However, the commercial potential of the illustrated editions cannot be denied either, partly because the serial publication of the illustrated editions plays on the hype and anticipation of the original series while addressing both a new younger readership and devoted older fans, partly because the illustrations are now part of the transmedia marketing strategy of *Pottermore* where Kay's illustrations become part of promotional material for new media works, as the example of the portrait of Dumbledore illustrates.

Based on the analysis of the illustrated book and its context, my claim is that it is not sufficient to make a straightforward distinction between transmedia storytelling and adaptation, contrary to, among others, Henry Jenkins' argument that "[A] simple adaptation may be 'transmedia' but it is not 'transmedia storytelling' because it is simply re-presenting an existing story rather than expanding and annotating the fictional world" (Jenkins, 2009). As Christy Dena has argued, drawing on Hutcheon, this notion of adaptation is too limited to account for contemporary practices as "a transmedia attitude [...] can be present in adaptation practices" (p. 147–48). As the illustrated *SS* demonstrates, adaptation is a process of interpretation and reconfiguration, not only reproduction, since adaptations may differ from the literal to the transformative. Generally, all shifts between media have the potential to offer new experiences and add new meaning and nuances to an art work, which is why adaptation needs to be considered one of many contemporary transmedia storytelling practices.

Notes

1. See Johnson (2013) and Jenkins (2006) for more on the historical development in media franchising and contemporary convergence.
2. In May 2017, Kay wrote in a blogpost on his website that he is currently on a break from illustrating the *Harry Potter* books, which will most likely affect the announced publishing schedule of the series (Kay, 2017a, n. pag.).
3. See Brummitt for a detailed analysis of *Pottermore*'s role in the development of the Harry Potter franchise and the difference between *Pottermore* 2011–2015 and 2015–present.
4. At the premiere for *Harry Potter and the Cursed Child* in July 2016, Rowling even stated that "Harry is done now" and "This is the next generation" (Flood, 2016, n. pag.).
5. It should be mentioned that a "Deluxe Illustrated Slipcase Edition" has also been published featuring "an opulent page size and an exclusive pull-out double gatefold of Diagon Alley; intricate foiled line art by Jim Kay on the real cloth cover and slipcase; gilt edges on premium grade paper; head and tail bands and two ribbon markers—the ultimate must-have edition for any fan, collector or bibliophile" (Bloomsbury, n. pag.).
6. The back cover holds an interesting detail in the illustration as an owl is sitting on an edge of the wall far above the busy platform. Next to the owl we distinctively see the characteristic blueish steel arches with circle ornaments from King's Cross Station in London. Set designer, Christine Jones has elaborated on the same arches for the set design for *Harry Potter and the Cursed Child* (Brochure, *Harry Potter and the Cursed Child, Parts One and Two*, 2016)
7. Later in the book (Rowling, 2015, p. 193), the reader will realize that this dog is indeed Fang, Hagrid's loyal but cowardly boarhound. In Kay's version, Fang is actually depicted as a boarhound (also known as a Great Dane) whereas in the movies Fang is a Neapolitan Mastiff. The detail of the eyes does not refer to Fang in either the written text or movie and must be part of Kay's own interpretation.
8. Jim Kay describes his technique and working process in the *Special Collector's Edition* of Patrick Ness' *A Monster Calls* (2016) relating that many of the images for his illustrations grew from ink blobs, smudges and his own mistakes (p. 232–251). These ink blots and the watercolor splashes have also been transferred to the movie (2016) where the opening credits are accompanied by animations showing running ink and watercolors mixing and forming images thus passing on Kay's visual style from the illustrated *A Monster Calls* (2011) to the movie and the illustrated Harry Potter books.
9. The same motion occurs in the published book version of the manuscript for *Harry*

Potter and the Cursed Child, which is written by Jack Thorne and not Rowling herself. The cover and title page reads: "Based on an original new story by J.K. Rowling/John Tiffany & Jack Thorne/A new play by Jack Thorne" (2016). The book also holds dedications made by all three "authors." Similar to her endorsement of Jim Kay, Rowling has made a dedication to Jack Thorne: "To Jack Thorne who entered my world and did beautiful things there."

10. "Cleg" is a common name for horsefly and "wig" could be borrowed from earwig.

11. In this way, the illustrated edition corresponds to Nikolajeva and Scott's (2001) category of "expanding" or "enhancing" picturebooks where "words and images provide alternative information or contradict each other" (p. 17).

12. This corresponds to Jason Mittell's (2009) idea of modes of forensic fandom in television, meaning productions that encourage viewers to dig deeper into the story world to better understand it.

13. Kay's troll cleg now has its own entry on the fan driven *Harry Potter Wiki*.

14. See Pottermore Limited 2017b for information about the next and yet-untitled movie in the Fantastic Beasts series.

REFERENCES

Bhaskar, M. (2016). *Curation: The power of selection in a world of excess*. London: Piatkus.
Bloomsbury (2017). Harry Potter and the philosopher's stone deluxe illustrated edition. *Harry Potter*. Retrieved from https://harrypotter.bloomsbury.com/uk/harry-potter-and-the-philosophers-stone-9781408871874/?ewid=1330
Brummitt, C. (2016). Pottermore. Transmedia storytelling and authorship in Harry Potter. *The Midwest Quarterly*, 58(1), 112–132.
Bryant, J. (2002). *The fluid text: A theory of revision and editing for book and screen*. Ann Arbor: University of Michigan Press.
Bryant, J. (2013). Textual identity and adaptive revision: Editing adaptation as a fluid text. In J. Bruhn, A. Gjelsvik & E.F. Hanssen (Eds.), *Adaptation studies: New challenges, new directions* (pp. 47–67). London: Bloomsbury Academic.
Dena, C. (2009). *Transmedia practice: Theorising the practice of expressing a fictional world across distinct media and environments*. Ph.D. dissertation. University of Sydney. Retrieved from http://www.christydena.com/phd/
Flood, R. (2016, August 1). J.K. Rowling: I think we're done with Harry Potter now. *The Guardian*. Retrieved from https://www.theguardian.com/books/2016/aug/01/jk-rowling-done-with-harry-potter-now-cursed-child
Freeman, M. (2017). *Historicising transmedia storytelling: Early twentieth-century transmedia story worlds*. New York: Routledge, Taylor & Francis Group.
Genette, G. (1997). *Paratexts: Thresholds of interpretation*. Cambridge: Cambridge University Press.
Hallberg K. (1982). Litteraturvetenskapen och bilderboksforskningen. *Tidskrift för litteraturvetenskap*, 3–4, 163–169.
Harry Potter Publishing and Theatrical Rights (2016). *West End premiere edition Harry Potter and the cursed child official souvenir brochure*.
Harry Potter Wiki (2017). Trollcleg. *Harry Potter Wiki*. Retrieved from http://harrypotter.wikia.com/wiki/Trollcleg
Hayles, N.K. (2002). *Writing machines*. Cambridge, MA: MIT Press.
Hutcheon, L. (2013). *A theory of adaptation*. 2d ed. New York: Routledge.
Jenkins, H. (2006). *Convergence culture: Where old and new media collide*. New York: New York University Press.
Jenkins, H. (2007, March 21). Transmedia storytelling 101. *Henry Jenkins. Confessions of an aca-fan*. Retrieved from http://henryjenkins.org/blog/2007/03/transmedia_storytelling_101.html
Jenkins, H. (2009, December 12). Revenge of the origami unicorn: The remaining four principles of transmedia storytelling. *Henry Jenkins. Confessions of an aca-fan*. Retrieved from http://henryjenkins.org/blog/2009/12/revenge_of_the_origami_unicorn.html
Jennette, J. (2016, July 15). Easter eggs in Jim Kay's illustrations for "Harry Potter and the

sorcerer's stone." Mugglenetwww. Retrieved from http://www.mugglenet.com/2016/01/easter-eggs-in-jim-kays-illustrations-for-harry-potter-and-the-sorcerers-stone/
Johnson, D. (2013). *Media franchising: Creative license and collaboration in the culture industries.* New York: New York University Press.
Jones, P. (2015, September 10). Pottermore readies radical relaunch. *The Bookseller.* Retrieved from http://www.thebookseller.com/news/pottermore-readies-radical-relaunch-312036
Kay, J. (2017a). Azkaban finished. *Jim Kay. Home of illustrator Jim Kay.* Retrieved from http://www.jimkay.co.uk/azkaban-finished/
Kay, J. (2017b). Harry Potter. *Jim Kay. Home of illustrator Jim Kay.* Retrieved from http://www.jimkay.co.uk/home/harry-potter/
Klastrup, L. & Tosca, S. (2004). Transmedial worlds: Rethinking cyberworld design. In *Proceedings of the 2004 International Conference on Cyberworlds* (pp. 409–416).
Lefebvre, B. (Ed.) (2013). *Textual transformations in children's literature: Adaptations, translations, reconsiderations.* New York: Routledge.
Mittell, J. (2009). Lost in a great story: Evaluation in narrative television (and television studies). In R. Pearson (Ed.), *Reading Lost* (pp. 119–138). London: I.B. Tauris.
Ness, P. (2016). *A monster calls: Special collector's edition.* London: Walker Books.
Newell, K. (2017). Adaptation and illustration. In T.M. Leitch (Ed.), *The Oxford handbook of adaptation studies* (pp. 477–493). New York: Oxford University Press.
Nikolajeva, M., & Scott, C. (2001). *How picturebooks work.* New York: Garland.
Paolone, M. (2015, January 15). Here are the first images from the fully illustrated edition of "Harry Potter." *BuzzFeed.* Retrieved from https://www.buzzfeed.com/meganp25/accio-new-harry-potter-editions?utm_term=.phXxxOyOq
Pottermore Limited (2017a). About us. *Pottermore.* Retrieved from https://www.pottermore.com/about/us
Pottermore Limited (2017b). Dumbledore and Newt will team up against Grindelwald in the new Fantastic Beasts film. *Pottermore.* Retrieved from https://www.pottermore.com/news/dumbledore-and-newt-will-team-up-against-grindelwald-in-the-next-fantastic-beasts-film
Pottermore Limited (2017c). News. *Pottermore.* Retrieved from https://www.pottermore.com/news
Pottermore Limited (2017d). What we learned about Professor Dumbledore from the Mirror of Erised. *Pottermore.* Retrieved from https://www.pottermore.com/features/what-we-learned-about-professor-dumbledore-from-the-mirror-of-erised
Rowling, J.K. (2001). *Fantastic beasts and where to find them. Newt Scamander.* London: Bloomsbury.
Rowling, J.K. (2005). *Harry Potter and the half-blood prince.* London: Bloomsbury.
Rowling, J.K. (2015). *Harry Potter and the sorcerer's stone.* New York: Arthur A. Levine Books.
Rowling, J.K. (2016). *Harry Potter and the chamber of secrets.* New York: Arthur A. Levine Books.
Rowling, J.K., Tiffany J., & Thorne, J. (2016). *Harry Potter and the cursed child: Parts one and two. Special rehearsal edition script.* New York: Arthur A. Levine Books.
Sims, A. (2017, May 5). Pottermore is launching its own Harry Potter Book Club to celebrate 20th anniversary. *Hypable.* Retrieved from https://www.hypable.com/official-harry-potter-book-club/
Warner Bros. Pottermore promotional clips (2015, October 5). Exclusive Jim Kay video release. Retrieved from https://www.youtube.com/watch?v=O1oRQhpfvFs

About the Contributors

Dr. Christopher E. **Bell** is an associate professor of media studies at the University of Colorado Colorado Springs. He teaches both theory and methodology courses in critical analysis of popular culture, rhetorical theory, representation theory and mass media. He specializes in the study of popular culture, focusing on the ways in which race, class and gender intersect in different forms of children's media. He is a TED speaker, a diversity and inclusiveness consultant for Pixar Animation Studios, a 2017 David Letterman Award winning media scholar, and the 2017 Denver Comic Con Popular Culture Educator of the Year. Recognized nationally for his expertise in the area of children's culture, he serves as the chair of the Southwest Popular/American Culture Association's *Harry Potter* Studies division.

Dr. Bronwyn E. **Beatty** is a senior lecturer at the New Zealand Broadcasting School, Ara Institute of Canterbury in Christchurch, Aotearoa/New Zealand where she teaches media ecology. Her research interests traverse transmedia storytelling, the political economy of the media, audience studies and community radio. She has published in various journals including *Postscript, The Electronic Journal of Communication*, and *Radio Journal*. Her research involves recording the history of community access radio in Aotearoa/New Zealand for a book on the sector to be coauthored with Dr. Brian Pauling.

Dr. Brian P. **Bernard** is an assistant professor of engineering at Schreiner University in Kerrville, Texas. With a specialty in nonlinear dynamics, he teaches a variety of mechanical engineering, mathematics, and physics courses, and promotes an engaging real-time classroom environment to remote students by offering a number of courses through synchronous distance education. A former submarine officer in the U.S. Navy, he is the principal investigator for Schreiner's Autonomous Systems Laboratory. He mentors technical undergraduate research projects in virtual reality, game theory, and control systems and won Schreiner's 2017 Faculty Award for Excellence in Research, Scholarship and Creative Activity. He has also published and given invited lectures in the fields of participatory fandom and technology in pop culture.

Caitlin **Boyle** completed her MA in children's literature from the University of British Columbia in Vancouver. Her research interests include adaptations, musical adaptations of children's novels and the transmediation of Harry Potter and its fandom culture. She's been a presenter at the Child and the Book, the Midwest Popular Culture Conference, UBC's Biennial Children's and YA Literature Conference and LeakyCon. She holds a bachelor's degree in education from the University of Texas at Austin, specializing in literacy education with English as a Second Language certification. She also holds a graduate certificate in youth services in information settings from the University of North Texas.

Bárbara **Cardoso de Souza** is an English teacher at Yázigi Cachoeirinha School, where she teaches English as a second language for Brazilian students. She holds an undergraduate degree in arts—letters, focused on English language and literature. She is always interested in popular culture, and has already coordinated a fan club of *A Song of Ice and Fire,* used to discuss literary aspects of the books with other fans in the national literature event, Odyssey of Fantasy Literature. She is an enthusiast of linguistics and the connection of popular culture, seeking a future specialization.

Jørgen Riber **Christensen** is an associate professor at the Institute of Communication and Psychology, Aalborg University, Denmark. His research is in the fields of narratology, quantitative content analysis, media, and media production. The wide scope of his research, which also includes museology and fantasy, rests on the foundation of semiotic cultural theory. His publications include books on media production, film analysis and television analysis. He has worked as a literary editorial consultant, and he is editor-in-chief of *Academic Quarter.*

Dr. Ana **Gruszynski** holds a Ph.D. in communication and is an associate professor in the Postgraduate Program in Communication and Information of the Federal University of Rio Grande do Sul (UFRGS), Brazil. Her area of expertise is the relationship between design and journalism. She teaches theoretical and applied disciplines such as image theories, editorial design, typography and multiplatform communication. She is a researcher at the National Council for Scientific and Technological Development (CNPq) and coordinator of the Editing, Culture and Design Laboratory (LEAD).

Dr. Alison **Halsall** is an assistant professor in the Department of Humanities at York University, Toronto, Canada. She holds a Ph.D. in English literature, with specialties in Victorian and Modernisms. Her research examines global "crisis comics" for and about children and youth. She is also coediting the first-ever collection of LGBTQ comics criticism with the University Press of Mississippi. She has published articles about H.D., the pre–Raphaelites, *Penny Dreadful, South Park*, and neo-Victorianism in contemporary graphic novels.

Dr. Thessa **Jensen** is an associate professor at InDiMedia–Centre for Interactive Digital Media at the University of Aalborg, Denmark. Her research focuses on the ontological theory of K.E. Løgstrup, paired with A. Honneth's work on recognition. She specializes in fandom and fan fiction studies, focusing on ethical challenges and possibilities in the use of social media platforms. Applying fandom research to design processes, she has worked on developing a theoretical and methodological approach to strategic design fiction.

About the Contributors 201

Kimberly D. **Martinez** is an undergraduate student at Schreiner University in Kerrville, Texas. She expects to graduate in spring 2019 with a B.A. in English with Honors and a teaching certification. While at Schreiner, she has been involved as a Mountaineer Mentor, a Freshman Resident Assistant, a Judicial Board member, and a Schreiner Ambassador. In addition, she holds the position of treasurer in the Sigma Tau Delta English Honor Society and is a member of Alpha Chi Honor Society. Upon graduation, she plans to pursue a master's degree in English while teaching high school.

Sergey **Medvedev** is a Ph.D. candidate and Fiosraigh scholar at Dublin Institute of Technology, Ireland. He is the author of more than a dozen of peer-reviewed articles, book chapters and conference papers, and a frequent speaker at the events of the UK Political Studies Association and International Communication Association. His primary research centers on the political dynamics between populist conservative movements and governing elites in the Western and Russian contexts. He is also interested in the aspects of Russian culture that constrain political participation.

Sarah Jayne **Mokrzycki** is a Ph.D. candidate at Victoria University in Melbourne. Her research examines the importance of inclusive children's literature, focusing on the benefits of diverse family representation in picture books. She is also a creative writer and poet, and has won First Prize and Highly Commended in Edith Cowan University's TALUS awards for her poetry, and published several short stories and articles. She was a top 10 finalist in the 2018 Asia-Pacific Three Minute Thesis competition, and presented her Ph.D. research at the 23rd annual Australasian Association of Writing Programs conference in Western Australia.

Dr. Sarah **Mygind** is a postdoctoral scholar at Aarhus University, Denmark. She holds a Ph.D. from the Centre for Children's Literature and Media, Aarhus University. Her doctoral dissertation focuses on transmedia relations in contemporary children's literature. She is an editor of the Danish literary journal *Passage* and a critic of digital literature at the Danish newspaper *Jyllands-Posten*. She works as a project manager and consultant in relation to game and digital storytelling development, and she teaches courses on literary culture, publishing, comparative literature, intermediality and children's texts and media.

Elena **Pronkina** is a senior lecturer at the National Research University Higher School of Economics, Russia. She teaches theory and methodology of contemporary communication studies and runs research seminars. She has authored peer-reviewed articles on various aspects of media culture. In particular, she studies user behavior on social media and the media representations of social issues.

Gabriela Gruszynski **Sanseverino** is a Marie Skłodowska-Curie ITN Early Stage Researcher at Laboratoire d'Études et de Recherches Appliquées en Sciences Sociales (LERASS) at University Paul Sabatier–Toulouse III. She is a full-time Ph.D. researcher, with a project focused on the politics and ethics of user generated content in journalism. She has a bachelor's degree in social communication from the Federal University of Rio Grande do Sul (UFRGS), Brazil, where she also got her master's degree in communication and information.

About the Contributors

Celina **Smith** is the author of two award-winning essays for the Harry Potter Conference at Chestnut Hill College. She was part of a leadership team that was a top ten finalist in the Harvard University KIND School Challenge. She served a two-year term as president of the Gender and Sexuality Association (GSA) and received awards for her work in the San Gabriel Valley Law Enforcement Explorer Academy. Her writing and social justice causes led her to pursue a major in performing arts musical theater at the American Musical and Dramatic Academy (AMDA) in New York City.

Kris **Swank** is a library director and honors instructor at Pima Community College, Tucson, Arizona. She has taught Harry Potter courses at Pima and Signum University. She holds a BA, summa cum laude, in humanities and English, and three master's degrees, including an MA in language and literature from Signum University. Her fantasy literature essays have appeared in *Tolkien Studies* and *Mythlore*, and several edited collections, including an essay on "Harry Potter as Dystopian Literature," in *Harry Potter for Nerds II* (Unlocking Press, 2015). She has also written for *Library Journal, American Libraries*, and other professional library publications.

Index

abandonment 56, 114, 161, 162
accents 89, 92, 93, 95–96, 99, 172
activism 72, 75, 81–86, 133
adaptation 2, 3, 5, 36, 44, 47, 62–65, 68–71, 91, 96–97, 100–103, 105–106, 116, 128–129, 146–149, 164, 181–185, 187–188, 191–192, 194–200
aesthetics 24, 36, 53, 56, 58, 63, 71, 90, 136, 152, 191
animagus 25, 51, 57, 60
anti-fandom 118–120
Aunt Marge 160
The Avengers 4, 42, 117

Bagshot, Bathilda 35
Barthes, Roland 8, 138
bibliotherapy 155, 157–159, 164, 165
Black, Sirius 43, 57, 60, 110
Brown, Lavender 35

canon 8, 31–32, 38, 40, 43–45, 61, 62, 66, 69, 71, 75, 111, 115, 116, 132, 188
Chang, Cho 54, 65, 87, 113
Crouch, Barty 145

Delacour, Fleur 112, 114, 143
Dobby 45, 55, 128, 168, 187
Dumbledore, Albus 21, 25, 34, 35, 55, 62, 66, 67, 82–83, 85, 93, 99, 105, 109, 110, 113, 135, 138, 144, 145, 147–151, 162–163, 189, 191–193, 195, 198
Dursley, Dudley 101
Dursley, Petunia 156, 160
Dursley, Vernon 17, 34, 43, 94, 101, 139, 155–156, 189–190

Goldstein, Queenie 167
Goldstein, Tina 167, 172, 174, 176, 178
Granger, Hermione 22, 35, 44, 48–49, 51, 54, 60, 66–67, 73–76, 81, 109–112, 114–115, 124, 136, 140, 142–145, 147, 167–168, 172, 178–179
Grindelwald, Gellert 151, 195, 198

Hagrid, Rubeus 25, 92–96, 99, 103, 108, 145

Jenkins, Henry 1, 2, 5, 8–11, 30, 39, 46, 53, 54, 57–60, 65–67, 71, 81, 83, 86, 106–107, 117–118, 121–123, 129, 133, 181, 188, 193, 196–197

Kowalski, Jacob 167, 171, 175, 178

Lestrange, Bellatrix 114
Lockhart, Gilderoy 108
Longbottom, Neville 84–87, 109–110, 114, 128
Lovegood, Luna 26, 75, 110, 114–115
Lovegood, Xenophilius 14, 19, 26
Lupin, Remus 42, 60

Malfoy, Draco 42, 44, 50, 65, 67, 74, 108, 110, 113, 137, 140, 142, 145, 148, 192
Malfoy, Lucius 108
McGonagall, Minerva 147
Mirror of Erised 99–101, 138, 195
Moody, Mad-Eye 109, 143

Obama, Barack 79, 166
Ollivander 126

Pettigrew, Peter 51, 60
Pigwidgeon 125
Potter, Albus 115
Potter, Harry 2, 4, 5, 8, 10, 12, 14, 16, 18, 20, 22, 24, 26, 28, 30, 32, 34, 36, 38, 40–42, 44, 46, 50, 52–54, 56, 58–66, 68, 70, 71, 74–78, 80–86, 88, 90, 92, 94, 96–98, 100, 102, 104, 106, 108, 110, 112–114, 116, 117, 119, 120, 122–128, 130, 132–134, 136, 138, 140, 142–144, 146, 148, 150, 152–165, 168, 170–172, 174, 176–180, 182–199, 202
Potter, James 60, 101, 115
Potter, Lily 35, 52, 101, 145

quidditch 10, 18–19, 24, 27, 49, 54, 102, 105, 109–111, 113, 144, 148, 153–154, 184
Quirrell, Quirinus 67, 191

Riddle, Tom 54, 82, 108, 111, 145
Rowling, J.K. 7–11, 14, 18, 20–22, 24–29, 33, 38, 44, 45, 47–60, 64, 71, 75, 77, 78, 82, 85–88, 92, 93, 98, 103, 104, 108, 112, 115–117, 121, 129, 136, 138–143, 145, 149, 151–155, 159–165, 167–169, 171–180, 182–189, 191, 192, 194–198

Scamander, Newt 144, 166, 174–177, 180, 184, 190–191, 195, 198
Slughorn, Horace 111, 145
Snape, Severus 35, 66, 71, 113, 138, 140–141, 144–146, 148–151, 192

The Tales of Beedle the Bard 143–144, 153, 184
Thomas, Dean 110–114

Umbridge, Dolores 81–82, 109–110

Voldemort 17–18, 23–24, 54–56, 60, 66–67, 70, 78–82, 87, 93, 105, 108–109, 113–114, 138–139, 141, 146, 148, 191

Weasley, Arthur 74, 115, 179, 198
Weasley, Fred 109, 110, 143, 145
Weasley, Ginny 9, 11, 14, 19, 26–27, 54, 105, 107–117
Weasley, Molly 114
Weasley, Percy 108
Weasley, Ron 35, 48, 49, 54, 60, 66–67, 105, 107, 109–112, 114–115, 136, 140–145, 167, 172, 178
Winky 168